# A THEATERGOER'S GUIDE TO
## *Shakespeare's Characters*

# A THEATERGOER'S GUIDE TO *Shakespeare's Characters*

## ROBERT THOMAS FALLON

*Ivan R. Dee*

CHICAGO

Library of Congress Cataloging-in-Publication Data:

Fallon, Robert Thomas.
   A theatergoer's guide to Shakespeare's characters / Robert Thomas Fallon.
     p. cm.
   Includes bibliographical references and index.
   ISBN 1-56663-570-5 (alk. paper)
    1. Shakespeare, William, 1564–1616—Characters—Handbooks, manuals, etc.
2. Characters and characteristics in literature—Handbooks, manuals, etc. I. Title.

PR2989.F26 2004
822.3'3—dc22

2003067414

*For Francie, Rob, and Bill,*
*whom I wear*
*"In my heart's core, ay in my heart of heart."*

# Contents

*For the convenience of readers, the characters are listed both individually and by play. A complete index may be found at the end of the book.*

# Contents by Play

*Some figures, of course, appear in more than one play.*

# Prologue

*"The play's the thing."*

THIS BOOK, like the two others in the series, *A Theatergoer's Guide to Shakespeare* and *A Theatergoer's Guide to Shakespeare's Themes*, is born of a desire to enhance the playgoer's enjoyment of a performance. The first *Guide* lays emphasis primarily on plot, the second on theme, the present volume on individual characters. Like the earlier works, this one is written in "plain though not inelegant English," avoiding the specialized terminology of the theater and scholarship. The reader will find only occasional footnotes, and those few offering helpful cross-references or matters of intriguing but only marginal interest. This is not to dismiss the importance of the generous annotation and commentary to be found in editions and works of scholarship, which are indispensable to understanding Shakespeare's poetry, his sometimes unconventional use of language, and his classical and contemporary allusions. But this is a book intended for readers who may not be intimately familiar with the plays, written in the hope that by knowing Shakespeare better they may enjoy him the more.

It has been estimated by those who have taken the care to count that Shakespeare's plays contain some eight hundred separate and distinct figures.* We shall examine only a few of them here: most of the central characters of the plays and a number of the significant supporting figures, those that have captured the imagination of playgoers over the centuries. It will inevitably be asked, then, why these few and not some other few from Shakespeare's vast array of characters? How can such a survey be considered complete without

---

*Having counted, I find, for example, more than a hundred dukes.

attention to Cordelia, Miranda, Pericles, or Cymbeline? I must confess to personal preferences among the characters, but I do so unapologetically, sharing in that regard the sentiments of any number of Shakespeare enthusiasts. Further, practical matters have a way of dictating the size and shape of a book, and to keep this one within reasonable limits while offering a comprehensive analysis of selected figures required that some choices be made.* An additional factor is the need to consider how often the average theatergoer will have an opportunity to see a particular play by Shakespeare, some of which are only infrequently produced. It seems reasonable to discuss those figures that patrons are most likely to encounter in performance. The astute reader will notice that I have ignored this practicality by including such characters as Timon of Athens, Margaret of Anjou, and Henry VI. But they fascinate me—again, a personal preference.

Broader and more objective factors are involved, however. Shakespeare's characters are often complex; they are torn by divided loyalties, inflamed with sudden passion, immobilized by melancholy, brightened with joy. These are the poet's most memorable figures because their trials and delights so closely mirror human experience, which is itself a compound of conflicting choices. What possesses Lear to divide his kingdom and disown his youngest daughter? What prevents Hamlet from fulfilling his vow to avenge his father's murder until the deed is forced upon him? Such questions do not have easy answers, and these figures excite interest because they reflect our own dilemmas, which themselves have no easy answers.

Further, of Shakespeare's host of characters many are what may be called "types," that is, stock characters that are subject to little development or complexity, figures familiar to any audience, readily recognized and enjoyed for what they are. This group includes, among others, smart-talking servants, inept policemen, common citizens or soldiers, court fops, and the various national figures who

---

*Several works in print cover all, or nearly all, of the characters, among them *Who's Who in Shakespeare*, eds. Peter Quennel and Hamish Johnson (Routledge) and *A Dictionary of Who, What, and Where in Shakespeare*, ed. Sandra Clark (Mc-Graw-Hill).

demonstrate the stereotypical, often comic, qualities of their origins, whether they be English, Welsh, French, Italian, or Spanish. They fill their roles ably, and Shakespeare fashions them with insight and variety, but they do not lend themselves to individual study except, that is, as types. In the final analysis, there is really not much to say about them, since in most cases they do not have much to say.

The figures examined in these pages may be grouped in several ways. In the very broadest sense it may be said that some of them undergo changes during the course of a play or series of plays, and others do not. Some evolve as they face challenges that cause a variety of character traits to emerge (Henry V, Mark Antony, Margaret). Some suffer abrupt shifts in personality, brought on by folly or intrigue (Lear, Othello, Timon). Others change little, as Shakespeare explores various qualities of a consistent character (Brutus, Richard III, Prospero). Some appear only in supporting roles but are uniquely memorable (Bottom, Caliban, Malvolio). Some are men, some women; some are strong, others weak; some are foolish, others wise; some are evil, others virtuous; some are comic and some are tragic.

The range, then, of Shakespeare's characters is extraordinary, and for each a diversity of description is called for. Again in the broadest sense, these essays address individual figures in two ways, depending on whether they undergo change or not. We follow those that evolve in some fashion through the narrative of unfolding events that act upon them to reveal character. King Lear, for example is at one time or another an imperious monarch, a pathetic father bartering for the favor of his daughters, a madman, and a sorrowing ancient who goes to his grave mourning the loss of love. Othello is transformed from a doting husband to a vengeful murderer, Timon from a generous patron to a bitter misanthrope, and many a young man in the comedies is reduced from a confirmed bachelor to a simpering suitor. Those that exhibit little or no change of character lend themselves to a more analytic approach, that is, a listing of qualities with illustrative episodes that demonstrate them. Richard III, for example, is as wicked at the end as he is at the beginning, Falstaff as devious and engaging in *Part 2* of *Henry IV* as he is in *Part 1*, and Thersites as vitriolic in his last appearance in *Troilus and Cressida* as in his first.

The overriding consideration is to render the figures accessible to readers who may be only marginally acquainted with them. Playgoers may consult this *Guide* in advance of a performance, or afterward to revisit a character that has captured their interest. Shakespeare's plays can be difficult, even for those who devote a lifetime of study to them, but they reward anyone who returns to them from time to time. Each new performance, each new reading uncovers something not noticed before; a single line or an entire speech that has escaped attention in the past can, when seen afresh, illuminate a puzzling episode or enigmatic figure.

Indisputably these characters are open to many different interpretations, hence the descriptions herein are by no means intended to exclude others. Where a figure is subject to a wide variety of readings, as with a Hamlet, Henry V, Prospero, or Shylock, I have suggested alternate strategies of portrayal, each of which depends ultimately on an imaginative director's vision of a play. But the purpose here is to clarify, not confuse. In most instances, I offer readers an interpretation that will provide them with a place to stand, a reasonably sound analysis of a character that will enable them to compare it to the one they see in a performance so that they may arrive at their own judgment about the meaning of the figure.

Some repetition is unavoidable in the descriptions of characters who appear in the same play but are considered in separate chapters. The outcome of a battle will have a different effect on the victor and the vanquished, and a death will cause some to rejoice and others to mourn. But an account of the battle or death must be given in each instance if the individual responses are to be appreciated. Again, a father and a son may look upon the young man's immature indiscretions very differently, as do Henry IV and Prince Hal, but in describing their individual points of view those indiscretions will necessarily bear repeating in chapters devoted to one and the other. Similarly, mothers and sons are often at odds, as in the case of Volumnia and Coriolanus or Gertrude and Hamlet, and the cause of their dissension must be made clear in each case.

Finally, these descriptions are based primarily on the evidence of the text, only infrequently on stage or screen productions. Of course, using the text as a source can itself prove hazardous; scholars debate endlessly about which quarto or folio edition most closely represents Shakespeare's final version of a play, disputing over which in the end is the ultimate distillation of his art. These are important matters; but the average playgoer, setting out in anticipation of a rewarding night at the theater, will be content to leave such controversies to the scholars.

I am indebted to my colleagues, James A. Butler and Kevin Harty, good friends both, for their counsel and encouragement over the years, and as ever to Ivan Dee, who has cleansed my sometimes muddy prose and guided me along the path to publication. And I am grateful again to the members of The Shakspere [*sic*] Society of Philadelphia, a varied group of learned bankers, lawyers, doctors, brokers, ministers, musicians, and entrepreneurs who over many convivial evenings have offered insights into Shakespeare's characters from points of view outside my own realm of experience.

# A THEATERGOER'S GUIDE TO
*Shakespeare's Characters*

# ANGELO

*"A deflowered maid,*
*And by an eminent hand that enforced*
*The law against it!"*

WHEN WE FIRST SEE Angelo in *Measure for Measure*, he seems nothing more or less than an upright, respectful deputy to the Duke of Vienna. In time, however, we learn more of him from others: To the duke he is "a man of stricture and firm abstinence," one who "scarce confesses / That his blood flows." To Lucio (called simply "a fantastic" in the cast of characters) he is "a man whose / Blood is very snow-broth; one who never feels / The wanton stings and motions of sense." All this we hear before even seeing Angelo again, but the reports define him as a man who is monklike in his habits, denying himself physical pleasures in favor of "the mind, study, and fast," as Lucio puts it. Today we might say of him that ice flows in his veins.

We may picture him as austere, humorless, highly moral, and reserved in manner, a man, in brief, ideally suited for a plan the duke has in mind. As he confesses later, he has "let slip" enforcement of the laws of Vienna until he has seen "corruption boil and bubble / Till it o'errun the stew." In consequence, regrettably, "Liberty plucks Justice by the nose," and something must be done about it. But the duke is devious. He announces that he will travel abroad for a time, and during his absence he deputizes Angelo to govern Vienna in his stead. He does not instruct the deputy to be more strict, only to "enforce or qualify the laws / As your soul seems good." But he knows his man and is confident he will fill the purpose, with the important added advantage that no blame for the sudden severity will fall on himself. Further, the duke will not in fact travel but will remain in the city disguised as a friar to keep an eye on developments.

Angelo lives up to the duke's expectations. Vienna, it seems, has a draconian law that prohibits, on pain of death, fornication outside of marriage. The deputy's first act is to close down all the brothels in the city suburbs, a drastic measure that he follows promptly with yet more deterrents. He later has a madam, Mistress Overdone, arrested when she attempts to relocate her business within the city limits, and he imprisons a young man, Claudio, for impregnating his betrothed before their marriage. Angelo intends to have Claudio executed as an example to others, and it is here that his troubles begin.

Shakespeare portrays Angelo as a puritanical figure, though he exhibits no evidence of religious fervor—such as might be expected, that is, of the stereotypical Puritan with a capital "P." He is a sternly moral man who has adopted an ascetic habit of life devoted to "the mind, study, and fast," and in consequence looks upon all demands of the flesh as base and corrupting. He finds it just and proper, therefore, to condemn those who cater to such demands and to punish any who succumb to them. His blind conviction is at once a strength and, as it turns out, a fatal weakness of character. Never having tasted of the pleasures of the flesh, he is hopelessly vulnerable to them.

The condemned Claudio pleads with his sister, Isabella, to intercede for him with the deputy. She, a novice in a convent and hence free to leave, gains an audience with Angelo and appeals to him for mercy. Unbending in his convictions, he refuses, but during the course of the interview he develops a prurient passion for Isabella, aroused, it seems, by her beauty and virtue. But he appears to be deeply disturbed by this sudden onrush of lust: "Dost thou desire her foully," he asks himself after she leaves, "for those things / That make her good?" "This virtuous maid / Subdues me quite," he concludes, and marvels at a sensation so alien to his nature: "Ever till now, / When men were fond, I smiled and wondered how."

Angelo, completely possessed by his desire, offers to pardon Claudio if Isabella will yield her "body to my will," and he insists that should she not, her brother will die. She refuses and, highly distraught, returns to Claudio, where she encounters the duke in his disguise as a friar. He has a plan. Some years earlier Angelo had treated a young woman, Mariana, dishonorably. Betrothed to her, he canceled the marriage when her dowry was lost at sea, but she has remained devoted to him. The duke proposes that Isabella agree to an assignation with Angelo but that Mariana take her place under conditions that will conceal the substitution. Mariana is content, and so it happens.

Afterward, Angelo treacherously breaks his bargain with Isabella by ordering Claudio's execution anyway, fearing, as he says, that the young man will seek revenge for his sister's shame. He seldom appears again until the final scene of the play, the intervening acts being largely taken up with comic episodes—this *is* a comedy— and the duke's design to prevent Claudio's execution. Angelo is convinced that he has had his way with Isabella and successfully disposed of Claudio, and the glimpses we have of him reveal a deeply remorseful man: Isabella is, he laments, "a deflowered maid, / And by an eminent hand that enforced / The law against it!" Of Claudio he says, "He should have lived" and again "would yet he had lived." In the final scene, once Angelo's duplicity has been unmasked, he passes judgment on himself; in keeping with the laws of Vienna, he says, justice demands that he receive "immediate sentence, then, and sequent death." He pleads that his "penitent heart [craves] death more willingly than mercy; / 'Tis my deserving, and I do entreat it." The duke is merciful, however, and passes sentence on him—he is to marry Mariana!

Angelo is a villain, but a villain with a conscience. He is possessed by a passion that lies outside his comprehension, that catches him entirely unawares, and his traverse from innocence to experience is indeed traumatic. He attempts to cover up his crime by ordering the death of Claudio, but he regrets the need to do so; and in keeping with his bloodless moral and legal code, he accepts death as the only just punishment for his supposed "deflowering" of Isabella. Angelo certainly does not arouse our sympathy, but we can acknowledge him as a pathetic creature who, having narrowed his human concerns to the stark demands of duty and the law, lies open to the unfamiliar heat of passion. Mercy is not in his code, but he receives it in the end—if marriage to Mariana so seems to him. Could Angelo, his sensibility once singed by the flame of passion and then soothed by the healing balm of mercy, possibly emerge from the experience a more complete man and prove a congenial husband? Well, probably not.

# BEATRICE AND BENEDICK

*"There is a kind of merry war betwixt Signior Benedick
and her: they never meet but there's a skirmish of wit
between them."*

THE "MERRY WAR" between Beatrice and Benedick is one of the
chief attractions—some would say *the* chief attraction—of Shakespeare's *Much Ado About Nothing*. Since so much of the character of
them both unfolds as a result of their interaction, it would be unre-
warding and needlessly repetitive to consider them separately. Audiences worldwide respond to their appeal as a couple—and so shall
we. The background to their history is briefly told. Don Pedro,
Prince of Aragon, leads a military expedition to put down a rebellion raised by his bastard brother Don John, and on the way to the
campaign his forces pause for a short visit in Messina, where they are
entertained by the governor, Leonato. The play opens on Don Pedro's return to Messina after a successful campaign. He is accompanied by his young officers Benedick and Claudio, and by Don John,
whom he has generously—and as it turns out unwisely—forgiven
for his revolt. Leonato, accompanied by his daughter Hero and niece
Beatrice, greets the party joyously, and we are immediately introduced to the caustic wit of Beatrice, who mocks Benedick's martial
prowess. She asks if he is in the returning company and then how
many he has dispatched in battle, adding sardonically that she could
probably "eat all of his killing."

Beatrice and Benedick are in fact very much alike. Both are
young, attractive, and much admired for their lively wit within
their separate circles of friends. Both are outspoken, self-assured, and
independent-minded. Both declare themselves determined never to
marry. When Claudio, Benedick's comrade-in-arms, reveals that he

has fallen in love with Hero, Benedick is appalled: "I hope you have no interest to turn husband, have you?" Claudio reveals that he does indeed so intend, despite the fact that he "had sworn the contrary," and Benedick looks upon his decision as a betrayal of the bond between them: "Is't come to this? . . . Shall I never see a bachelor of threescore again?" Later he confirms his resolve to remain single in a declaration of his attitude toward all women:

> Because I will not do them the wrong to mistrust any, I will do myself the right to trust none: and the fine [conclusion] is, for which I may go the finer, I will live a bachelor.

Don Pedro predicts that some day he will see Benedick "pale with love," and the young man replies confidently, "with anger, with sickness, or with hunger, my lord, not with love." Beatrice is equally as adamant, praying that God will

> . . . send me no husband, for the which blessing I am at him upon my knees every morning and evening. Lord, I could not endure a husband with a beard on his face! I had rather lie in the woollen.*

The two meet, and as predicted verbal sparks soon fly between them. A short excerpt will give some flavor of their barbed exchanges in the play:

> *Beat.* I wonder that you will still be talking, Signior Benedick: nobody marks you.
> *Bene.* What, my dear Lady Disdain! Are you yet living?
> *Beat.* Is it possible disdain should die, while she hath such meet food to feed it as Signior Benedick? Courtesy itself must convert to disdain, if you come in her presence.
> *Bene.* Then is courtesy a turncoat. But it is certain I am loved of all ladies, only you excepted; and I would I could find in my heart that I had not a hard heart, for truly I love none.
> *Beat.* A dear happiness to women, they would else have been troubled with a pernicious suitor. I thank God and my cold blood,

---

*That is, under a rough, scratchy blanket without sheets.

I am of your humour for that; I had rather hear a dog bark at a crow than a man swear he loves me.

*Bene.* God keep your ladyship still in that mind, so some gentleman or other shall scape a predestinate scratched face.

*Beat.* Scratching could not make it worse, and 'twere such a face as yours were.

And so on.

There is a history to their apparent animosity, though Shakespeare alludes to it only indirectly. They had met on the army's outward march, it seems, and engaged in a brief, unsatisfactory affair. The subject comes up when Don Pedro remarks to Beatrice that she has "lost the heart of Signior Benedick," and she replies, "Indeed, my lord, he lent it me awhile, and I gave him use [interest] for it, a double heart for his single one." She leaves the impression that she had declared her affection only to have him ride off indifferent to it. Thus there is always an undercurrent of regret in her dismissal of romantic involvement and assertion of independence. It surfaces during the masked ball given by Leonato for the entertainment of the visitors. Beatrice and Benedick meet again and under the anonymity of their masks exchange oblique insults. Each is aware of the other's identity, but he is apparently unaware that she knows who he is. In a revealing moment she glances about the room, as if in search of him, and remarks wistfully, "I am sure he is in the fleet [among the dancers]; I wish he had boarded me." He is so incensed by her insults, however—she had referred to him as "the Prince's jester, a very dull fool"—that the broad hint of her affection and disappointment escapes his notice entirely.

So this charming, quick-witted young woman, having been once disillusioned by Benedick, now keeps him at a distance with her sharp tongue. There is no comparable sign of affection on his part. He seems entirely unaware that he has done anything to distress Beatrice and is obliviously dense about the whole affair. His sole concern is to avoid her, since whenever they do meet he is stung by her wit. At one point, seeing her approach, he exclaims, "O God, sir, here's a dish I love not! I cannot endure my Lady

Tongue," and dashes off. It does appear that she more often than not has the edge in their "merry war"; she always seems to have the last word at any rate.

The couple's friends are convinced that despite their outward aversion to each other they are actually very much in love. Don Pedro devises a charade in which they will discuss the matter so that each of the two, concealed nearby, will overhear the conversation. The men profess that Beatrice loves Benedick but is reluctant to reveal her affection because, having heaped scorn on him for so long, she fears that he will only scoff at her. And none of his friends will tell him because "he would make but a sport of it and torment the poor lady worse." The women in turn affirm that Benedick loves Beatrice but they dare not tell her for fear that she, with her "swift and excellent wit," will only laugh at the teller. It works! On hearing their friends' exchanges, both become convinced of the other's love and exult in the realization that each loves in return. She: "And, Benedick, love on, I will requite thee, / Taming my wild heart to thy loving hand." And he: "When I said I would die a bachelor, I did not think I should live till I were married."

We await the moment, surely the most tender in any love's progress, when they reveal their affection for each other. But events threaten to cloud the promise of that happy encounter. Briefly, the villainous Don John deceives Claudio into believing that his Hero is a wanton woman. The young man waits until they are approaching the altar to accuse her openly, claiming then that "she knows the heat of a luxurious bed." Hero faints, and Beatrice is incensed at the egregious insult to her cousin's virtue.

When Beatrice and Benedick finally do meet again, they circle one another warily, each bearing the scars of the other's stinging wit. He is the first to blurt out his affection: "I do love nothing in the world so well as you—is not that strange?" Beatrice is less forthcoming, reasonably so since he has already rejected her once, but apparently no less willing. She veils her sentiments, however, in an ambiguous admission: "It were as possible for me to say I loved nothing so well as you, but believe me not; and yet I lie not; I confess nothing, nor I deny nothing." So the courtship takes a familiar turn, with the man pressing his suit and the woman responding with customary reluctance. Beatrice does so, however, not with a display of coyness or maidenly modesty but with the edge of her tongue.

Benedick adopts the traditional stance of the chivalric lover eager to prove himself in service to his lady, "Come, bid me do anything for thee," but he is stunned when she suddenly erupts: "Kill Claudio." He refuses to consider this startling command at first, torn between the conflicting demands of loyalty to his friend and love for his mistress, but she accuses him of pretense, "There is no love in you," and, stung by her heated reproaches, he finally agrees to challenge Claudio to a duel. When they next meet, he informs her of his challenge; there is more evasive banter between them, as she refuses a kiss and he claims, "I love thee against my will." Benedick strikes at the heart of their contentious courtship when he remarks to her, "Thou and I are too wise to woo peaceably." And so it seems.

Don John's malicious plot is unmasked in time, Claudio and Hero are reconciled, and there is no need for a duel. In the final "skirmish" of their "merry war," Beatrice and Benedick discover the trick their friends have played on them and acknowledge that nonetheless they will accept one another, though only, each insists, to ease the other's suffering:

> *Bene.* Come, I will have thee, but by this light I take thee for pity.
> *Beat.* I yield upon great persuasion, and partly to save your life, for
> I was told you were in a consumption.

She as usual manages to have the last word, but he silences her finally with a kiss.

Shakespeare's richly varied survey of love ranges from the youthful passion of Romeo and Juliet to the "raging fires" of Petruchio and Kate to the mature sensuality of Antony and Cleopatra. The list includes couples shattered by jealous husbands—Othello and Desdemona, Posthumus and Imogen in *Cymbeline*, Leontes and Hermione in *The Winter's Tale*—as well as women who betray their lovers, as Cressida does Troilus. Add to the list now the unique instance of Beatrice and Benedick, who are attracted to one another on the basis of mutual aversion. In their contest of wills they seem a perfect match, both of them confident, bold, intelligent, independent, strong-minded, and engagingly witty. The only difference between them is that she appears to harbor a lingering affection for him, one that initially he does not seem to share; but in the end both find qualities in the other that they most value in themselves. It is difficult to imagine either assuming the role of a submissive spouse; theirs is a union that is by any measure a convergence of equals.

# BOTTOM

*"I have had a dream, past the wit of man to say what
dream it was."*

AMONG THE MANY engaging characters in *A Midsummer Night's
Dream*, perhaps the most appealing is Nick Bottom the weaver. He
is one of a number of simple artisans, called in the play "mechanicals," a group that includes Starveling the tailor, Snug the joiner,
and Snout the tinker. Peter Quince the carpenter calls them together
to assign parts in a play, "The most lamentable comedy, and most
cruel death of Pyramus and Thisbe," which they hope to perform at
the nuptial celebration of Theseus, the Duke of Athens, and his
Amazonian queen, Hippolyta. Bottom, the most robust and vocal of
the group, insists confidently, and impractically, that he play all the
key roles—Pyramus, Thisbe, and the lion; and Peter Quince must
point out firmly that he is to be Pyramus and none other. Later,
when it is decided that the play requires a Prologue, Bottom announces that he would be perfect for that part as well. Once the cast
has been determined, the group adjourns to learn their parts. They
agree to assemble the following night in the forest to prepare the
play, and as they leave an ebullient Bottom, who is given to malaprops, encourages them: "We will meet, and there we may rehearse
most obscenely and courageously."

Bottom is to play another role, however, one not of his choos-
ing. Unwittingly he has a personal encounter with the forest's fairy
kingdom, one in which the boundary between the human and the
supernatural realms becomes blurred.* Briefly, Oberon and Titania,
the king and queen of the fairies, are engaged in a marital tiff over

---

*For more on this effect, see pp. 27–28.

a "little changeling boy," a human child, that is, who has come into
their possession. He is, in short, a part of Titania's court; Oberon
wants him for his, but the queen stubbornly refuses to surrender
him. Oberon decides to play a prank on her, one involving the magical properties of "a little western flower," whose juices, if dropped
on a sleeper's eyelids, will cause the victim on awakening to fall in
love with the first creature that comes into view. Oberon applies
the potion to a sleeping Titania, and his mischievous servant Puck
provides the creature. The mechanicals have met in the forest for
their rehearsal as planned, and Bottom as Pyramus exits momentarily. Puck, finding him alone, seizes the opportunity and, using
the powers fairies are said to have, crowns him with a donkey's
head. Bottom, entirely unaware of his transformation, reenters on
cue, only to be greeted by his stunned friends who, terrified by the
spectacle, all run off. Titania, sleeping nearby, awakens, sees him,
and as Puck reports to Oberon, "straightway loved an ass."

Bottom is soon comfortably settled in fairyland where, beguiled
by the sight of the small airy spirits Titania places at his service (often delightfully played by young children), and apparently unfazed
by the experience, he assumes the role of a gentle giant and addresses
them courteously:

> *Bot.* I cry your worship's mercy, heartily. I beseech your worship's
> name?
> *Cob.* Cobweb.
> *Bot.* I shall desire you of more acquaintance, good Master Cobweb.
> . . . Your name, honest gentleman?
> *Peas.* Peaseblossom.
> *Bot.* Good Master Peaseblossom, I shall desire you of more ac-
> quaintance too. . . . Your name, I beseech you sir?
> *Mus.* Mustardseed.
> *Bot.* Good Master Mustardseed, I know your patience well. . . . I de-
> sire you of more acquaintance.

Bottom seems to take his strange circumstances as a matter of
course, as Shakespeare explores the comic possibilities of a figure
both human and animal who is transported to the spirit world. He
asks the small fairies to scratch his head, for as he says, "methinks I

am marvellously hairy about the face." When asked what he desires
to eat, he replies, "Truly a peck of provender; I could munch your
good dry oats" and drink "a bottle of hay." Titania finally leads him
off to her bower, where they fall asleep as she professes her passionate attraction to him: "O how I love thee! How I dote on thee!"*

Oberon has his way in the end. Titania is so besotted with Bottom that she surrenders the changeling child without thought, so
the king releases her from the spell and directs Puck to relieve Bottom of his "ass-head." Bottom awakens, bewildered by the experience: "I have had a dream, past the wit of man to say what dream it
was." He expresses his perplexity in nonsense lines that reflect his in-
comprehension but which at the same time are an artful evocation of
the confusion of the senses that often accompanies a dreamlike state:
"The eye of man hath not heard, the ear of man hath not seen, man's
hand is not able to taste, his tongue to conceive, nor his heart to report, what my dream was." "It shall be called 'Bottom's Dream,'" he
concludes, "because it hath no bottom."

His brief sortie into fairyland is not mentioned again, as Bottom,
now quite himself, rejoins his companions to report that their play
is "preferred." The performance of *Pyramus and Thisbe* portrays the
distance between the unsophisticated artisans, who are confident
they are portraying high drama, and their cultured audience, who see
their performance as farcical and respond with witty ridicule. Fortunately the players are oblivious to the commentary of their critics.
Shakespeare is obviously having fun with these simple men, but he
is also obliquely mocking the histrionic exaggerations of actors of his
time who insist upon butchering his carefully composed speeches.
There are few occasions in these plays where we can be confident that
we hear the authentic voice of the poet himself, but when he writes
of those who tread the stage we can be sure it is Shakespeare speaking. In *Pyramus and Thisbe* he chides them for their excesses.

We are put in mind of another occasion when Shakespeare artic-
ulates his discontent with immoderate actors: Hamlet's advice to the

---

*Shakespeare leaves them sleeping, but modern productions carry the matter
further, strongly implying and sometimes openly featuring events in the bower,
during which one thing leads to another.

players. He counsels them to "speak the speech" as it is written, "trippingly on the tongue," rather than "mouth it," that is, draw the lines out with exaggerated emphasis; nor should they "saw the air too much with their hand" in overly athletic gestures. It offends him, he goes on, to hear "a robustious periwig-pated fellow tear a passion to tatters, to very rags." "Suit the action to the word, the word to the action," he advises further, for anything "o'erdone is from the purpose of playing." He has heard actors, he says, who "have so strutted and bellowed [that] they imitated humanity . . . abominably."

As Pyramus, Bottom displays all these excesses. He struts and bellows, "mouths" his lines, tears them "to rags," and waves his arms about. In balance, it must be said in his defense that Shakespeare's lines openly invite excess. The poet may indeed be mocking his fellow dramatists as well when he has Bottom exclaim:

> O grim-looked night! O night with hue so black!
> O night, which ever art when day is not!
> O night, O night! alack, alack, alack,
> I fear my Thisby's promise is forgot!

Such speeches confirm that Shakespeare could write bad verse when he put his mind to it.[*] As for suiting "the action to the word," Bottom is clearly meant to render his lines "o'erdone" when he discovers Thisbe's body and stabs himself: "Thus die I, thus, thus, thus!" And he takes an unconscionably long time dying: "Tongue, lose thy light; / Moon, take thy flight! / Now die, die, die, die, die." Actors delight in death scenes, of course, and Bottom is encouraged to take full advantage of the occasion.

Bottom is not only a vehicle for Shakespeare to mock the more egregious excesses of the stage, however. He is a generous, well-meaning, simple man engaged in an enterprise beyond his modest talents, though not above his irrepressible confidence in them, and he is as well an unwitting pawn in a matrimonial spat between two

---

[*]Also worth mentioning are the comic alliterations in the Prologue's speech: "Whereat with blade, with bloody, blameful blade, / He bravely broached his boiling bloody breast," and Bottom's "Quail, crush, conclude, and quell."

powerful supernatural figures. Further, we find him an endearing character as he deals graciously with the denizens of his "dream" and later is convinced that his portrayal of a doomed lover is genuinely moving to the duke and his sophisticated courtiers. In his simplicity he is blissfully unaware that he is ridiculous in both roles and emerges unshakably confident that he is worthy of the praise and affection lavished upon him by all.

Bottom's unself-conscious assurance may well be the source of his sympathetic appeal to audiences of this popular play, for we can recognize in him the familiar figure of one who looks on his world with innocent eyes, unaware of how its more cynical and contentious inhabitants may see him. We laugh at Bottom, but with uneasy apprehension. He suggests that we consider how we are perceived by others, whether, as all prefer, we are seen to be a much admired and respected figure, or as a clown adorned with donkey's ears visible to all but those who wear them, as Bottom is in one episode, or as an uncomprehending innocent, happily ignorant that he is making a fool of himself, as he is in another.

# BRUTUS

*"This was the noblest Roman of them all."*

AUDIENCES may find that, aside from Hamlet, the Marcus Brutus of *Julius Caesar* is Shakespeare's most exasperating tragic character. We cannot but admire his finer qualities, "noble, wise, valiant, and honest," as Mark Antony acknowledges, to which we might add decent, loyal, kind, and honorable. The poet's tragic figures usually end up defeated by some flaw in character—Othello's passion, Macbeth's ambition, or Lear's blind arrogance—but if there is a flaw in Brutus, it can only be his inherent nobility. He falls not because of some error or frailty in his nature but by the very quality that makes him most admirable, his unassailable virtue.

Brutus is highly respected by all. The conspirators against Caesar, of whom Cassius is chief, insist that his inclusion in the plot is essential to its success, and on joining them he becomes the undisputed leader of the group. Cassius shows no resentment at this, and when disagreements arise between them he invariably bows to Brutus's judgment. To emphasize the high regard in which Brutus is held, Shakespeare inserts a brief episode in which he enlists Ligarius in the conspiracy. He does so, however, without revealing its purpose, and the man joins without hesitation, declaring, "I follow you / To do I know not what: But it sufficeth / That Brutus leads me on."

We want to admire Brutus, but he repeatedly dilutes our sympathy with his blindly impractical idealism. When the conspirators meet at his house on the night before the assassination, Cassius makes several proposals, each of which Brutus rejects on various grounds. Responding to the suggestion that they swear an oath, the high-minded Brutus dismisses the idea on the basis that they are already bound together, and he asks what more assurance they need "than honesty to honesty engaged / That this shall be or we will fall for it?" Cassius proposes that Cicero be included, but Brutus rejects that as well. When Cassius finally insists that Mark Antony be killed along with Caesar, Brutus objects with an impassioned defense of their mission as a sacred cause which the murder of Antony would only sully. "Let us be sacrificers, but not butchers," he urges, "let's kill him boldly, but not wrathfully; / Let's carve him as a dish fit for the gods," so as to ensure that when the deed is done, "we shall be called purgers, not murderers." Brutus conceives of Caesar's death as a sacrificial offering on the altar of Roman liberty, not an act of vengeance or envy—otherwise, of course, he could not in conscience take part in the plot.

Later, when the bloody conspirators are standing over the body of Caesar, Mark Antony comes before them, feigning acceptance of the murder. Brutus assures him that "Our reasons are so full of good regard / That were you, Antony, the son of Caesar, / You would be satisfied," and he offers him an opportunity to speak to the populace after he has addressed them. Cassius is appalled at the idea. Drawing Brutus aside, he protests, "Know you how much the people may be moved / By that which he will utter?" but Brutus is blindly confident that "It shall advantage more than do us wrong."

In time these decisions prove disastrous to their cause. It is soon evident that they have need of an accomplished orator like Cicero to justify the assassination. The survival of Mark Antony proves to be their undoing, and allowing him to speak is a fatal blunder. But Brutus seems to think that everyone is as fair-minded as he and shares the same exalted vision of their purpose.

When Brutus addresses the troubled Roman people who have gathered in the Forum on hearing of Caesar's death, his speech is disappointingly flat, an impression that Shakespeare conveys by rendering it in prose. Further, his appeal is largely personal, in defense of his own role in the assassination, as if he is confident that in justifying himself he will justify the murder: "As Caesar loved me, I weep for him; as he was fortunate, I rejoice at it; as he was valiant, I honour him; but as he was ambitious, I slew him." His words seem to have the desired effect, however, as the citizens are swayed by his sincerity, some heard to cry out, "Let him be Caesar." But Brutus, for all his fine qualities, is undistinguished as an orator, far less eloquent than Cicero, who would have been useful here, or Antony, who follows him with an impassioned speech transforming the citizens into a howling mob that rushes off to lynch the assassins.

Brutus is in many ways a reflection of the philosophy of the Roman Stoics, meaning in the modern sense that he is unemotional, sober-minded, and moved by reason and principle alone. He is akin to Horatio, whom Hamlet values as "a man that Fortune's buffets and rewards / Hast ta'en with equal thanks." On two occasions, however, we see passion disturb Brutus's impassive, philosophical shell, both involving his love for his wife Portia. On the night the conspirators agree to assassinate Caesar, she pleads with her husband to confide in her the cause of what she has observed as his recent distraction. Brutus, anxious that the plot remain secret and determined to shelter his wife from the brutal realities of Roman politics, is evasive. To prove herself trustworthy, Portia has inflicted a wound on her thigh, and when she displays it Brutus is overcome: "O ye gods, / Render me worthy of this noble wife." In response he promises to take her into his complete confidence.*

On the second occasion, during the days leading up to the crucial Battle of Philippi, he receives word that Portia has taken her own life, and in an especially gruesome manner—she is said to have "swallowed fire." The news seems to color his entire state of mind during the preparations for and conduct of the battle, and so deserves special attention. First, he seems uncharacteristically quarrelsome with Cassius. The two generals meet and retire to a tent so that their soldiers will not witness their disagreements. Cassius is incensed that Brutus has condemned one of his officers for accepting bribes, and the exchange becomes heated as Cassius makes a veiled threat: "Do not presume too much on my love, / I may do that I shall be sorry for." Brutus replies self-righteously that he is "armed so strong in honesty" that he is impervious to such threats, and then complains that Cassius had denied him gold to pay his legions, a charge that the general refutes. It cannot escape notice that Brutus chastises Cassius for securing funds through bribery, but he has no reservations about accepting the tainted money once it has been collected.

*He proves justified in his concern, for there is a leak. Artemidorus discovers the plot and attempts to warn Caesar.

After more recriminations, the two are reconciled and Brutus reveals the cause of his distemper: "Portia is dead." Cassius is stunned: "How scaped I killing when I crossed you so?" But Brutus stoically brushes aside all expressions of sympathy: "Speak no more of her." "No more, I pray you." Messala enters and discreetly inquires if Brutus has heard from his wife. Satisfied by his answers that he is ignorant of her fate, Messala finally reports that "for certain she is dead, and by strange manner." In response Brutus seems outwardly unperturbed by the news, answering not as one would expect with "yes, I know" but with a staple of Stoic philosophy: "Why, farewell, Portia. We must die, Messala: / With meditating that she must die once / I have the patience to endure it now."

What sort of man is this? He is obviously distraught, inciting a meaningless quarrel with Cassius, but now he seems to be trifling with the sentiments of a loyal follower by adopting a pose of unconcern upon the receipt of devastating news. Admittedly, as a general he wants to convey the impression of confidence and composure to anxious subordinates on the eve of an impending battle, but with this pretense of stoic acceptance one must wonder if he has become dehumanized by his ideals. His response at any rate has the desired effect on Messala: "Even so great men great losses should endure."

Subsequent events imply that Brutus is not so unaffected by the loss of Portia as he attempts to project. A shadow of fatalistic sadness seems to descend upon him as he turns his attention to the coming campaign. The first implication is another debate with Cassius over their strategy in the face of the advancing forces of Antony and Octavius. Cassius proposes that they conserve their strength by conducting a delaying operation to wear down the enemy,* but Brutus insists that the moment is ripe for an immediate confrontation. He argues strategy and then adds the weight of philosophy:

There is a tide in the affairs of men
Which taken at the flood leads on to fortune;
Omitted, all the voyage of their life
Is bound in shallows and in miseries.

---

*Cassius proposes what is known as the "Fabian defense," named for Quintus Fabius Maximus, who wore down the army of Hannibal in 217 B.C. with such a strategy.

Brutus as usual prevails, and there is nothing in the play to indicate that his strategy is faulty, except, of course, for the fact that they suffer defeat in the battle. But the scene leaves the unmistakable impression that Brutus is so disheartened by Portia's death that he simply wants the question of victory or defeat quickly decided one way or the other. It is as if, compared to her loss, he finds their cause of small consequence—he just wants the matter settled.

This impression is enhanced by the atmosphere that pervades the parting of Brutus and Cassius once the decision has been reached. They bid each other a moving farewell in which they both seem resigned to defeat. Cassius observes that "If we do lose this battle, then is this / The very last time we shall speak together," and Brutus replies that "Whether we shall meet again I know not. / Therefore our everlasting farewell take." It is a well-known adage that whether it be in sports, or commerce, or war, the side that enters competition with thoughts of losing, invariably does.

And so it happens here. Cassius, mistakenly interpreting a scene reported to him as a sign of defeat, takes his own life; and Messala has the final word on his death: "Mistrust of good success hath done this deed." Brutus responds to the sight of the corpse with stoic reserve. "I shall find time, Cassius, I shall find time" to mourn the loss, he says, but for the moment he must return to the battle.

That battle lost, Brutus searches among his men for someone to help him end his life, but as one replies for them all, "That's not an office for a friend, my lord." Finding one willing at least to hold his sword, he impales himself upon it, his final words implying that, in balance, his death is only just: "Caesar, now be still: / I killed thee not with half so good a will."

Our sympathy for this great, good man is impaired by the impression that his virtues tend to cloud his common sense. We admire his honesty, his idealism, and his high-minded devotion to his country, but we cannot help but feel that he is perhaps too ready to proclaim his moral probity. He is given to self-serving utterances, such as "I love / The name of honour more than I fear death," "I am armed so strong in honesty," and as he approaches death, "My heart doth joy that yet in all my life / I found no man but he was true to me"; and his display of stoic composure to Messala is too obviously a pose. Only his wife is able to penetrate that surface of imperturbable reserve to touch the core of human vulnerability at the center of his being, and her death leaves him adrift in a despair that his philosophy cannot answer to. He is indeed "the noblest Roman of them all," in the words of Antony's moving epitaph, but in the final analysis that is precisely his problem.

# CAESAR

*"But I am constant as the northern star."*

SHAKESPEARE'S *Julius Caesar* has more to say about Brutus and Mark Antony than Caesar himself, since he is assassinated less than halfway through the play, but any work that includes him as a significant character must, it seems, have his name in the title. This is not to say that he disappears as a presence in the play, since his body is in view for some time, he appears briefly as a ghost later, and he remains in the thoughts and on the tongues of the other figures for the balance of the performance. But none of these instances add to the impression we receive during the early scenes, except to confirm that he was much loved by some of the Roman people and greatly feared by others.

In effect, Shakespeare's Caesar is more of a caricature than a character. Of course, his death is legendary, and it is safe to say that the patrons of the Globe were well aware of how he died and even why, as are just about all modern theatergoers well before they take their seats. Shakespeare plays upon that knowledge, filling the early scenes with dramatic irony in anticipation of the event. But Caesar is portrayed as a one-dimensional character, a pompous, overbearing, self-important, and at times comic figure, whose death, however dramatic and visually gory it may be, seems unlikely to impress a playgoer as tragic.

Caesar is enormously popular with ordinary Roman citizens. His first appearance is preceded by a scene in which the tribunes, the people's voice in the Senate, who have little affection for him, scold a group of commoners that has assembled in excited anticipation of a sight of him in public procession. Each time we see him in the streets of Rome he is surrounded by adoring retainers who have to clear a path for him through a jostling crowd, eager for a glimpse of the great man. He seems to bask in his popularity, sublimely assured that he is loved by all—except, that is, for Cassius. In a glimpse of the political acumen that has brought him to the pinnacle of power in Rome, he confides in Antony that he mistrusts such men as Cassius, who have "a lean and hungry look." They are "never at heart's ease," he explains, "whiles they behold a greater than themselves, / And therefore are they very dangerous."

Caesar is ambitious. With the death of Pompey he has emerged as the sole dictator of Rome, and members of the Senate fear that he aspires to be elevated to the prestige of a king. Shakespeare does not elaborate on the political implications of that office—that is, to what degree it would enhance Caesar's powers beyond those he already has as dictator—but the senators are obviously convinced that were he to assume a crown, he will prove tyrannical and undermine the traditional authority of the Senate. Cassius is especially concerned:

> Why, man, he doth bestride the narrow world
> Like a Colossus, and we petty men
> Walk under his huge legs and peep about
> To find ourselves dishonourable graves.

The noble Brutus decides to join the conspiracy, not because he is convinced that Caesar will necessarily abuse his powers but simply because of the possibility that he might.

Caesar has a flair for the dramatic gesture. We hear of a scene he stages in the Forum, where before a cheering crowd he refuses the offer of a crown when it is offered to him symbolically three successive times. In another instance, on his way to the Senate on that fateful day, Artemidorus attempts to deliver a letter to him warning of the conspiracy. Artemidorus presses it upon him, insisting that "mine's a suit / That touches Caesar" personally; but, seizing upon the occasion to play again to the crowd, he dismisses the letter, declaring that his first concern is the public good and "what touches us ourself shall be last served."

In a single long scene we are afforded an insight into the private man, only to find that the private Caesar acts and sounds much like the public one. In the early morning hours of the Ides of March, Caesar's wife, Calphurnia, awakens him with an account of her dream, which presages terrible things for him. She begs him not to attend the Senate on that day, but he is adamant, answering her imperiously, "Caesar shall go forth; for these predictions / Are to the world in general as to Caesar." The first thing that strikes us is that even when talking to his wife in the privacy of their home, he refers to himself by his name, rather than the more customary and personal "I."* He speaks to her as if he were addressing the Senate and follows his announcement with a bit of philosophical bluster: "Cowards die many times before their deaths; / The valiant never taste of death but once." The entire episode is ludicrous. He is not speaking to a crowd of impressionable citizens; this is an intimate conversation held between a man and his wife while they are standing about in their nightgowns!

Caesar takes the precaution of consulting the priests, however, who return with the disturbing news that they have examined the organs of a sacrificial animal and found that it had no heart. Swayed by this ominous sign and his wife's further entreaties, Caesar changes his mind and decides to "stay at home."

Decius, one of the conspirators, enters, his mission to ensure that Caesar will be present in the Senate house on that day, and he is confronted with their intended victim's troublesome decision to absent himself from the session. Asking his reason, Decius receives the peremptory reply, "The cause is in my will: I will not come; / That is enough to satisfy the senate." But Caesar goes on to confide in Decius that his wife has had a dream in which "she saw my statua, / Which like a fountain with an hundred spouts / Did run pure blood," and he has decided to stay at home to calm her fears. Decius tempts him deviously with the news that "the senate have concluded / To give this day a crown to mighty Caesar," and he asks how it would look to them if he is not present to receive the honor simply because his wife has bad dreams. Will they wonder perhaps if "Caesar is afraid"? The challenge to his vanity and his valor is enough; Caesar commands: "Give me my robe, for I will go."

---

*One can readily imagine the reaction of a modern wife faced with a husband who announces, "Jones must leave for work" or "Johnson will have his dinner now."

The scene is ironically comic in tone, conveying the image of a pompous, self-righteous Caesar, blinded by his exalted concept of himself, easily manipulated by a superstitious belief in omens, by the pleading of his wife, and finally by the subtle appeal to his honor and ambition. That same tone pervades his later meeting with the senators, though the occasion is more ominous. Caesar doesn't sound much different in the stately dignity of the Senate house than he did speaking to his wife in his nightgown. One senator kneels before him to petition for the return of his banished brother, and Caesar dismisses him disdainfully: "These couchings and these lowly courtesies / Might fire the blood of ordinary men," he proclaims, but not him. "I could be well moved, if I were as you," he continues, "but I am constant as the northern star" and like it am "unshaked in motion." Thus asserts the man whom we have just witnessed change his mind twice within minutes. His haughty demeanor lends substance to the senators' fears that he will abuse his powers if elected king. So they murder him to end that threat—in vain as it happens, for they have yet to deal with Mark Antony.

This is the last we see of Caesar, alive at any rate, and it cannot be said that he ever arouses our sympathy. We never pierce that imperious surface to catch a glimpse of the man himself, though we do hear of his weaknesses from others. Cassius, for example, in his attempt to enlist Brutus, dwells at length on Caesar's vulnerability, describing occasions when he saved him from drowning and saw him helpless with fever; and, again from others, we learn that he is subject to epileptic fits, the "falling-sickness," as it was called. He may indeed be but a man, but we never witness the human dimension of the character, and so his death, however dramatic, is not likely to strike us as tragic.

# CALIBAN

*"You taught me language, and my profit on't
Is, I know how to curse."*

THE MEDIEVAL WORLD embraced a system of belief that conceived of all existence arrayed in a divinely designed hierarchical order. God presided at the top, of course, and below him ranged the multitude of spiritual beings, several levels of angels, and farther down the countless unseen guardians of forest and sea. Next came the visible domain—mankind, animals and fishes, the lush greenery of plants and trees, and lastly the apparently lifeless minerals. It was a belief that prevailed into the eighteenth century, at least as an image in the poetry of the age.

At the boundaries of these various orders of existence were elements that seemed to possess qualities of those both above and below them, representing subtle transitions between levels. The oyster, for example, was clearly an animal, but like a plant it was rooted on underwater rocks and died when detached. Flying fishes could be observed as well as waterfowl that were at home on or beneath the surface; seals lived on both land and sea; bats retired to caves like burrowing creatures in daylight and took to the sky by night; and in the mineral world magnets were seen to have the power of attraction. The human imagination enlarged this catalogue with a variety of mythological figures, including the centaur, part man, part horse, and the harpy, who had the features of both a woman and an avaricious vulture. It would not have surprised people of the time, had they known, that the whale is a mammal or that certain flowering plants devour insects. All this, so went the belief, was part of God's intricate design of our infinitely varied world.

Modern science explores these same borders. Following Darwin's revolutionary discoveries in the mid-nineteenth century, evolutionary biologists speculated about the existence of a "missing link" between the human and animal worlds. Anthropologists today prod alluvial deposits in Africa's desert gullies in search of evidence to reveal when mankind first experienced the blossoming of conscious thought. And zoologists test chimpanzees and dolphins for signs of human intelligence.

Whether Shakespeare shared in these beliefs of his time we shall never know, but he drew on this popular perception in fashioning the character of The Tempest's Caliban. He is a complex figure, to whom we respond with a contradictory mixture of revulsion and sympathy, depending on what qualities of his character are evident at any single time. Some of these qualities may be seen as unique to the animal world. Others, we find, are common to both human and animal, blurring the boundary between the two levels of existence. Still others mark him as distinctly human. In many respects Caliban's human qualities are most in evidence, but their prominence may simply be a consequence of the dramatist's need to place before us on the stage a recognizable character, one that can at times utter moving poetry and act in ways familiar to a playgoer.

First, then, Caliban has character traits that identify him as a being who lives at a level below the human. In our very first impression of him, strikingly, he enters from a hole in the ground, like some burrowing animal emerging from his lair. The impression is enhanced when we learn that before the arrival of Prospero and the infant Miranda on this exotic island, he lacked language. Prospero reminds him that early in their exile, "I pitied thee, / Took pains to make thee speak"; at first, he goes on, he "wouldst gabble like / A thing most brutish [and] I endowed thy purposes / With words that made them known." Caliban acknowledges that Prospero "took pains" with him, teaching him "language" and how "to name the bigger light, and how the less, / That burn by day and night." It is possible that Caliban's "gabble" was another tongue, but Prospero identifies his "brutish" utterances as a sign that he did not "know thine own meaning."

Caliban pleads that when the two first arrived, he showed them "all the qualities o'th'isle, / The fresh springs, brine-pits, barren place and fertile"; and later, in an effort to engage the alliance of Trinculo and Stephano, the King of Naples's jester and his drunken butler, he promises to show them "the best springs: / I'll pluck thee berries: / I'll fish for thee." Pathetically, these are the only gifts he can offer to those whom he seeks to please, the simple animal's knowledge of the island's sources of food and water:

I prithee, let me bring thee where crabs grow;
And I with my long nails will dig thee pig-nuts,
Show thee a jay's nest, and instruct thee how
To snare the nimble marmozet.

Perhaps the most notable evidence of Caliban's lower nature is his response to Prospero's accusation that he "didst seek to violate / The honour of my child." He makes no effort to deny or justify the act. Instead he acknowledges his desire, unapologetically insisting that given the chance he would do it again: "O ho! O ho! Would't had been done! / Thou didst prevent me—I had peopled else / This isle with Calibans." His approach to Miranda, in brief, arose from an instinctive animal desire to procreate, and he sees nothing morally amiss in molesting a child held dear by his generous benefactor, whom he considers a god. Indeed, he is indignant at the restrictions Prospero imposes on him to prevent a recurrence, puzzled that he should be punished for such a natural act.

In the blurred boundary between the animal and human, Caliban displays qualities of both levels.* Most prominent, of course, is his physical appearance, which stage directors are at liberty to depict as their imaginations incline them. Stephano and Trinculo address him throughout only as "monster," and Alonso observes, "This is as

---

*Shakespeare exploits elsewhere the comic possibilities of these borderlands between the animal, human, and spirit worlds. In *A Midsummer Night's Dream*, Bottom is both donkey and man in his encounter with the forest fairies. And Falstaff, his head ridiculously adorned with deer antlers, is terrified when he is assaulted by what appear to be forest spirits, the citizens of Windsor disguised as fairies and elves.

strange a thing as e're I looked on." Shakespeare leaves the matter up to inventive costume designers, and to us, implying only that Caliban is indeed bizarre. Early productions depicted him as half-man, half-fish, based on allusions in the text that he "smells like a fish . . . a strange fish," a "debauched fish," and "a plain fish." In modern performances, however, he is often portrayed as a lower-order primate, a hairy figure, low browed, muscular, and near naked, one whose characteristic posture is a crouch, supporting himself at times on his knuckles.

Like both man and beast, he is territorial, complaining to Prospero that "this island's mine . . . which thou tak'st from me." And he is suspicious of learning: "You taught me language, and my profit on't / Is, I know how to curse: the red-plague rid you, / For learning me your language." Living on that contradictory cusp between mankind and animal, he has acquired the intelligence of the one only to find that he has been deprived of the placid oblivion of the other.

In any number of ways, however, Caliban is distinctly human. Prominently, of course, is the very fact that he can learn, assimilating Prospero's teaching of language and some elementary astronomy, the nature of "the bigger light" and the lesser. Further, he can conceive of a higher essence, though he confuses spiritual and corporeal beings. Prospero is more powerful, he realizes, than his primitive god Setebos, and he looks upon Stephano as a deity—"I prithee be my god"—though this may be the effect of the "celestial liquor" he has imbibed. He is nonetheless convinced that this "brave god" has "dropped from heaven."

Caliban has, in addition, an incipient social consciousness. He is angrily aware that he is kept subservient, forced by the threat of punishment with "cramps" and "pinches" to perform menial tasks: in Prospero's words, "he does make our fire, / Fetch in our wood, and serve in offices / That profit us." Caliban also displays some of the more malicious qualities of human nature: he can plot murder. Persuading Stephano and Trinculo to kill Prospero, he urges them sensibly "first to possess his books." In other respects, however, he is more benignly human, displaying, for example, a sensitivity to music. When, in response to the sound of Ariel's mysterious instruments, Stephano is momentarily cowed, Caliban attempts to reassure him:

> Be not afeared—the isle is full of noises,
> Sounds and sweet airs, that give delight and hurt not:
> Sometimes a thousand twangling instruments
> Will hum about my ears; and sometimes voices,
> That, if I had waked after long sleep,
> Will make me sleep again.

Some commentators detect in him the dawning of a moral consciousness. Rebuked by Prospero in the closing scene and ordered "Go, sirrah, to my cell [and] trim it handsomely," a contrite Caliban replies: "Ay, that I will: and I'll be wise hereafter, / And seek for grace. What a thrice-double ass / Was I, to take this drunkard for a god!" It has been suggested that his words imply a state of "redemption."

Despite Caliban's animal features and his all-too-human malice, it must be said that our revulsion is mixed with equal measures of sympathy. He is in effect a slave to Prospero, forced into servitude by the threat of physical punishment and reduced to labors that "profit" his master. In response to this image, some modern scholars suggest that the play represents Shakespeare's condemnation of slavery, his ideological testament against the practice. Perhaps. But as we see so often, Shakespeare is not concerned with taking a position on ideological issues. His avowed purpose in these plays is to "hold as 'twere a mirror up to nature," not to pass judgment on his characters; he presents them whole with all their blemishes and virtues. Prospero is not an unduly harsh master; he treated Caliban kindly at first, showing a certain fondness for the "monster." Caliban is reduced to service out of necessity, to protect Miranda's "honour," and in the end Prospero is merciful, forgiving the design on his life. It must be said, however, that the spectacle of forced labor is disturbing. We may not condemn those who harness a horse, an ox, or a camel to haul and plow in service of their "profit," but Caliban has so many marks of the human that we wish him free. And in the end, as the lords prepare to leave the island, we can rejoice that, like Ariel, he is.

We may wonder, however, again in sympathy, about the lasting effect of learning and language on Caliban. Before the arrival of the exiles he lived in an innocent state of nature, subsisting on crabs and berries, giving no thought to the daily movement of the bigger and the lesser light that divided his day from night. He was comfortable with his primitive god Setebos and a life that left him unconscious of a world beyond his island shores. Naples and Milan were unknown to him, places where the vicious lords of Italy scheme for advantage and murder without scruple. The island was a kind of Eden before Prospero and Miranda intruded upon it, bringing with them the corrupting knowledge of good and evil—and language taught him only "how to curse." What good will all this learning do him once they depart, leaving him troubled with the memory of wickedness and a power of speech for which in his solitude he will have no use?[*] We cannot help but sympathize with this innocent creature awakened now to the evil in the world. He was better off in his state of natural ignorance.

---

[*]It has been suggested that Caliban accompanies Prospero on his return to Milan, but the play is silent on the matter.

# CLAUDIUS

*"O, my offence is rank."*

THE NEWLY CROWNED KING of Denmark assumed the throne on the death of his royal brother by promptly marrying his widow, Queen Gertrude—this despite the existence of an able and popular prince, young Hamlet, the dead king's son and heir. The swift transition was precipitated by a number of factors, prominent among them the threat of an invasion by Norway, an emergency that immediately required a firm hand at the helm of the Danish state. Then too, the prince was absent at the time, pursuing his studies in Wittenberg. And not to be ignored is the implication of a close affectionate bond between the widow and her brother-in-law.

Hamlet arrives home to attend his father's funeral to find Claudius in command of the kingdom. Shakespeare leaves the sequence of events before the opening of the play necessarily vague; Hamlet himself is ambiguous about the timing, complaining at one point that the marriage took place when his father was "but two months dead, nay not so much, not two," and at another that it came only "a little month" after the funeral. The essential fact is that Claudius, not the prince, is king.

Once on the throne, Claudius gives the impression of an able, politic, and decisive ruler. Faced with the threat of an invasion by Fortinbras, he sends envoys to the King of Norway, requesting that he curb his headstrong young nephew, a strategy that, as it turns out, is entirely successful. Next he receives Laertes' request to return to his studies in Paris, and before granting the young man leave he courteously asks if he has his father's permission. The king then turns to Hamlet, whose persistent melancholy troubles both him and the queen. Offering stepfatherly counsel, he first calls it "sweet and commendable" that the son should mourn his father's death but chides him for persevering in his "unmanly grief." Observing that Hamlet is "the most immediate to our throne," he prefers, he says, that the prince remain in Denmark rather than return to Wittenberg.

Thus on first impression Claudius seems a competent monarch, presiding effectively over the kingdom's domestic and foreign affairs, and a concerned father dealing kindly with a sullen stepson. And, depending on the staging of the scene, he may be seen as an attentive husband, exchanging affectionate glances and gestures with the queen.* All is well, it would appear, in the state of Denmark. This impression is compromised later, however, when Hamlet and Horatio, awaiting the appearance of the ghost of the dead king on the ramparts of Elsinore castle, hear the sound of revelry in the court below. "The king doth wake to-night and take his rouse," Hamlet explains, a custom, he goes on disapprovingly, "more honoured in the breach than the observance." This is the only indication in the play that Claudius is anything other than a sober, responsible king. Once Hamlet hears the ghost's tale of his father's murder, he is understandably more virulent toward his stepfather. He later abuses his mother for her precipitous marriage, characterizing Claudius as "a murderer and a villain, a slave [and] a vice of kings, / A cutpurse of empire and the rule." We certainly cannot warm to Claudius, but nothing in the play, aside from Hamlet's tirades, depicts him as in any way dissolute or depraved.

Shakespeare withholds confirmation of the king's guilt until almost halfway through the play, when Claudius in an aside laments the "heavy burden" of his crime. In brief, the king has a conscience. Deeply disturbed after he witnesses the incriminating *Murder of Gonzago* (the play within the play), which depicts the murder, he retires to pray in private and in a soliloquy voices what is in effect a full confession:

> O, my offence is rank, it smells to heaven,
> It hath the primal eldest curse upon't,

---

*John Updike speculates about events before the play in his engaging and imaginative novel *Gertrude and Claudius*. He portrays a wife neglected by a distant, unfeeling husband, who is frequently absent on affairs of state. As a consequence she finds herself in the constant company of an attractive and attentive brother-in-law. Love blossoms.

A brother's murder. Pray can I not,
Though inclination be as sharp as will.

He fears that his desire for repentance will be to no avail—"O wretched state! O bosom black as death!"—but he kneels nonetheless, hoping that "all may be well." Hamlet steals upon Claudius and prepares to kill him; but, seeing him at prayer, he withholds his sword, reasoning that the king may be in a state of grace, a condition that would ensure his entrance into heaven while his father continues to burn in purgatory. No revenge there, he concludes, and passes on. Hamlet's concern proves groundless, for Claudius rises unrepentant, lamenting, "My words fly up, my thoughts remain below. / Words without thoughts never to heaven go."

So, having abandoned his soul, Claudius sets out to protect his life. In his schemes to murder Hamlet he is briskly decisive, in contrast to the prince, whose contemplative nature seems to render him powerless to act. Earlier, eavesdropping on Hamlet's abuse of Ophelia, the king perceives that he could present a danger to the court and promptly decides to send him to England. There is no indication that he intends harm to Hamlet at this stage; he simply wants him out of the way. Later events, however—the performance of *The Murder of Gonzago* and the murder of Polonius—alert him to the fact that the prince presents a danger to him personally, and it is then that he plots the prince's death. He promptly engages Hamlet's fellow students, Rosencrantz and Guildenstern, to accompany him to England, supplying them with sealed letters to the king there that order the prince's immediate death.

Thus Hamlet, because of his delay, has managed to signal his intentions. Both he and the king face the same challenge: How are they to do away with their adversary so as to avoid the charge that they are cold-blooded killers? Hamlet has only the word of the ghost that Claudius is a murderer, evidence that would carry little weight in a court of law or public opinion; and the king has only his political instincts to convince him that the prince is a danger to him, a judgment fed by Hamlet's violent behavior toward Ophelia and Polonius. The two of them, then, each aware that the other seeks his death, circle one another warily. They come face to face in a tense moment, during which Claudius informs Hamlet that he will leave immediately for England:

> *Hamlet.* For England.
> *King.*                                         Ay, Hamlet.
> *Hamlet.*                                                          Good.
> *King.* So is it if thou knew'st our purposes.
> *Hamlet.* I see a cherub that sees them.

When this scheme fails, Claudius quickly devises another, enlisting Laertes, who seeks vengeance for his father's murder, to engage Hamlet in a friendly duel. The king is politically astute. As he explains to Laertes, because of "the great love the general gender bear him," he realizes that he cannot move against the prince overtly. And there is another consideration: "The queen his mother / Lives almost by his looks" and "she is so conjunctive to my life and soul," he goes on, that he must not act in a way to arouse her suspicion. So Hamlet's death must seem an accident. Claudius leaves nothing to chance this time: in the duel Laertes will have "a sword unbated," that is, without the customary protective tip used in practice, so that "no wind of blame shall breathe upon" them. Laertes adds that he will poison the tip; and for good measure the king will offer Hamlet a poisoned cup of wine when the two pause between bouts. Thus Claudius devises successive schemes to eliminate Hamlet, this while the prince delays, pondering his options.

Claudius does not impress us as an outright villain. Murdering his brother was a treacherous act, to be sure, but *during the course of the play* he comes across as an able monarch, decisive and politically judicious. He is certainly ruthless, a necessary attribute in kings of the day, but his devious schemes to do away with Hamlet do not arise from any malice toward the prince, rather an instinct of self-preservation, another essential asset to a medieval monarch. Claudius senses that Hamlet intends to kill him, so the king attempts to kill the prince first.

Shakespeare takes few pains to explain why his villains are evil. He simply sets them before us in all their multicolored wickedness, confident that we will recognize them for what they are and not wonder too much how they got that way. His villains are moved by familiar passions—ambition, envy, lust—and they act in a manner appropriate to their twisted nature. We watch them plot their crimes, relish the outcome, manipulate others to provide the occasion, and then destroy their victims with stony unconcern for the suffering they inflict.

King Claudius is a departure from this pattern, however. As the play opens, his crime is behind him, so we do not witness the events leading up to and away from it, except in the stylized reenactment of the players. He can plot and manipulate, to be sure, as his schemes to eliminate Hamlet attest; but he does so to remove a threat to his life, not out of hatred or malice toward the prince. This villain comes before us, then, as an able king, decisive, resolute, resourceful, and at the same time as a stepfather who, outwardly at least, seems sincerely concerned about his son's state of mind, and a husband openly affectionate toward his wife. Shakespeare fashions a man whose public demeanor belies his secret gnawing guilt for the murder, a crime, moreover, that no one in Denmark, save for Hamlet and Horatio, suspects even took place—and the prince has only the ghost's word for it. Plagued by chronic indecision, Hamlet tests the ghost's legitimacy—"The spirit that I have seen / May be a devil, and the devil hath a power / T'assume a pleasing shape"— and, until just moments before his death, he is still questioning the justice of his cause: "Is't not perfect conscience / To quit him with this arm?"

Were Hamlet opposed by an absolute, unrepentant villain, his hesitation would be inexplicable. Thus Shakespeare lends credence to his indecision and delay by matching him with an antagonist who, in all respects other than the manner in which he came to the crown, appears to be a devoted husband and a competent ruler. As mentioned, we do not witness his crime, hence are less repulsed by his iniquity. We may not sympathize with Claudius, nor can it be said that his manifest qualities are in any way redeeming, but we can identify with him, since the character before us has many of the marks of a decent human being. Hamlet certainly doesn't see him as such, but the very ambiguity of the figure helps make credible to us the prince's frustrating inability to bring himself to avenge his father's death until the act is forced upon him.

# CLEOPATRA

*"Age cannot wither her, nor custom stale*
*Her infinite variety."*

THE QUEEN OF EGYPT is Shakespeare's portrait of the consummate woman, endlessly alluring, at once passionate and shrewdly calculating. Of course, on the Elizabethan stage she was portrayed by a prepubescent boy, suitably gowned and padded, so it was difficult for him to convey the depth of her passion and the appeal of her person. It is in the lines of Shakespeare's matchless poetry, as various characters record their impressions of her, that we learn of Cleopatra's legendary attraction. We catch the strength of Antony's enthrallment in his responses to her and in the frowning disapproval of his fellow Romans; but the chief source of our knowledge is the emperor's close friend and aide, Enobarbus. In the play he acts in the manner of a chorus, a trustworthy voice that guides us through the complex plot and describes the various characters with unerring insight.

Shakespeare's Cleopatra is a queen, but she is also an enchantingly sensual woman. She is, moreover, a woman in love[*] and in time must face a conflict between that love and her obligation to Egypt. As a queen she is a proud, imperious monarch, conscious of her heritage as the heiress of a centuries-long line of Ptolemy monarchs and devoted to maintaining her kingdom's independence within the Roman orbit. As such she is aware of the symbolic power of ceremonial display, and she has a flair for the dramatic gesture. Her theatrical command of the moment is evident both in her first meeting with Antony and in her last farewell, which we shall come to in due course.

[*]Or at least the age saw her as such. When John Dryden rewrote the play for performance some eighty years later, he entitled it *All for Love.*

When Enobarbus accompanies Antony to Rome, he finds himself a center of attention in a circle eager for firsthand accounts of the legendary opulence of the Egyptian court and its fabled queen. He warms to the task of describing that oriental splendor to down-to-earth Roman generals and begins with an account of how the famous couple first met. Antony had established a court at Cydnus in Asia Minor, where he called together all the monarchs of his domain to acknowledge him as their emperor. They dutifully appeared and were properly submissive—except for Cleopatra, who made a memorable entrance. She sailed up the river, Enobarbus explains, in a vessel that defies description:*

> The barge she sat in, like a burnished throne
> Burned on the water: the poop was beaten gold,
> Purple the sails, and so perfumed that
> The winds were love-sick with them: the oars were silver,
> Which to the tune of flutes kept stroke and made
> The water which they beat to follow faster,
> As amorous of their strokes.

Enobarbus is obviously enjoying himself as he goes on to picture Cleopatra herself:

> For her own person,
> It beggared all description, she did lie
> In her pavilion—cloth of gold of tissue—
> O'er-picturing that Venus where we see
> The fancy outwork nature.

And so on. Antony invited her to supper, but she suggested that he dine with her instead. He accepted, and the rest, as they say, is history.

Aside from her attraction as a reigning queen, Cleopatra is a sensuous, seductive woman who exudes an air of irresistible appeal. She had enmeshed Julius Caesar "in her strong toil of grace," bearing him a son, as well as Pompey the Great, who, she recalls with delight,

---

*Any attempt to describe the character of Cleopatra by paraphrase of Shakespeare's lines would do an injustice to her and to the poet, hence we must resort to quotations more so than usual in these pages.

"would stand and make his eyes grow in my brow." This appeal, as Enobarbus describes it, is paradoxical. He gives an account of seeing her once

> Hop forty paces through the public street;
> And having lost her breath, she spoke, and panted,
> That she did make defect perfection,
> And breathless, power breathe forth.

Further, Enobarbus goes on, Antony is not the only man he has seen fall under her spell: "For vilest things / Become themselves in her, that the holy priests / Bless her when she is riggish [wanton]." And indeed, it seems as if he is a bit in love with her himself. In famous lines he sums up her contradictory attraction:

> Age cannot wither her, nor custom stale
> Her infinite variety; other women cloy
> The appetites they feed, but she makes hungry
> Where most she satisfies.

Shakespeare portrays Cleopatra's hold over Antony in this same contradictory vein, as a woman in whom "the vilest things / Become." She attracts by contrarity. We first meet her in the company of Antony, who has received word of the arrival of a messenger from his fellow emperor, Octavius Caesar. The empire is threatened on all sides, by Parthian armies overrunning Asia Minor and the forces of Pompey's son encroaching on Rome itself, but Antony is reluctant to interrupt his Egyptian idyll to attend to matters of state and refuses to receive the messenger. Cleopatra, fearful that Caesar has called Antony to Rome, employs all her wiles to prevent his departure. She does so perversely, however, urging him to hear the messenger, in the process trivializing the message and ridiculing her lover as a man always at the beck-and-call of others: "Fulvia [Antony's wife] perchance is angry; or, who knows / If the scarce-bearded Caesar have not sent / His powerful mandate to you." The knife is in, she twists it: "That blood of thine / Is Caesar's homager; else so thy cheek pays shame / When shrill-tongued Fulvia scolds."

When Antony later shows signs that he will indeed answer the summons to Rome, Cleopatra sends her serving-woman, Charmian, to seek him out and "if you find him sad, / Say I am dancing; if in mirth, report / That I am sudden sick." Charmian chides her, advising that she should rather "in each thing give him way, cross him in nothing," to which Cleopatra replies sharply, "Thou teachest like a fool: the way to lose him." Shakespeare thus portrays Cleopatra as a woman who holds sway over her lover with a paradoxical combination of passionate attachment and deliberate perversity.

Her perversity has the desired effect for the moment. Antony declares grandly, "Let Rome in Tiber melt, and the wide arch / Of the ranged empire fall! Here is my space." Even in her petulant moods, he finds her endlessly enchanting:

> Fie, wrangling queen!
> Whom everything becomes, to chide, to laugh,
> To weep; whose every passion fully strives
> To make itself, in thee, fair and admired!

Nonetheless, on sober reflection Antony decides to return to Rome, and at his departure we catch sight of Cleopatra's love, a passion for him as deep as his for her. On hearing his decision, this "wrangling queen" scoffs at his love, accusing him of betrayal by returning to Fulvia. When, despite all her efforts, it appears that he is determined to leave, she abruptly changes tone to bid him farewell. But she finds herself incapable of voicing her dismay, stumbling over a love that is all but unutterable:

> Courteous lord, one word.
> Sir, you and I must part, but that's not it:
> Sir, you and I have loved, but there's not it:
> That you know well: something it is I would,—
> O! my oblivion is a very Antony,
> And I am all forgotten.

And once he is gone, she is beside herself, desolate at his absence:

> O Charmian!
> Where thinkest he is now? Stands he, or sits he?
> Or does he walk? Or is he on his horse?
> O happy horse, to bear the weight of Antony!

In a later scene we see another side of Cleopatra. This "enchant-ing queen" has a temper. In an effort to heal the breach between the two emperors, Antony, whose wife Fulvia has died in the interim, agrees to marry Caesar's sister Octavia. When an innocent messen-ger brings news of the marriage to Cleopatra, she flies into a rage and attacks the man, threatening to have him "whipped with wires, and stewed in brine." When he protests "I that do bring the news made not the match," she draws a knife and is prevented from killing him only when restrained by members of her court.

Consumed by curiosity, however, she calls the messenger back to describe Octavia. In the interim he has apparently been coached in how to address this queen, so when she asks, "is she as tall as me?" he answers that she is not; and when asked about the manner of her speech he replies that "she is low-voiced." Cleopatra is satisfied, con-cluding that Antony "cannot like her long" since she is "dull of tongue and dwarfish." Warming to his task, the messenger then re-ports that when Octavia walks it is as if "she creeps," that her face is "round, even to faultiness," her hair brown, and her forehead "low." Cleopatra is pleased, apologizes for her abusive behavior, and con-cludes, "I will employ thee back again: I find thee / Most fit for business."

Shakespeare's portrayal of a woman in love has another critical dimension, however. Cleopatra is a queen and Antony an emperor, powerful offices that inevitably complicate their life together. He apparently abandons her, after all, in the interest of imperial unity, and she must be ever conscious of the welfare of Egypt. In the dan-gerous world of ancient Rome, during a time when the empire is torn by civil wars, Cleopatra's position is perilous. The continuation of the long line of Ptolemy monarchs and the survival of the coun-try itself as an autonomous kingdom depend on the goodwill of Rome. And the fabled Egyptian treasury is a strong temptation for ambitious emperors under constant pressure to pay their widely scattered legions. Thus her hold over Antony assures her reign, and his departure for Rome and subsequent marriage to Octavia, while a disappointment in love, are also a threat to the security of Egypt.

The dramatic tension in the figure of Cleopatra arises from a conflict between her love for Antony and her devotion to Egypt. The two allegiances are not at odds in the early scenes when their love enhances the independence of her kingdom. But what will be her response when Antony is no longer in a position to ensure her reign? Which will prevail then, love or duty? Shakespeare provides no answers; he presents her as an enigma, so that we are never quite sure which prevails as the play proceeds. The poet raises the question in three later episodes when Antony's power is threatened and Cleopatra's motives are more ambiguous, episodes that are left unexplained in the poet's historical sources and remain so in the play.*

The first of these episodes occurs during the climactic sea battle between the forces of Caesar and Antony at Actium. Cleopatra accompanies Antony on the campaign, though Enobarbus rebukes her sternly for her presence, which he says will "take from his heart, take from his brain, from's time, / What should not then be spared." Shakespeare strongly implies that she influences Antony's ill-conceived decision to fight Caesar by sea rather than on land where he has a clear advantage. Despite his soldiers' urgent plea that he change the order, he remains adamant, prompting one of his captains to remark in dismay, "so our leader's led, / and we are women's men."

In the midst of the battle the Egyptian fleet, apparently at Cleopatra's command, abruptly hoists sail and deserts, dooming Antony to defeat. He impulsively abandons his navy and rushes after her.† They retreat to Alexandria, where he agonizes over what he perceives as her betrayal, not so much of his honor as their love. When he finally confronts her, she pleads her innocence: "O lord, my lord, / Forgive my fearful sails! I little thought / You would have followed." He replies, "you did know / How much you were my conqueror, and that / My sword, made weak by my affliction, would / Obey it on all cause." In the end, persuaded by her appeal for pardon, he submits: "Fall not a tear, I say; one of them rates / All that is won or lost. Give me a kiss; / Even this repays me."

---

*Shakespeare's chief source is Plutarch's *Parallel Lives of Greeks and Romans*. Antony and Cleopatra do in time marry and have children, though Shakespeare makes no mention of it or them until the closing scene and Cleopatra's "Husband, I come!"

†Roman historians disagree on the event. Dio Cassius insists that their flight was a contingency agreed upon before the battle. Shakespeare follows Plutarch.

Caesar pursues Antony on his retreat to Alexandria but is checked there by the city's defenses and a still defiant Antony, setting the stage for another of these ambiguous episodes. In an effort to divide his foes, Caesar sends an envoy, Thidias, to Cleopatra with instructions to promise her anything if she will abandon her husband. She hears Thidias out, not committing herself, and when on his departure he asks to kiss her hand, she graciously accepts the courtly gesture. Antony bursts upon the scene at that moment and, flying into a rage at the sight, he has Thidias whipped for, as he says, undue familiarity with "my playfellow, [her] hand." Suspecting duplicity, he accuses Cleopatra of flattering Caesar to ensure her safety and again of betraying their love. She pleads her devotion and once again he forgives her, though this time more curtly: "I am satisfied."

The third episode, like the others unexplained by Shakespeare or his historical sources, occurs during the final battle between Antony and Caesar. The Egyptian fleet on this occasion yields to Caesar and to make matters worse celebrates its surrender. Antony has no doubts now that Cleopatra has betrayed him, not only here but in the former episodes as well: "Triple-turned whore! 'tis thou / Hast sold me to this novice, and my heart / Makes only wars on thee." He vows to kill her, and she, hearing of his intent, meets the challenge with a device that has served her in the past. She sends word that she has taken her own life, and we recall her earlier, "If in mirth, report / That I am sudden sick." Here, however, the evasion has a tragic consequence as Antony, despondent over the loss of empire and now devastated by the death of his love, attempts to kill himself by falling on his sword. The wound, though ultimately fatal, leaves him alive, and he is borne to a final farewell with Cleopatra. At his death she laments that she still lives "in this dull world, which in thy absence is / No better than a sty," and that without him "there is nothing left remarkable / Beneath the visiting moon."

Cleopatra is not in such despair, however, that she is prepared to die for love. She had in her time, after all, enmeshed two emperors in the web of her allure, Julius Caesar and Antony, and captured the eye of the "great Pompey." So why not try her chances with yet another! Octavius Caesar is a different breed, however; he has but one goal in mind—the Roman Empire—and though not without compassion he has no taste for the erotic attractions of Egypt. The only temptation that Cleopatra offers is her treasury—and her person in captivity. He sees her as a means to add luster to his victory by parading her as a prisoner on his triumphal return to Rome, and his only concern is that she will defeat that design by taking her own life.

Caesar's troops force their way into Cleopatra's tower refuge in Alexandria and, as instructed, assure her of his goodwill. Before they meet, however, a sympathetic Roman informs her of Caesar's intention to display her as a trophy of war on his triumphal return to Rome, a knowledge that forms a backdrop to their eventual encounter. She is deceptively submissive to this "sole sir o'th'world" and he is full of courtly courtesy, but their exchange of mutual assurances is interrupted by a revealing incident. She gives him an accounting of her treasury, surrendering it to him; but her treasurer, who knows where his interests now lie, discloses that she has concealed half of it from him, retaining it for her own use. So, we may surmise, she has fully intended to survive and, confident of her allure, to persuade Caesar to retain her on the throne of Egypt. He dismisses the revelation as of no consequence and, assuring her of his "care and pity," takes his leave.

Cleopatra knows emperors, and she reads this one shrewdly: "He words me, girls, he words me, that I should not / Be noble to myself." Her thoughts now turn to her husband as she prepares herself for death: "Methinks I hear / Antony call; I see him rouse himself / To praise my noble act." She calls for her robes and crown so that she will appear in all her regal splendor when she meets him; and as she applies the fatal asp to her breast she affirms her love: "Husband I come: / Now to that name my courage prove my title." Caesar comes upon the death scene, observing that "she looks like sleep, / As she would catch another Antony / In her strong toil of grace"; and he directs that "she shall be buried by her Antony. / No grave upon the earth shall clip in it / A pair so famous." And indeed Shakespeare's words have proven prophetic. In all of history and legend there is no other "pair so famous."

Thus Antony's "enchanting queen," Shakespeare's picture, unequaled in literature, of the ultimately seductive woman. She is regal, passionate, volatile, manipulative, sensuous, and possessed of an irresistible allure. She is a woman in love but also a survivor, able to recover from her tragic loss to confront a new challenge to her person and her throne. In the end, unwilling to endure the humiliation of a disgraceful public display, she rejoins her husband in a final dramatic gesture of defiance at the forces that have robbed her of her love and her kingdom. We cannot fault, indeed must admire, Cleopatra for using her charms to retain her throne, and her love for Antony engages our full sympathy. The lingering irony of the play, however, is that the "infinite variety" that binds Antony to her is the very quality that distracts him from the affairs of empire, disarms the soldier in him, and leads in the end to the death of them both.

# CORIOLANUS

*"Would you have me / False to my nature?"*

CORIOLANUS is Shakespeare's portrait of the arrogant warrior. The opening scene sets the tone and introduces the three contending factions in the city of Rome. First we meet the common citizens. It is apparently a time of want, and they are insistent that, to feed the hungry people, the wealthy distribute the grain they are reputed to be hoarding for future profit. Resentful of the uncaring aristocracy, they are prepared to take the grain by force, and they focus their anger on the person of Caius Martius, the "chief enemy of the people," whom they intend to kill in the uprising.*

The second force in the city is the Senate, the ancestral governing body of Rome, its membership open only to the better families, those who by wealth or public service are said to merit seats. The exceptions to this oligarchic arrangement are the tribunes, elected by the people to look after their interests in the lofty body. The Senate is seen as a moderating influence in the play, represented in the opening scene by the aged Menenius, who attempts to placate the angry citizens with ineffectual argument and an obscure parable comparing the Senate to the human stomach.

The third force in the city is Coriolanus himself, who comes upon the scene spitting contempt for the citizens: "What's the matter, you dissentious rogues?" He goes on at some length, reviling them as "curs," "fragments," and "rats." "He that trusts you," he rages, "where he should find you lions, finds you hares; / Where

---

*He is not named "Coriolanus" until later in the first act, but for the sake of clarity we shall so call him from the outset. The tribunes refer to him only as "Martius."

foxes, geese." His tirade, which effectively silences the citizens, is interrupted by news that the Volces, troublesome enemies of Rome,
are in arms, and the Senate calls upon Coriolanus to defend the city.

The figure arouses little sympathy in an audience on first meeting; he seems a thoroughly unpleasant man. Shakespeare's tragic figures, we find, are torn by conflicting emotions, and Coriolanus
seems to have none; they are, moreover, brought low by some destructive flaw in their character, and he appears to have many. The
poet is invariably able to arouse sympathy for these figures by confronting them with choices familiar to any audience, those between
love and duty, reason and passion, and the like, and endowing them
with weaknesses endemic to humankind—Othello's jealousy, for example, or Macbeth's ambition. If there is a single prominent flaw in
the character of Coriolanus, it is his intemperate arrogance, evident
in his harshly intolerant contempt for his fellow citizens. Our first
response to him may well be the conviction that he richly deserves
any misfortune that fate may have in store for him.

Coriolanus is essentially a soldier, and Shakespeare portrays him
as a man who well deserves his reputation for unequaled courage and
martial prowess. In the war with the Volces he leads an assault on
the gates of their stronghold city of Corioli and is trapped alone
within its walls. He fights his way out and, inspiring the army by
his example, returns to take the city. Later, coming upon Roman
forces in full retreat, he rallies them to achieve a decisive victory, and
during the course of the battle he routs the formidable Volcian general, Tullus Aufidius, in single combat. In recognition of his valor,
the Roman commander, Cominius, announces that henceforth he
will be known as Coriolanus, after the city he has conquered.

As a soldier, Coriolanus has but one measure of a man, his bravery in battle, and he has good reason to question the martial quality
of the Romans. He finds himself alone within the gates of Corioli
because his soldiers fail to follow him, one protesting "Foolhardi-
ness, not I," and another echoing him, "Nor I." He comes upon Roman armies in timid retreat on two occasions and has to shame them
into standing against the Volcians, taunting them in one instance as
"you souls of geese / That bear the shape of men," and in another as
mice who "ne're shunned the cat as they did budge [flee] / From ras-

cals worse than they." Coriolanus scorns those who fall short of his devotion to Rome, admiring only those who "think brave death outweighs bad life, / And that his country's dearer then himself."

Coriolanus exhibits a contradictory mixture of pride and modesty about his achievements. When Cominius offers him a tenth part of the spoils taken during the conquest of Corioli, he refuses, declaring, "I cannot make my heart consent to take / A bribe to pay my sword," and he claims only the "common part" allotted to all. Later, when the Senate meets to elect him consul, he prefers to leave the chamber rather than sit and listen to praise of his deeds, his "nothings" as he calls them. He does not seek the consulship—"It is not mine own desire" he later says—but will accept it as his duty to Rome and as an honor appropriately bestowed because his service has merited it. And so this blunt soldier becomes enmeshed in the tangled politics of his native city.

While the Senate finds merit in Coriolanus, the common people see only menace. At first the citizens are divided over his election to consul, some arguing that he deserves it, others fearing he will prove despotic. The tribunes, Sicinius and Brutus, are unalterably opposed to the appointment, insisting that he despises the people and once in power will silence them, their advocates in the Senate. They plot to discredit him by challenging his fitness for the office, a tactic they are confident will incite him to intemperate remarks revealing his contempt for the baseness of the Roman people.

It is the custom in Rome that a candidate for consul, having received the full accord of the Senate, appear before the people to seek their approval as well, in the case of a deserving soldier to display the wounds he had received on their behalf. Coriolanus asks that he be excused from the ceremony, claiming that his service speaks for itself. To parade his wounds before the citizens, he says, would be to demean that service, the equivalent of showing "th'unaching scars which I should hide, / As if I had received them for the hire / Of their breath alone!" He finally agrees, however, but his haughty demeanor is such that the tribunes are able to arouse the citizens against him, persuading them to deny him the consulship.

The two civic forces of Rome now come into contention, focusing their efforts on Coriolanus. The Senate urges him to meet with

the people once more, but this time "to answer mildly." He reluctantly agrees but is faced by an aroused mob that has been incited
by the tribunes to refuse "a consul that will from them take / Their
liberties." He is incensed and replies with more abuse—"Thou
wretch" and "Hence, rotten thing!"—providing a pretext for the
tribunes to call for his arrest, prevented only when the senators rise
to his defense.

How came Coriolanus to this disdain for the people and his resolute devotion to Rome? The chief influence in his life is Volumnia,
a familiar figure in life and literature—the ambitious mother (there
is no mention of a father). She raised him, she declares proudly, to
be a soldier and "was pleased to let him seek danger where he was
like to find fame." "Had I a dozen sons," she proclaims, "I had rather
had eleven die nobly for their country" than have one shirk his duty.
When Coriolanus is injured in the repulse of the Volcians, she is
elated: "O, he is wounded; I thank the gods for't," and reports
proudly that before that engagement "he had twenty-five wounds
upon him." They are "large cicatrices [scars] to show the people,
when he shall stand for his place." One episode is illustrative of her
child-rearing practices: she remarks that she once observed the
young son of Coriolanus as he chased a butterfly, repeatedly captur-
ing and releasing it until finally in a fit he crushed it. The child's
impulsive cruelty confirms him in her eyes as truly his father's son,
showing promise of future greatness. Volumnia, aside from encouraging such behavior in her son, continually reviled the common citizens to impress him with his uniqueness. He recalls that she

> was wont
> To call them wollen vassals, things created
> To buy and sell with groats, to show bare heads
> In congregations, to yawn, lie still and wonder,
> When one but of my ordinance stood up
> To speak of peace and war.

From such instruction, Shakespeare implies, grew the low opinion
Coriolanus harbors for the people of Rome.

After his second disastrous encounter with the people, the sympathetic senators urge Coriolanus to yet a third; they entreat him to

return to the marketplace and address them with "a gentler spirit," apologizing for his behavior. He adamantly refuses, demanding of them, "Would you have me / False to my nature?" Volumnia enters and attempts to resolve the impasse. She scolds him for his stubbornness and argues at length that he should address the people with humility rather than jeopardize "your fortune and / The hazard of much blood." "I would dissemble with my nature," she insists, "where / My fortunes and my friends at stake required / I should do in honor." He remains determined—"I will not do't"— and she resorts to the time-honored appeal of a mother faced with grown sons and daughters who disregard her counsel. She accuses him of disrespect, ingratitude for her sacrifices on his behalf, and, most heinous of all, a failure to return the love she has lavished on him. In the face of his refusal she turns away, lamenting that "to beg of thee, it is my more dishonor" than it is for him to appeal to the people. "Do as thou list [please]," she concludes, as if to say, "you never listen to me anyway."

Stung by her dismissal, he reluctantly agrees; but he is unable to muster the necessary humility. Responding to the tribunes' inflammatory accusation that he has aspired to "power tyrannical" and is therefore "a traitor to the people," he lashes out at them. The charge of "traitor" is an egregious insult for a man who has fought for the freedom of Rome from an early age and bears wounds "two dozen odd" suffered in battles "thrice six" for his country, and Coriolanus responds in a rage: "the fires i'th'lowest hell fold in the people! / Call me their traitor, thou injurious tribune!" The citizens at first call for his death but in the end are satisfied with his banishment, and he leaves obsessed with a fierce desire to avenge the indignity.

Bent on revenge, he makes his peace with the Volcians, is greeted warmly by Aufidius, and leads their armies in a fresh attack on Rome, threatening to lay waste the city which, deprived of his leadership, appears to be defenseless. Various figures whom he respects plead with him to withdraw his forces, among them his old comrade-in-arms, Cominius, and his revered friend Maninius, all to no avail. Finally he is confronted with his wife, his young son, and his mother, who kneel before him and entreat him to relent. When he refuses, Volumnia adopts the same stance as before, the long-suffering mother neglected by her children. She attempts to shame him: "There's no man in the world / More loved to's mother, yet here he lets me prate / Like one i'th'stocks," and, she goes on, "thou hast never in thy life / Showed thy dear mother any courtesy." Once again she turns away in dismissal: "So we will home to Rome, / And die among our neighbors." An anguished Coriolanus finally relents but he is well aware of the consequences for him: "O mother, mother! / What have you done?" He withdraws his army and as a result is executed by the Volcians for, as Aufidius charges, "breaking his oath and resolution."

We can sympathize with Coriolanus on those occasions when he insists that he must be direct and honest about himself, however impolitic the stance may be. He is surrounded by those who present themselves falsely. The tribunes are one thing to the Senate and another to the people. They pretend deference to the senators while scheming to undermine their choice of consul. They plan to anger Coriolanus publicly—to "put him to choler"—and they rehearse the people on how to respond to their charges. The senators are concerned only with placating the citizens and urge Coriolanus to conceal his mistrust, to "speak to 'em fair." But he refuses to compromise his integrity, to be "false to [his] nature," thinking it dishonorable to conceal his true feelings under a cloak of humility. He would have them know him no matter how distasteful he may be to them and damaging to his candidacy for consul. It is of no consequence to him how imperious he may appear or threatening to their interests; he will offer himself to them only as the man he is. The fact that he is insufferably proud, arrogant, and openly contemptuous of the common people notwithstanding, that is in effect who he is, and he thinks it dishonest to present himself as anything other. Ironically, "who he is" precludes him from serving his country in any role other than that of a soldier.

Shakespeare portrays a man instilled with a narrow concept of devotion to his country, one limited to martial duty. He is dedicated to the service of his country, but "Rome" to him is a lofty abstraction, one that does not seem to include its citizens, who quite rightly claim that "the people are the city." True, he lived in a time when Rome was surrounded by enemies and its survival depended on the martial prowess of its people; but Coriolanus has scant sympathy for, or understanding of, the other civic values that enrich a society: concern for the people, respect for their rights, and the need to include them in the dynamics of governing. His elevated sense of duty is as shortsighted as the citizens' fearful self-interest.

Shakespeare is as critical in this play as he is in others of the people as a mob, easily swayed from one side to the other by whoever speaks to them last. Neither an intransigent Coriolanus nor the malleable people come across as entirely admirable in the play, and the Senate is again, as it is so often in Shakespeare, a hotbed of cold feet. Indeed, the only figures that arouse our admiration are the ancient Menenius, who seems a throwback to a more civilized time, and the generous Cominius, who manages to strike a wise balance between the soldier and the civil servant. Coriolanus falls victim to his own nature, a tragic martyr to a militant code, when he is confronted in the end by the mother who shaped him to it.

It is illuminating to compare the figure of Coriolanus to Henry V, another famous soldier portrayed by Shakespeare some years earlier, for the two have much in common. Both are valiant warriors and inspiring leaders who achieve victory over a formidable foe. Both lead an assault against a city, the one through the gates of Corioli, the other into a breach in the walls of Harfleur. Coriolanus is left stranded by his soldiers, and in response to Henry's rousing speech urging "Once more into the breach, dear friends," we see the reluctant soldiers of his Boar's Head days scrambling to avoid the battle. Both fight against daunting odds, Coriolanus in the streets of Corioli and Henry at Agincourt, where the French outnumber him five to one. Both dismiss soldiers unwilling to fight, Coriolanus who selects only those that think "his country's dearer than himself," and Henry who offers free passage home to those that "hath no stomach to this fight." Neither covets power. Coriolanus does not desire the consulship, and Henry regrets that he must in time assume the crown, both looking upon high office as a duty.

The crucial difference between the two is the contrast in their sympathy toward the common people. Coriolanus, having engaged in "thrice six" battles for Rome, has nothing but scorn for the citizens who shirk their duty, while Henry in his youth has consorted with the lowly tenants of Eastcheap and there developed a respect for and understanding of his ordinary English subjects. This difference lies at the heart of their separate fates: the one is a dishonored warrior, the other a triumphant king.

# EDMUND

*"Now, gods, stand up for bastards!"*

AS THE ILLEGITIMATE SON of the Earl of Gloucester, Edmund has an unpromising future. In the opening scene of *King Lear*, his father introduces him to the Earl of Kent with the dismissive remark that "He hath been out nine years, and away he shall again." Gloucester goes on rather thoughtlessly to assure Kent that Edmund's mother was "fair; there was good sport in his making, and the whoreson must be acknowledged." He has another son, he goes on, who is legitimate but "yet is no dearer" to him than Edmund. In this brief exchange, then, we learn that Gloucester in his rough way is fond of Edmund; and though an illegitimate son has no claim to his father's fortunes, the earl provides for him generously, preferring, however, that he keep his distance from the ancestral home.

Edmund is unfailingly courteous and respectful to his elders, and we cannot assess his response to his father's insensitive remarks until later, when he voices his thoughts in a revealing soliloquy. He complains about his status, questioning why he should "stand in the plague of custom" since he is as much his father's son as his brother Edgar. "Why bastard? Wherefore base?" he asks indignantly. He does not, however, look upon his father with rancor, nor does he seem jealous of Edgar. He holds no grudges; he simply wants to improve his prospects, and the most practical means of doing so is to discredit his brother in his father's eyes. He states his purpose with unapologetic directness—"Legitimate Edgar, I must have your land"—and he ends lightheartedly with a prayer, part in earnest, part in jest: "Now, gods, stand up for bastards!"

Edmund emerges as a thoroughly engaging villain who captures our interest, though not necessarily our approval, because of his single-minded determination to advance his fortunes. As each opportunity presents itself he quickly seizes it, unmindful of the harm he may inflict on others, but again without malice toward any of his victims. Each of them unfortunately stands in his way, an obstacle to his ambition, and therefore must be eliminated. And with each success and each new opportunity, his ambition mounts. He cuts his way to the top, greeting each occasion for villainy with a cavalier air of surprise and delight.

Edmund has to devise a scheme, of course, to acquire "legitimate Edgar's" land, but a gullible father and an ingenuous brother who are readily deceived by his devices make his task easy. Displaying as evidence a forged letter and a self-inflicted wound, he convinces his father that Edgar is plotting to kill him so as to inherit his title and wealth. The young man is forced to flee when Gloucester orders him captured and put to death. The distraught father then turns to his sole remaining son, promising that he will "work the means / To make thee capable," that is, to designate him as his heir. So far, so good.

A brief exchange of views between father and son offers a glimpse of Edmund's philosophical guides. Gloucester has just returned from the tumultuous scene where Lear angrily disowns Cordelia and divides his kingdom between his other daughters, Goneril and Regan, and the earl detects an ominous pattern to the discord in his own family and that within the royal court: "There's son against father . . . there's father against child." To his mind, schooled in the belief in a divine order of the universe, this disruption of family bonds on earth can be traced to unnatural events in the heavens, to "these late eclipses in the sun and moon," which he fears, "portend no good for us." Edmund outwardly agrees with his father, but once the earl has taken his leave, he privately scoffs at his quaint notions:

> This is the excellent foppery of the world, that, when we are sick in fortune, often the surfeit of our own behaviour, we make guilty of our disaster the sun, the moon, and the stars. . . . Fut, I should have been that I am, had the maidenliest star in the firmament twinkled on my bastardizing.

In what has every appearance of a generational divide, the son rejects the father's adherence to traditional teaching, preferring to think that as an autonomous being he is entirely responsible for his own destiny. He professes, in brief, a more modern view of history, a practical, materialistic philosophy that rejects any role for the otherworldly in human affairs. Shakespeare offers both sides of this ancient controversy, here and elsewhere in his plays. In *Henry IV, Part 1*, Hotspur scoffs in a similar vein at Owen Glendower's insistence that at his birth marvelous manifestations of his future greatness appeared in the heavens and on earth. And Cassius refuses to attach any importance to the strange sights that trouble his fellow Romans on the night before Caesar's death. We can only speculate where Shakespeare stood on the issue, but it is possibly significant that all three—Edmund, Hotspur, and Cassius—fall in the end.

An unexpected opportunity for advancement comes Edmund's way when he intercepts a letter his father has received informing him that Cordelia is en route with a French army to rescue Lear. Edmund reveals the letter to the Duke of Cornwall, confirming in effect that his father is in collusion with the enemy, a betrayal that costs the earl his eyes and eventually his life. But it also enhances Edmund's prospects. As a consequence of his father's apparent defection, Cornwall designates him Earl of Gloucester. He is now in possession of not only Edgar's "land" but his father's as well.

Then, in another unanticipated turn of events, Edmund discovers that both of Lear's treacherous daughters have fallen in love with him. He is bemused by their passion for him, jauntily relishing his good fortune while caring little which of them he chooses, since either will bring him power and riches. Regan would seem to have the better claim since she is widowed, Cornwall having been killed by a servant outraged at the duke's cruelty in gouging out the eyes of Gloucester. But the ravenous Goneril has a device of her own, a scheme to rid herself of her husband, the Duke of Albany. She writes to Edmund, proposing that he arrange for the duke's death during the battle with the French. This promising prospect fades, however, as Edmund's designs begin to unravel. Goneril poisons Regan, and when her plot to dispose of her husband is discovered, she kills herself.

Edmund assumes command of the English forces, and his victory over the French provides him with a final fortuitous opportunity to mount still higher. He has captured Lear and his daughter Cordelia, the last surviving members of the royal family. Disposing of them will leave him the most powerful figure in the kingdom, save only for the singularly unwarlike Duke of Albany. The prospect proves too tempting to resist, so he orders their execution, not again from any animosity toward them but simply because they stand in his way.

Edmund is finally defeated in a ceremonial "trial by combat," an episode that brings to mind his earlier disdain for his father's belief in a supernatural influence in human affairs. It was a conviction of the time that in a contest of arms, God would favor the side whose cause was just. Should two men bring charges against each other, in the absence of evidence on either side, it was said, a trial of mortal combat between them would reveal which one was truthful, since God would surely not permit a liar to prevail.

A fully armored figure enters the scene, his identity hidden by his helmet. In a formal, ritual recital of charge and countercharge, he accuses Edmund of treason, and the two clash in a struggle that leaves Edmund fatally wounded. His opponent reveals himself as his wronged brother Edgar, who voices judgment on him: "The gods are just, and of our pleasant vices / Make instruments to plague us." So justice is served as Edmund falls, a victim of his own iniquity, though in a larger sense his fate is an ironic answer to his ridicule of Gloucester's belief in the role of the heavens in human affairs. But justice is not for all. As he lies dying, Edmund experiences a sudden spur of deathbed remorse—"Some good I mean to do, / Despite of mine own nature"—and he confesses to ordering the death of Lear and Cordelia, urging Edgar to prevent the execution. He is too late, however; Cordelia has been hanged, and her father dies of grief at her loss.

Edmund is not evil in the same way that Iago and Richard III are evil, gloating over the destruction of those they hate or envy. Certainly he schemes to discredit his brother, but afterward he simply plays the hand that fortune deals him, often in surprised delight at the opportunities that come his way. He is not malicious, nor does he revel in his wickedness. He pursues his goals with a care-free, almost casual air in a spirit of "nothing ventured, nothing gained" until his final defeat, when he accepts judgment on his deeds and in a last redemptive gesture attempts to remedy the wrongs he has caused. Edmund is not a likeable figure by any means, but we cannot entirely condemn his spirited efforts to break the mold in which "the plague of custom" confines him, nor can we unreservedly fault his determination to assert his individual worth. Shakespeare has once again given us a villain for whom we can summon a measure of sympathy.

# ENOBARBUS

*"That truth should be silent I had almost forgot."*

ENOBARBUS PLAYS a number of roles in *Antony and Cleopatra*. As a Roman soldier, he serves as Mark Antony's friend, counselor, and lieutenant. At times he acts as a detached observer who stands off from events and comments wittily, often ironically, on them. In this respect he acts much in the manner of a chorus, guiding our response to the shifting alliances, ambitions, and emotions of the figures who shape the unfamiliar world of pre-Augustan Rome. His analysis of characters informs our understanding, especially in his eloquent lines describing the captivating allure of Cleopatra.

Enobarbus is a sympathetic companion to Antony, accompanying him in his Alexandrine revels. When we first see him, he seems a worldly man, a bit decadent himself, agreeably comfortable in the opulent court of Cleopatra and obviously at ease with her handmaids and servants, joining them in their erotically witty banter. Although Antony's captains deplore their emperor's passionate attachment to the Egyptian queen, Enobarbus seems to find it mildly amusing. When Antony confides in him that he is determined to return to Rome, Enobarbus advises lightheartedly against it. Were he to do so, he responds with witty irony, "then we kill all our women," that is, they will proclaim pitifully that in the men's absence they will die. Cleopatra especially, he says, on "catching but the least noise of this, dies instantly"; and when an exasperated Antony declares his wish that he had never met her, Enobarbus replies, "O, sir, you had then left unseen a wonderful piece of work." Antony reveals that his wife, Fulvia, has died, and the pragmatic Enobarbus counsels that he is now free to marry Cleopatra; but, intent now upon departure, Antony dismisses his lieutenant's levity: "No more light answers."

Before the battle of Actium, Enobarbus, acting again as his emperor's friend and counselor, takes it upon himself to rebuke Cleopatra for accompanying her lover on the campaign, warning her that her "presence needs must puzzle Antony; / Take from his heart, take from his brain, from's time / What should not then be spared." And he joins the other captains in pleading with Antony to abandon his plan to challenge Caesar by sea, a strategy urged by Cleopatra, rather than on land where his forces have the advantage. After the defeat Enobarbus remains loyal, though, as he admits, his reason counsels against it: "I'll yet follow / The wounded chance of Antony."

Enobarbus, though a minor figure in the play, is an engaging and perceptive voice, guiding, choruslike, our response to various characters and often confirming with ironic accuracy our judgment of unfolding events. When Caesar and Antony meet in an effort to resolve their differences in the face of Pompey's threat to Rome, Enobarbus reminds them, with undiplomatic candor, that once Pompey is disposed of they will "have time to wrangle" once again. Antony commands him to hold his tongue, and he responds ironically, "That truth should be silent I had almost forgot." When Antony agrees to marry Caesar's sister Octavia, a union designed to cement the tenuous amity between the two emperors, Enobarbus predicts to others that the marriage will have the opposite effect. "Octavia is of a holy, cold, and still conversation," he observes, and in time Antony "will to his Egyptian dish again," thereby angering Caesar and enflaming the dissension between the two proud men. And this, of course, is exactly what happens.

In later scenes Enobarbus can only comment wryly on Antony's fading fortunes. Watching Cleopatra's courteous reception of Caesar's envoy, Thidias, he is convinced that she means to betray her husband: "Sir, sir," he mutters to himself, "thou art so leaky / That we must leave thee to thy sinking, for / Thy dearest quit thee." This is a troubling observation. To this point Enobarbus has been a trustworthy voice, one that we have come to rely upon for insight into the motives and qualities of the principal characters. Could he possibly be right about Cleopatra's intentions here? Witnessing the reconciliation of the lovers and Antony's vaunted resolve to continue the fight against Caesar's vastly superior forces, he concludes that "a diminution of our captain's brain / Restores his heart," and he decides to "seek / Some way to leave him." He crosses into Caesar's camp, where, struck with sorrow at his betrayal, he dies of remorse with a final plaintive cry: "O Antony! O Antony!"

The most memorable of Enobarbus's lines, and perhaps of the entire play, are those in which he describes the fascinating attraction of Cleopatra. On Shakespeare's stage, of course, she was played by a "squeaking" boy (Cleopatra's scornful phrase), who no matter how artfully gowned and padded could not hope to project the legendary allure of a queen who dazzled three emperors, Pompey, Julius Caesar, and Mark Antony, bearing children by the latter two. Antony describes her as a woman "whom every thing becomes, to chide, to laugh, / To weep," and Enobarbus echoes his words in his account of her paradoxical appeal. He once saw her running through the street, he tells a group of spellbound Roman captains, "and having lost her breath, she spoke, and panted, / That she did make defect perfection, / And, breathless, power breathe forth." "Age cannot wither her," he continues, "nor custom stale her infinite variety"; other women may

cloy

The appetites they feed, but she makes hungry
Where most she satisfies: for vilest things
Become themselves in her, that the holy priests
Bless her when she is riggish [wanton].

Thus Enobarbus, with his acute asides and penetrating irony, clarifies the rivalries and alliances that determine the destiny of the Roman Empire, and he defines the passions of those who aspire to rule it. He knows Antony well and has an intuitive appreciation for Cleopatra's hold on him, insofar, that is, as anyone can fathom her contradictory appeal. For all his worldly cynicism, however, he is a man in turmoil, torn between loyalty to his friend and emperor and dismay at the man's self-destructive infatuation for the Egyptian queen. In the end he betrays Antony's trust and dies lamenting the loss.

# FAIRIES AND WITCHES

AMONG Shakespeare's contemporaries there prevailed a widespread belief in supernatural forces at work, for good or ill, in human affairs. In his plays, gods descend to earth and lesser spirits—fairies, elves, and witches—inhabit forbidden places—the deep forests, isolated islands, and desolate heaths of the earth. When these creatures come in contact with human beings, they use their strange powers as their fancy directs to work mischief or outright harm, often for motives that defy understanding. They can change shape, appear and disappear suddenly, and lurk in dark corners to await unsuspecting victims. People of the time attributed to them the inexplicable accidents of everyday life—a dropped dish, a lost hammer, or a stool mysteriously displaced so as to trip up its owner—as well as more serious mishaps that could cause bodily harm—the weakened step of a ladder or a tree's falling branch. Such things happen, hence, it was thought, something or other is causing them to happen. Shakespeare's otherworldly figures come in a variety of shapes and sizes, prominently among them the fairy kingdom of *A Midsummer Night's Dream*, the elusive Ariel of *The Tempest*, and Macbeth's malignant witches.

## Oberon and Titania

*"Think no more of this night's accidents
But as the fierce vexation of a dream."*

The king and queen of the fairies in *A Midsummer Night's Dream* are engaged in a marital dispute. Titania has abandoned her husband's "bed and company," and Oberon is indignant: "Am I not thy lord?" They are at odds over possession of a little changeling boy, that is, a human who has crossed into their world.* The two realms were said to intermix at times, and the boy is the son of a human mother whom Titania had befriended before she died, leaving him in the queen's care. Oberon wants him as a member of his own court, and Titania refuses to surrender him.

The quarrel between the powerful fairies, as Titania explains, has had a devastating effect on the lives of humans. Because of their discord, the winds "have sucked up from the sea / Contagious fogs," causing floods on land, rotting crops, "rheumatic diseases," and other hardships. Summer has turned to winter and spring to fall "from our debate, from our dissension." Oberon is determined to have the boy, however, and plans to "torment" Titania with the magic properties of "a little western flower," whose juice, if dropped on sleeping eyelids, will cause the victim on awaking to fall in love with the first creature to come in view.

Oberon anoints Titania with the juice of the flower, and his servant Puck arranges for a suitable figure to greet her when she opens her eyes. Coming upon the simple weaver Bottom in the forest, Puck replaces his head with that of an ass, and Titania wakens to dote on the monster, much to the bemusement of Bottom, who is unaware of his transformation, and to the delight of Oberon. The prank has the desired effect, for Titania is so besotted with Bottom that she becomes indifferent to the changeling boy and readily surrenders him to her husband, with the result that concord returns once more to the fairy kingdom. Fortunately, Oberon has an antidote to the flower's charm, and, gazing sympathetically on Titania and Bottom asleep wrapped in each other's arms, he decides to release them from the charm in such a way that they will "think no more of this night's accidents / But as the fierce vexation of a dream." Titania awakens, puzzled that she had been "enamoured of an ass," and Bottom is restored to his former shape, waking in bewilderment at what he can only conceive of as a marvelous dream.

Thus the fairies do not intentionally distress humans, though their tricks and pranks may cause consternation among them. Indeed,

---

*When a child inexplicably disappeared, it was often thought to have been stolen by the fairies.

they often show compassion for hapless humans, a concern that may again cause more trouble than it cures. Oberon takes pity on four young people who wander into the forest. Two lovers, Demetrius and Hermia, take refuge there, pursued by Lysander, who also loves Hermia. But Lysander is in turn pursued by Helena, whose love he harshly rejects. A sympathetic Oberon sends Puck to anoint the sleeping Lysander with the magic flower's juice so that he will awake and, seeing Helena, return her love. Puck mistakenly applies the juice to Demetrius, creating much distress among the four, all of which must be remedied by additional doses of the juice and its antidote.

So the fairies, though well meaning, will often cause mischief among humans. Oberon and Titania are benevolent, however, and at the close of the play, when the lovers are married and retire to bed, the fairies bestow blessings on them, dispatching attendant spirits about the palace with instructions to protect the loving couples so that their children will be born without blemish.

## Puck

*"Lord, what fools these mortals be!"*

Oberon's servant Puck is the legendary mischief-maker among fairies. We first see him in conversation with another spirit, who recognizes him as "that shrewd and knavish sprite / Called Robin Goodfellow," known widely for his pranks. Among other escapades, he "frights the maidens of the villagery," prevents cream from churning into butter despite the labors of "the breathless housewife," and leads "night-walkers" astray. Puck acknowledges his reputation and expands on it. He can also, he says, turn himself into an object that appears unexpectedly in "a gossip's bowl," causing the surprised drinker to spill its contents; and he can become a stool that disappears when "the wisest aunt" attempts to sit on it, so that she falls on "her bum" to the hilarity of all. These are all harmless tricks that, since it is said that Robin is responsible for them, help to explain the unaccountable accidents that could happen to anyone on any day.[*]

---

[*]It would appear that for the most part the victims of his pranks are women.

Puck has many talents. He can fly from place to place at dazzling speed, "swifter than arrow from a Tartar's bow," as he claims. When Oberon sends him from Athens to India to collect the "little western flower," he promises to return promptly, boasting that he can speed "round about the earth / In forty minutes." Further, he has the power to transform the shape of humans, as he does when he crowns Bottom with an ass's head, and he can change his own form at will: "Sometime a horse I'll be, sometime a hound, / A hog, a headless bear, sometime a fire." He can also imitate human voices, as he does those of Demetrius and Lysander when they become rivals for Helena and he leads the rivals astray to prevent them from harming one another.

Shakespeare's fairies seem unmoved by the highs and lows of human passion. They are subject to a degree of envy, anger, and desire, as are Oberon and Titania, but never in excess, never with the heat that drives the lovers in the play to distraction (Titania is under a spell when she dotes on Bottom). Puck, as he watches the four lovers dash about the forest in mad pursuit of one another, can only shake his head in disbelief: "Lord, what fools these mortals be!"

# Ariel

*"Where the bee sucks, there suck I.*
*In a cowslip's bell I lie."*

*The Tempest*'s spirit, Ariel, has many of Puck's qualities. He can appear and disappear at will, and he has the ability to imitate voices, as he does in mimicking the jester Trinculo's, angering Caliban and Stephano. He can change shape, dwindling in size to fit within "a cowslip's bell" and swelling to become the fearful harpy that terrifies the shipwrecked lords of Italy. And he seems to share Puck's lack of feeling toward human beings, by his very nature remaining untouched by their joys and sorrows. Indeed, he says as much. When Prospero reduces his enemies to a painfully paralyzing trance, Ariel describes their plight:

*Ariel.* Your charm so strongly works them,
That if you now beheld them, your affections
Would become tender.

*Prospero.*                              Dost thou think so, spirit?
*Ariel.* Mine would, sir, were I human.

Prospero responds, "and mine shall," concluding that if a spirit who is "but air, [has] a touch, a feeling / Of their afflictions," then he as a human being must "be kindlier moved" toward them.

Ariel is no Robin Goodfellow, playing tricks on unsuspecting housewives. Aside from a brief episode of levity, when he toys with the comic conspirators by mimicking Trinculo's voice, he is all business, performing Prospero's tasks and keeping him informed of conditions on the island. As a spirit, he is clearly more powerful than Puck, but it is never quite clear which of his powers are his own and which he employs as an agent of his master's magic. The storm at sea seems his work, since Prospero asks him if he has "performed to point the tempest I bade you," though later the wizard says, "I raised the tempest." In the aftermath of the storm, Ariel shows remarkable talents: he ensures that all the passengers on the ship, who jumped overboard in terror, reach shore safely, with their clothing dry and fresh, and he brings the vessel securely to harbor with its crew all sleeping soundly. But again, the spell that paralyzes the lords is Prospero's work, since Ariel reports that they are still "just as you left them."

Ariel can also create music, the "sounds and sweet airs" that comfort Caliban, including at times "a thousand twangling instruments" and the "marvelous sweet music" that accompanies the mysterious appearance of the feast set out for the Italian lords. His songs are hypnotic, compelling various figures to follow their sound, as does his air, "Full fathom five thy father lies," which leads young Ferdinand to his rendezvous with Miranda.

Again in contrast to Puck, Ariel is an unwilling servant to his master, kept in thrall by fear of him. On arriving at the island, Prospero liberated him from a tree where he had been imprisoned, in return for which the spirit was bound to his service for a year. When Ariel reminds him that the year is up and asks for his freedom, the wizard threatens angrily to "rend an oak" and confine him once more if he doesn't behave. Two more days, Prospero promises, and "I will discharge thee."* Ariel, then, is moved by only two emotions

*The action of the play actually encompasses a single day.

common to humanity, the fear of Prospero and a strong desire to be free—but not pity, it would seem, since he is not "human."

## Macbeth's Witches

*"Double, double, toil and trouble."*

Witches are another matter, however. Fairies may be sympathetic, playful, or indifferent toward humans as their mood strikes them, but Macbeth's witches mean him harm, or in the words of their conjuring chant, they intend "toil and trouble." They live on the boundary between the natural and supernatural, possessing qualities of each realm. They are human, and women, though Banquo on first seeing them remarks, "your beards forbid me to interpret / That you are so." At the same time he observes that they "look not like th'inhabitants of the earth," and indeed it is their occult powers that most distinguishes them. Like the fairies, they can appear and disappear at will, but they have the additional ability to see into the future. Further, they seem to be able to peer into the minds of humans, perceiving, for example, Macbeth's secret ambition to be king. And they make use of their gift to undo him.

Of the witches' first three revelations to Macbeth, the first is no more than a statement of fact—he is the Thane of Glamis. But they go on to predict that he will become the Thane of Cawdor and "king hereafter." Their prophecies are both a promise and a snare, for the later news that King Duncan has indeed awarded him the title and lands of the Thane of Cawdor only fuels Macbeth's ambition to wear the crown. How the witches know these things we never learn— they are said to have such powers—but in the case of Macbeth the prophecy in effect fulfills itself.

But why do the witches single out Macbeth as a victim? Shakespeare provides oblique clues to the reason for their malice toward him. One of the witches gives an account of her recent encounter with a woman eating chestnuts, who refused rudely to share them with her. In retaliation for the indignity, the witch will make life miserable, she says, not for the woman but for her husband, the master of a ship bound for Aleppo. She will "thither sail" and deprive him of sleep, causing him in time to "dwindle, peak and pine," and further she will render his vessel "tempest-tost." It would appear that witches share Puck's ability to fly swiftly "round about the earth" and Ariel's power to raise a tempest. The account suggests that their vendetta against Macbeth may have arisen for reasons remote from any act of his, rather from something his wife or other relative might have done to incur their anger, an event left unmentioned, however, in the play. Their effect upon Macbeth bears comparison to their plans for the sea captain—he does indeed lack sleep, causing him to "dwindle, peak, and pine," and he becomes in time "tempest-tost."

On the other hand, there is no need to attribute a plausible motive to the witches. They are traditional enemies of mankind, creatures of the netherworld who owe allegiance to Hecate, the queen of that realm,* and they inhabit forbidden places of the earth, a barren heath and a darkened cavern. Their intentions toward humanity may be seen in the fruit of their labors: the temptation of Macbeth gives rise to a reign of blood in the kingdom of Scotland.

Macbeth is plagued by another of the witches' prophecies, that Banquo, his comrade-in-arms, will not himself wear the crown but will "get kings." He has Banquo killed, the first of many barbarous acts in a campaign of terror he inflicts on Scotland. Banquo's son escapes unharmed, however, adding to Macbeth's distemper, and he decides to question the witches once again.

Before this second meeting, Shakespeare treats his audience to a colorful description of the grizzly ingredients of a "witches' brew." The three are tending a boiling cauldron that contains, among other things,

> Eye of newt, and toe of frog,
> Wool of bat, and tongue of dog,
> Adder's fork, and blind-worm's sting
> Lizard's leg, and howlet's wing,

---

*Although Hecate's lines are said to be a later addition to the play, composed by Thomas Middleton.

as well as "scale of dragon, tooth of dog" and "finger of birth-strangled babe." Three heads appear from the cauldron, and it is they, not the witches, that address Macbeth. They first offer a warning, "beware Macduff," and follow with two prophecies, one that "none of woman born / Shall harm Macbeth" and another that he will not be vanquished until Birnam Wood comes to his castle at Dunsinane. The witches predictions are delphic in nature, that is, they prove to be true but in unanticipated ways, often provoking the inquirer to self-destructive behavior, in Macbeth's case his slaughter of Macduff's family.* They also instill in him a false sense of security, which dissolves when he sees Birnam Wood on the move, causing him to curse "the fiend / That lies like truth." And it time he falls to Macduff, who, as it turns out, was "not of woman born."

But Macbeth's purpose in confronting the witches is to demand confirmation of their prophecy that Banquo will "get kings," and we are entertained by yet another of the witches' talents. In response they conjure up a ghostly procession of kings, all descendants of his dead comrade-in-arms.

The question surrounding the witches' role in the play is how much they are responsible for Macbeth's rise and fall. Their prophecies, as mentioned, are both a promise and a snare; they are outwardly fair but have a hidden hook. They trigger his ambition and instill in him a false sense of security, but at the same time they arouse his anxiety. This is not to imply that the witches are the sole cause of his downfall, since in that regard their powers are limited. As we learn earlier, in seeking vengeance on the rude woman who refuses to share her chestnuts, they acknowledge that they cannot sink her husband's ship, only render it "tempest-tost." But if the witches had not appeared to Macbeth, would his fate have been any different? Would *Macbeth* have been another play entirely without their provocative prophecies? If these creatures are empowered to know the future and they reveal it, for whatever motive, good or ill, and with whatever delphic obscurity, do they

---

*Hence the tragic tale of Oedipus. The Delphic Oracle predicts that he will kill his father and marry his mother. Unaware that he is a foster child, he leaves the only family he knows to avoid that terrifying fate, and in so doing fulfills the prophecy.

then bring it about? When the question is so put, we cannot help but conclude that, regardless of their enticements, Macbeth brings his tragic end upon himself. In this sense the witches are not only the embodiment of mystical forces at work in the world, they are at the same time an evocation of the dark side of the human spirit, the underworld of humanity.

# FALSTAFF

THE CHERISHED FRIEND of Prince Hal's misspent youth, Sir John Falstaff, is a corpulent, old (admitting to sixty or thereabouts), irrepressibly merry companion who drinks, dances, sings, and delights in an exchange of wit and raillery. Accompanied by a group of devoted followers—Bardolph, Nym, Peto, Gadshill, and others—he holds court at the Boar's Head Tavern, an establishment run by Mistress Quickly in the ill-famed sector of London known as Eastcheap. Hal loves Falstaff's company, joining him in a battle of wits in which he disparages the fat knight's ample girth, his age, and his insatiable thirst for sack (sherry) while Falstaff constantly reminds him that he is a sorry specimen of a royal prince. They spar with amiable insults, old friends confident that no offense will be taken, each attempting to outdo the other with the ingenuity of his barbs. They play tricks on one another and engage in impromptu skits mocking the country's powerful figures, all in a joyous celebration of life.

Falstaff appears in three of Shakespeare's plays, *Henry IV, Parts 1* and *2*, and *The Merry Wives of Windsor*, and we hear of his death in *Henry V*. The figure in *The Merry Wives* is quite different in some respects from the one we meet in the history plays, hence we shall reserve the comedy for separate commentary and focus at first on the character of Hal's festive companion. It has been suggested that Shakespeare originally intended to write one play but that the figure of Falstaff took control of his pen and he ended up with enough material for two. Or possibly the actor Will Kempe, who performed in the role, insisted that he be given more lines.

## *". . . that old white-bearded Satan."*

Falstaff, however, is not the ideal companion for a prince of the realm. For one thing, he is a thief, a highwayman who robs travelers by night. At one point he jokingly requests that when Hal is king he and his like should be called "Diana's foresters, gentlemen of the shade, minions of the moon" rather than the distasteful "thieves." When Poins, Hal's companion from court, suggests that they rob pilgrims on the road to Canterbury, Falstaff eagerly agrees.

In the events of that night we find that Falstaff is also an inveterate liar. Poins persuades Hal to join in the robbery by describing the scheme as a joke on the fat knight. The two of them will agree to participate but fail to appear. Instead, hiding nearby, they will wait until the theft has taken place and then fall upon the thieves, chase them off, and secure the loot. "The virtue of this jest," Poins concludes, "will be the incomprehensible lies that this same fat rogue will tell us when we meet for supper."

Falstaff does not disappoint them. He enters the Boar's Head muttering about cowards and calling for a cup of sack. When asked what happened, he launches into an elaborate account of his martial prowess in the encounter, insisting that he and his band were attacked by "a hundred upon poor four of us" and at each stage of his tale increasing the number of assailants he had killed:

*Prince*. Pray God you have not murd'red some of them.

*Falstaff*. Nay, that's past praying for, I have peppered two of them. Two I am sure I have paid, two rogues in buckrom suits. . . . Here I lay, and thus I bore my point. Four rogues in buckrom let drive at me—

*Prince*. What four? Thou saidst but two even now.

*Falstaff*. Four, Hal, I told thee four.

*Poins*. Ay, ay, he said four.

*Falstaff*. These four came all afront, and mainly thrust at me. I made no more ado but took all their seven points in my target, thus.

*Prince*. Seven? Why, there were but four even now.

*Falstaff*. In buckrom?

*Poins*. Ay, four in buckrom suits.

*Falstaff*. Seven, by these hilts, or I am a villain else.

*Prince* (aside). Prithee let him alone, we shall have more anon.

*Falstaff*. Dost thou hear me, Hal?

*Prince*. Ay, and mark thee, Jack.

*Falstaff.* Do so, for it is worth the listening to. These nine in buckrom that I told thee of—

*Prince.* So, two more already.

*Falstaff.* Their points being broken—

*Prince.* Down fell their hose.

*Falstaff.* Began to give me ground; but I followed me close, came in, foot and hand, and with a thought seven of the eleven I paid.

*Prince.* O Monstrous! Eleven buckrom men grown out of two.

It has been suggested that Falstaff is well aware of the trick being played upon him and is simply joining in the dance of friendship between himself and Hal, offering these playful fabrications for his amusement. Perhaps. Later, however, in what is perhaps his most brazen falsehood, he is truly outrageous. Hal kills Hotspur at the Battle of Shrewsbury and leaves his body on the field. Falstaff comes upon the corpse, runs it through the leg to bloody his sword, and carries it off intending to lay claim to the deed. He encounters Hal, who, dumbfounded at the effrontery, exclaims, "Percy I killed myself." Falstaff, deploring "how this world is given to lying," insists that he fought Hotspur "a long hour by Shrewsbury clock" until he was finally able to subdue the rebel, and as a reward, he says further, "I look to be either duke or earl."

Further, Falstaff drinks to excess, continually calling for a "cup o'sack." Though we never witness him actually inebriated, on at least two occasions he is seen sleeping off the effects of an immoderate intake of spirits. He also shows evidence of cowardice, as when he takes to his heels on the night of the robbery. Again, when he encounters the fiery Douglas at the Battle of Shrewsbury, he falls down and plays dead, later justifying the deception: "The better part of valor is discretion, in which better part I've saved my life."

Falstaff at one time or another either scoffs in lengthy monologues at the civic qualities admired in a public figure, or he demonstrates disdain for them by his actions:

*Honor*: He has little regard for those seeking fame in battle:

What is honor? A word. What is that word honor? What is that honor? Air. A trim reckoning! Who hath it? He that died a' Wednesday. . . . Therefor I'll none of it, honor is a mere scutcheon.

And, coming on a dead nobleman on the battlefield, he observes: "There's honor for you!" He is not so contemptuous that he fails to pursue reputation by other, more deceitful means, however. In claiming credit for killing Hotspur, as mentioned, he hopes to be elevated to "either duke or earl." In *Part 2*, this aspiration apparently unrealized (Shakespeare does not pursue the matter), he turns a prisoner over to Prince John, expressing the expectation that the prince will give a "good report" of him at court.

*Sobriety*: In that same encounter with Prince John, Falstaff detects a certain coldness in the man and attributes it to the fact that "he drinks no wine." Such "demure boys," he concludes, never "come to any proof, for thin drink doth so over-cool their blood, and making many fish-meals, that they fall into a kind of male green-sickness, and when they marry, they get wenches."

*Frugality*: The fat knight is consistently short of funds. Hal defrays the cost of their revels, and when Falstaff incurs debt to others, he avoids payment by one device or another, usually blatant bluster. In *Part 2* it appears that he has played upon the sentiments of Mistress Quickly (called "Hostess" in the play) by promising marriage to her in return for credit at the Boar's Head and frequent loans, so extensive that, as she complains, "He hath eaten me out of house and home." Later he borrows a thousand pounds from Justice Shallow on the basis of his high expectations of royal favor once Hal is king. When the newly crowned Henry V rejects his old friend, Shallow asks for his money back; indeed he pleads that he will be satisfied with half of it. Falstaff, optimistically anticipating that his rejection will be short-lived, responds, "I will be as good as my word," a pledge that Shallow has reason to doubt.

*Integrity*: Falstaff exploits Hal's trust in him for personal gain. In the coming campaign against the rebels, the prince secures "a charge of foot" for him, an appointment as captain in the king's forces. The process of recruiting a medieval army was subject to wide corruption. The king called upon his nobles to raise forces, and they entrusted the actual imposition of "the king's press" to captains who were provided with funds to equip recruits. In practice, however, captains were often inclined to pocket the funds, called "coat and conduct" money, and accept bribes to exempt obviously able-bodied men from service.

In *Part 1* Falstaff admits to having "misused the King's press damnably." He has earned over three hundred pounds by releasing potential recruits, and as a result, he admits, his company is a group of "slaves as ragged as Lazarus," among whom "there's not a shirt and a half." When Hal meets him on the way to battle, he is appalled: "I never did see such pitiful rascals." Falstaff responds with his usual bluster: "Tut, tut, good enough to toss, food for powder, food for powder." In the ensuing battle his inept company is wiped out, "for there's but three of my hundred and fifty left alive," and the few survivors are "for the town's end, to beg during life."

In *Part 2* we are witness to Falstaff's corruption of his office. Arriving in Gloucestershire to recruit another company, he secures the aid of Justice Shallow in assembling candidates. In selecting from among them, he accepts bribes from those who can pay for exemption and enlists those who cannot, in the end enlisting a motley group who by their names—Wart, Shadow, Feeble—Shakespeare implies, are singularly unfit for military service.

Despite Falstaff's many faults, of which Hal is all too aware, it is clear that these two share a close bond of friendship. They enjoy one another's company enormously, delighting in exchanges of wit, an ambience of carefree gaiety, and the ingenuity of spontaneous skits which they improvise to satirize public figures, called in their discourse "plays extempore." Hal at one point proposes one on Hotspur but is diverted by Poins's scheme to subvert the robbery and catch Falstaff in "incomprehensible lies." That episode ends in convivial hilarity, but the enjoyment is interrupted by a message from the king summoning Hal to court because of a looming threat of a dangerous rebellion in the kingdom. Falstaff playfully proposes that Hal "practise an answer" before he must confront his irate father, and the prince readily agrees.

Falstaff, in the role of the king, rebukes Hal wittily for "the company thou keepest," with the exception of one, that is, "a goodly portly man, i'faith, and a corpulent, of a cheerful look, a pleasing eye, and a most noble carriage." Banish all the others, he continues, but "him keep with" for "there is virtue in that Falstaff." He ends with mock severity: "Tell me, thou naughty varlet, tell me, where hast thou been this month."

Hal insists that they exchange roles, and, now as the king, he reproaches his son for his associates, one in particular: "There is a devil haunts thee in the likeness of an old fat man, a tun of man is thy companion." And who is this? It is "that villainous, abominable misleader of youth, Falstaff, that old white-bearded Satan." The fat knight, in the role of the prince now, defends himself inventively and repeats his proposal that his associates be banished, with the exception once again of himself: "Banish him not thy Harry's company—banish plump Jack, and banish all the world." Hal's terse reply, "I do, I will," shatters the conviviality for the moment, but it soon revives.

Hal's reply also foreshadows the final scene of *Part 2*. His father dead, he is crowned king, and Falstaff rushes to London to reap the rewards of their long friendship. The king, however, rejects him— "I know thee not, old man"—and does indeed banish him from the royal presence. In *Henry V* we learn of Falstaff's death, brought on, his friends are convinced, by Hal's rejection. In Mistress Quickly's words, "The king has killed his heart."

Thus Sir John Falstaff is a thief, a coward, a chronic liar, a heroic imbiber of "sack," a spendthrift who defaults on his debts, and a man who betrays his public trust for gain. He demeans all of what may be called civic virtues—integrity, sobriety, frugality, and devotion to duty. And he has nothing but scorn for those who seek "honor," though in constant pursuit of it himself, consorting with a royal prince in expectation of high favor and deceitfully claiming credit for killing the formidable Hotspur.

On the other hand, Falstaff is what one of his time would have called affectionately a "mad rogue," a man of extravagant and highly entertaining behavior, and it is not difficult to appreciate Hal's affection for him. Despite numerous faults, his infectious gaiety, his eternal optimism, his incisive wit, and his exuberant joy of life would be irresistible to any young man of spirit. But these faults loom large for a prince who is called upon to assume the responsibilities of the crown, and Hal must inevitably put his cherished, profligate friend behind him.

## Sir John in Love

It is said that Queen Elizabeth, delighted with the figure of Falstaff in the *Henry IV* plays, expressed a desire to see the fat knight "in love," and, so goes the tale, Shakespeare as a result labored for two frantic weeks to compose *The Merry Wives of Windsor*. The play is essentially a farce, and though a highly popular one, it suffers in comparison to the histories. Nor does Falstaff have the stature of Prince Hal's merry companion, though he retains many of the qualities of that figure. He is still fat, still profligate, still ready for a jest—even one on him—and he still calls for sack.

We do not in fact ever see Falstaff "in love," as the queen requested. His motive for wooing the wives is the old familiar one—*gain*. He is as usual short of funds, so much so that he has to release his retainers, Bardolph, Peto, and Pistol, known to us from the earlier plays. Eager to restore his fortunes, he learns that of the two wives, Mistress Ford "has all the rule of her husband's purse" and Mistress Page "bears the purse too," and he means to woo them so that "they shall be exchequer to me."

He is still witty, though his complaints lack the satiric sting we have become accustomed to, where he disparages honor, scorns sobriety, and holds all civic virtues in despite. Here, in much briefer monologues, the scope of his disdain has shrunk; he complains chiefly about the rough treatment he has suffered, rather than ridicule public figures and extol the virtues of sack.

He is still exuberantly optimistic, as confident of his manly appeal to the ladies as he is of his martial prowess, despite abundant evidence to the contrary. Rather than the simple Mistress Quickly, however, and the prostitute Doll Tearsheet of the *Henry IV* plays, he is up against two proper, resourceful wives who are indignant to discover that he has sent identical love letters to them both. They are appalled at the insult to their virtue and are determined to have revenge for this effrontery. They devise not one but three separate hoaxes to humiliate him; and Falstaff, so full of vanity that he fails to see through their designs, returns again and again to what he is confident are amorous assignations, only to find himself debased. In the first he has to hide from a furiously jealous Master Ford in a basket of soiled clothes, and is unceremoniously dumped into the Thames. In the second he assumes a ridiculous disguise as the witch of Brainford and suffers a beating by Ford, who hates the woman. In the third he is lured into a forest glen and terrified by a charade in which the entire community takes part.

Thus Falstaff is still corpulent, still thirsty, and still out of pocket. And he still commands the stage, despite the presence of a rich array of comic characters: the dim-witted Alexander Slender and the irrepressible Mistress Quickly, both given to prodigious malaprops; the Welsh parson, Sir Hugh Evans, whose broad accent confounds the ear; and the irascible Dr. Caius who, according to Mistress Quickly, abuses "God's patience and the King's English." Even Nym's protestations, sprinkled liberally with his customary allusions to "humours," are said to "fright English out of its wits." This play is a comic assault on the language, no less so by those who mangle it as by Falstaff's bombastic eloquence. Hear him pay court to Mistress Ford:

> Have I caught thee, my heavenly jewel? Why, now let me die, for I have lived long enough. This is the period of my ambition. O this blessed hour!*

Falstaff, then, is a much diminished figure in *The Merry Wives of Windsor*, in contrast to the dissolute knight of the *Henry IV* plays, who pursues his own way in a flawed society, exploiting its inequities to his material advantage.† He is here, rather, a figure of folly, falling into traps devised by others more inventive, and more virtuous, than he. Blind to the tricks played upon him, he is no longer gifted with the ready wit by which the fat knight of the history plays was able to talk his way out of "incomprehensible lies" to the delight of all. On the other hand, he is still a joy to watch in this spontaneous farce as he is victimized by those cunning wives who outdo him in indignation and ingenuity.

---

*And compare his speech to Othello's lines on his reunion with Desdemona:

> If I were now to die,
> 'Twere now to be most happy; for I fear
> My soul hath her content so absolute
> That not another comfort like to this
> Succeeds in unknown fate.

†Harold Bloom dismisses him as "a nameless imposter masquerading as the great Sir John Falstaff" in his *Shakespeare: The Invention of the Human*. Bloom is inordinately fond of Falstaff and deeply resents this "tiresome exercise" of a play.

# FAULCONBRIDGE

*"That smooth-faced gentleman, tickling commodity,*
*Commodity, the bias of the world."*

PHILIP FAULCONBRIDGE, "the Bastard," is a lively presence in
*King John*, an otherwise disappointing play. He is an illegitimate son
of the deceased Robert, and he appears before the king and his
mother, Queen Elinor (Eleanor of Aquitaine), to contest the claim of
his legitimate, but younger, brother to his father's estate. All questions of inheritance are forgotten, however, when Elinor notices a
striking resemblance between Philip and her dead son, Richard I,
the renowned *Coeur de Lion*. "I like thee well," she says, and suggests
that he dismiss his claim to his brother's estate and join the royal
court, then preparing to embark on a campaign against France. He
readily agrees, and the king knights him "Sir Richard and Planta-
genet."* Later his mother confirms that he is indeed the son of the
great *Coeur de Lion*, the result of a dalliance with the king during her
husband's extended absence abroad.

Thus begins the career of the engaging Faulconbridge, which
sees him advance from the standing of a penniless knight in the royal
court to commander of the English armies defending the kingdom
from a French invasion. The Bastard is in the unenviable position of
illegitimate or younger sons of the English nobility who were victims of the tradition of primogeniture, which mandated that only
the oldest son could inherit the family title and lands. In medieval
times the quickest route to fame and riches for such unfortunates was

---

*Shakespeare identifies the speaker of his lines throughout the play simply as
"Bast." and so shall we. He is occasionally referred to as "Richard," his knighted
name.

to attract the royal favor by exemplary acts of daring and prowess on the field of battle; and the Bastard is eager to make a name for himself. He is sardonically hopeful about his prospects: "This is a worshipful society, and fits the mounting spirit like myself," so though he will not "practice to deceive," he says, "yet to avoid deceit, / I mean to learn; for it shall strew the footsteps of my rising."

The opportunity for the Bastard to distinguish himself arrives as the result of a dispute over the English crown. King John leads an army into France to oppose the claim to the throne of his young nephew Arthur, who is supported by the French king and his ally, the Duke of Austria. The two armies converge on the besieged city of Angiers, and both kings demand its surrender. The citizens reply that they will open their gates only to the rightful King of England, and they'll not do so until their majesties have sorted out the matter between themselves.

The Bastard is elated; battle impends. He proposes that the kings put aside their differences for the moment and join forces to reduce the city. That once accomplished, he counsels, they can then turn their armies on one another to decide who will reign over the ruins. The notion pleases, but before the attack can be launched, the citizens of Angiers offer a compromise: Let Lewis, the Dauphin of France, marry King John's niece, Blanche of Castile, a union that would put to an end the animosity between the two kingdoms. The match is arranged, and peace is restored.

The Bastard is contemptuous of all this talk of compromise and amity: "I was never so bethumped with words / Since I first called my brother's father dad." And he is disgusted when the kings agree to the proposal. They are reconciled and depart, leaving him to his thoughts: "Mad world, mad kings, mad composition!" he rails, all of it attributable to "that smooth-faced gentleman, tickling commodity, / Commodity, the bias of the world." His disgust with "commodity" is the age-old complaint of the soldier when his dedication to honor and homeland is compromised by the merchant's hunger for profit or what he sees as the politician's vacillation in pursuit of self-interest. It is this, the Bastard concludes, that has led "from a resolved and honourable war / To a base and vile-concluded peace." In the end, however, he is resigned; if he can't fight them, he will join them: "Since kings break faith upon commodity, / Gain, be my lord, for I will worship thee."

The reconciliation between the kings has the effect of denying Arthur's claim to the throne, however, and his mother, Lady Constance, reproves the French for abandoning his cause. To complicate matters, the papal legate Pandulph arrives, demanding that the French king, under a threat of excommunication, break his oath of friendship and attack England. The Bastard, impatient with the lengthy exchanges on these issues, is preoccupied with the Duke of Austria. To commemorate his victory over *Coeur de Lion*, during which the king is killed, the duke has adopted the provocative habit of wearing a lion's skin, an ostentatious display that irritates the Bastard (who, it will be recalled, is Richard's son).* He picks up on the remark of Lady Constance when she rebukes Austria: "Thou wear a lion's hide! Doff it for shame, / And hang a calve's-skin on those recreant limbs." Thereafter, every time the duke opens his mouth, the Bastard insults him with the same challenge to exchange his lion's hide for a calve's-skin. Austria is furious at his incessant nagging insolence, but he can do nothing to interrupt the critical exchanges between the kings and Pandulph. The legate eventually has his way and the two kingdoms resume the war, during which the Bastard has the satisfaction of killing the duke and displaying his head.

France invades England and John's nobles desert him, crossing over to join the French. The Bastard comes into his own, placed in command of the English forces, but he must contend with a weak-willed king who can do nothing but lament his fate as the French overrun the county. The Bastard attempts to rally a despondent John: "But wherefore do you droop? Why look you sad? / Be great in act, as you have been in thought. . . . Show boldness and aspiring confidence. . . . Let us, my liege, to arms." In this same temper he defies the French: "The King doth smile at, and is well prepared / To whip this dwarfish war, this pygmy arms. / From out the circles of his territories." Events move swiftly to a conclusion: the Bastard

---

*Shakespeare conflates two historical events here. The Duke of Austria held Richard I captive for a time but was not responsible for his death, which took place on a separate occasion some years later.

holds his own in battle, the English lords rejoin the king, John dies, and the French supply fleet is shipwrecked, forcing them to abandon the invasion. The Bastard has the final word, with an oblique reference to the turncoat lords:

> This England never did, nor never shall,
> Lie at the proud foot of a conqueror,
> But when it first did help to wound itself.
> . . . . . . . . . Naught shall make us rue,
> If England to itself do rest but true.

*King John* has some moving moments—the young Arthur pleading to save his eyes, his mother Constance despairing over the French betrayal of her son's cause, and the plaintive John lamenting his losses. But in the midst of a convoluted plot and thinly drawn characters, the Bastard Faulconbridge shines, a blunt, irreverent, and witty figure who in the end proves himself a worthy son of the valiant *Coeur de Lion.*

# HAMLET

*". . . you would pluck out the heart of my mystery."*

*"That would be scanned."*

THE PRINCE OF DENMARK is a young man of perhaps thirty years of age, as we learn from the gravedigger late in the play. Hamlet has been pursuing a course of studies at Wittenberg, a famous medieval center of learning, where it would appear he is highly regarded. He seems an extraordinary young man, one who readily attracts the affection and admiration of those about him. His fellow students, Rosencrantz and Guildenstern, who have come to Elsinore castle at the request of Claudius, the king, greet Hamlet with the deference due a prince of the realm—"My honoured lord!" "My most dear lord!"—but they immediately drop into the companionable banter of longtime friends, and he welcomes them warmly. Horatio, also from Wittenberg, is an unreservedly loyal and devoted confidant. The king remarks on "the great love the general gender bear" the prince, and further that "the queen his mother / Lives almost by his looks." Polonius's daughter Ophelia remembers him in earlier times as

> The courtier's, soldier's, scholar's eye, tongue, sword,
> The expectancy and rose of the fair state,
> The glass of fashion and the mould of form,
> Th'observed of all observers.

As the play unfolds, we find that Hamlet is indeed the center of all eyes, "th'observed of all observers," and even when absent he is on everyone's tongue. Gifted with a sharp intelligence, he dominates those about him, talking rings around the ponderous Polonius, toying with the uncomprehending Osric, compelling Rosencrantz and

Guildenstern to admit they have come at the king's request, and overwhelming Ophelia and his mother. He is quick-witted and clever, devising a scheme to punish Rosencrantz and Guildenstern for their collusion with Claudius, and improvising a play "to catch the conscience of the king."

Further, Hamlet is bold, fearlessly leading the assault on the pirate ship that interrupts his voyage to England, and as agile in body as in mind, besting Laertes in a duel in the final scene. He can be reckless, impulsively leaping into Ophelia's grave, and at times openly affectionate, confiding in Horatio that he holds his friend "in my heart's core, ay in my heart of heart." And he is deeply meditative, pondering such matters as life and death, justice and injustice, action and inaction, providence, destiny, and love.

When we first see Hamlet, however, it is clear that this altogether admirable young man is not himself. Deep in gloomy contemplation, he is an isolated figure in an otherwise busy court scene where his stepfather, King Claudius, is engaged in affairs of state, dispatching envoys to the King of Norway and releasing Laertes to return to his studies in Paris. Hamlet is dressed in black, a display of mourning for the recent death of his father. As we learned in the previous scene, his mother, Queen Gertrude, promptly remarried, her new husband the dead king's brother Claudius, who immediately assumed the crown, thus excluding the prince from the throne.

Hamlet clearly resents Claudius. Once the public business has been dispatched, the king and queen turn to their melancholy son, concerned with what they assume to be his prolonged bereavement over his father's death. Claudius asks, "How is it that the clouds still hang on you?" and Hamlet replies sharply, "Not so, my lord, I am too much in the sun." We learn at the outset, then, that he has a biting wit, here employing a double-edged pun to express his discontent that he is still the son of a king and must bask in the reflected glory of his stepfather's royal "sun."

The court moves on, leaving Hamlet to himself, and in an impassioned soliloquy he pours out his distress at what really troubles him. It is not so much that he has been denied the throne as it is his mother's hasty remarriage: "O God, a beast that wants discourse of reason / Would have mourned longer." Further, he deeply resents the fact that Claudius and Gertrude so openly display their affection for each other. His anger erupts as he condemns his mother for her "most wicked speed to post / With such dexterity to incestuous sheets!"

The depth of Hamlet's distress at his mother's remarriage bursts out again when he confronts her later in her bedchamber. He forces her to acknowledge that her precipitous marriage to Claudius was shameless and urges her to repent by abandoning his bed. "Assume a virtue," he insists cruelly, "if you have it not." In badgering her to avoid her husband, he heaps scorn on their lovemaking, though at the same time he seems almost to relish describing it:

> Nay, but to live
> In the rank sweat of an enseamed bed
> Stewed in corruption, honeying, and making love
> Over the nasty sty.

Do not do this "that I bid you do," he says:

> Let the bloat king tempt you again to bed,
> Pinch wanton on your cheek, call you his mouse,
> And let him with a pair of reechy kisses,
> Or paddling in your neck with his damned fingers.

Hamlet is a sorely troubled young man, but his mother's precipitous marriage is only the beginning of his troubles. He is confronted by his father's ghost, who gives an account of his suffering in purgatorial fires and reveals the manner of his sudden death. He died, he says, at the hand of his treacherous brother, who poured poison into his ear as he lay sleeping in his garden. The ghost pledges Hamlet to "revenge his foul and most unnatural murder," and the prince vows that "Thy commandment all alone shall live / Within the book and volume of my brain, / Unmixed with baser matter." "O most pernicious woman," he rages, and "O villain, villain, smiling damned villain!" Shortly thereafter, however, once he has sworn his friends to secrecy about the ghost's appearance, he seems already to regret his vow: "The time is out of joint, O cursed spite, / That ever I was born to set it right!"

To add to his distress, Hamlet is cut off by his lover, Ophelia, who rejects him, bowing to the will of her father, Polonius, the trusted counselor to the king. Hamlet, it appears, has been paying court to her, showering her with presents and sentimental poems; but her father, finding the relationship unsuitable, has ordered her to end it, and she has complied. Hamlet later encounters Ophelia on four separate occasions, in three of which he displays erratic behavior. The first of these we hear of in Ophelia's tearful report to her father: he came upon her, she says, seized her wrist, and stared wordlessly at her face. Then "He raised a sigh so piteous and profound / As it did seem to shatter all his bulk, / And end his being." And, wordless still, he took his leave, gazing back at her over his shoulder as he did so.

Ophelia's account convinces Polonius that Hamlet's melancholy arises from "the very ecstasy of love," and he intends to prove the point to the king. He places his daughter where the troubled prince will encounter her while he and Claudius conceal themselves to overhear the exchange. Hamlet does come upon her, and when, after a curt greeting, she attempts to return his gifts, he flies into a rage. "Get thee to a nunnery," he exclaims, "why wouldst thou be a breeder of sinners?" and again "get thee to a nunnery, go, farewell." He rails at all women, "You jig, you amble, and you lisp, you nickname God's creatures, and make your wantonness your ignorance," and at wedlock itself, "I say we will have no moe marriage." Polonius remains convinced that "his grief / Sprung from neglected love," but Claudius is not so sure: "Love! His affections do not that way tend."

In his next encounter with Ophelia, at the performance of *The Murder of Gonzago*, Hamlet is singularly composed. He seems his old self, addressing her with lighthearted, erotic banter:

*Hamlet*. Lady, shall I lie in your lap?
*Ophelia*. No, my lord.
*Hamlet*. I mean, my head upon your lap?
*Ophelia*. Ay, my lord.
*Hamlet*. Do you think I meant country matters?
*Ophelia*. I think nothing, my lord.
*Hamlet*. That's a fair thought to lie between maids' legs.

His final encounter is at her funeral, where he again flies out of control. Stung by the sudden revelation of her death and the sight of her brother, Laertes, leaping into her grave for a final embrace, he bursts from concealment and jumps in after him. He is incensed, grappling with Laertes and crying out, "O I loved Ophelia, forty thousand brothers / Could not with all their quantity of love / Make up my sum."

But while Hamlet reacts violently to a series of events that could be expected to unhinge any young man—the death of a revered father, his mother's abrupt remarriage which denies him his inheritance, an encounter with a ghost, the obligation to commit murder, the rejection of a lover—he is strangely unaffected by, even callous toward, other events we might expect would excite similar distress. When confronting his mother in her bedchamber, he treats her roughly, prompting a cry from Polonius, who is concealed behind a set of draperies. Hamlet impulsively runs his sword through the draperies, killing the old man; but the murder leaves him completely unmoved. As he takes his leave, he tells his mother with cold disdain that he will "lug the guts into the neighboring room"; and when later confronted by Claudius, he informs the king with sardonic wit that if he doesn't find the body "within this month, you will nose him as you go up the stairs into the lobby." He displays not the slightest hint of remorse that he has killed his lover's father, a deed that, as it happens, leads to her death.

Later, as he wrestles with Laertes in Ophelia's grave, he exclaims, "What is the reason that you use me thus? / I loved you ever." Again, he is oblivious to the possibility that Laertes may hold him responsible for his sister's death and is as determined as he to be avenged for his father's murder. Hamlet's insensitivity leaves him vulnerable to the king's plot. Blind to Laertes' hatred, he agrees to a friendly duel with him and falls victim to his inability to attribute his own passion to others.

Hamlet's seemingly heartless indifference to his murder of Polonius is matched by his callous disregard for the fate of Rosencrantz and Guildenstern, whom he sends to certain death. They are entirely innocent accomplices in the king's scheme to rid himself of the threat Hamlet poses by sending him on a voyage to England in the company of his two fellow students, who bear sealed letters to the English king ordering the immediate death of the prince upon arrival. Hamlet uncovers the plot and, unknown to them, substitutes letters calling instead for the death of the bearers. Providentially he manages to escape and return to Denmark, where he gives an account of his adventure to Horatio. He has no regrets that he has condemned his two former friends to death. They were the king's uncomprehending tools, certainly, but "'Tis dangerous when the baser nature comes / Between the pass and fell incensed points / Of mighty opposites." They ventured out of their depth, in brief, when they became involved in the dynastic conflicts of royalty, and as far as he is concerned they have paid the price for their presumption.

Hamlet, then, is pitilessly indifferent to the fate of those he kills or plots to kill. Indeed, the only time he shows remorse for any of his actions is his regret that he "forgot himself" in his outburst against Laertes at Ophelia's funeral. Curiously, he feels an affinity with the young man, "For by the image of my cause I see / The portraiture of his"; but again he is oblivious to the possibility that the son of Polonius may hate his father's murderer as much as he despises Claudius. As a result, he offers an apology to Laertes and allows himself to be drawn into that last, fatal duel.

The pervasive question of the play is why Hamlet fails to fulfill his oft-repeated, fervent vow to avenge the murder of his father until events force it upon him. At one point he compels Rosencrantz and Guildenstern to confess that they have been summoned to Elsinore by the king to keep an eye on him; and he accuses them angrily of attempting to "pluck out the heart of my mystery." To the court of Denmark, Hamlet's "mystery" is his unnatural melancholy, the result, it is thought at first, of his excessive grief at the loss of his father. His elders debate his condition. Polonius is convinced that Ophelia's rejection has caused his despondency, but Claudius has his doubts: "There's something in his soul, / O'er which his melancholy sits on brood." Ophelia and Gertrude are bewildered by his behavior. His former love can only despair at his abuse of her: "O, woe is me! / T'have seen what I have seen, see what I see!" His uncomprehending mother can only attempt to shame him for putting on a play that has so disturbed her husband: "Hamlet, thou hast thy father much offended."

Hamlet's "mystery" is something quite different, however, to a theater audience. This highly intelligent, physically vigorous, widely admired young man, who has every reason in the world to kill Claudius, cannot bring himself to act. He is himself at a loss to explain his reluctance: "I do not know / Why yet I live to say 'This thing's to do'" and still fail to do it. "How stand I then," he asks himself, "that have a father murdered, a mother stained, / Excitements of my reason and my blood, / And let all sleep?" He doesn't know, and neither do we.

Some productions emphasize the physical obstacles—the king constantly surrounded by an attentive court, hard to get at. But Hamlet's resolution is called into question by the one occasion when he comes upon the king alone, deep in apparently repentant prayer. He approaches Claudius stealthily with a drawn sword and is within an instant of killing him: "And now I'll do't, and so a' goes to heaven, / And so am I revenged." But he pauses—"That would be scanned"—and withholds the avenging stroke, reasoning that to kill him in the act of prayer would indeed dispatch him "to heaven" while his father continues to suffer the pain of purgatorial fires. No justice there, he concludes, and passes on.

This climactic encounter with Claudius at prayer suggests an alternate reason for Hamlet's delay—he thinks too much. He intellectualizes his options, meanwhile philosophizing on all manner of subjects: On life: "What is a man, / If his chief good and market of his time / Be but to sleep and feed?" On death: "The undiscovered country, from whose bourne / No traveller returns." On fortune: "There's a divinity that shapes our ends, / Rough-hew them how we will," and "There is special providence in the fall of a sparrow." On the deception of appearance: "Meet it is I set it down / That one may smile, and smile, and be a villain." On friendship: "Give me that man / That is not passion's slave, and I will wear him / In my heart's core, ay in my heart of heart." On humanity: "What a piece of work is man, . . . the beauty of the world, the paragon of animals."

Hamlet repeatedly rationalizes his resolve. Despite his fervent vows to his father's ghost, he insists on some tangible evidence of the king's guilt, reasoning that "the spirit I have seen / May be the devil, and the devil hath power / T'assume a pleasing shape." After witnessing the king's violent reaction to the reenactment of his crime in *The Murder of Gonzago*, Hamlet is exultant: "I'll take the ghost's word for a thousand pound." But he still passes up the opportunity to kill Claudius and instead vents his anger and frustration on his mother. He seeks assurance of the justice of his cause to the very end. Moments before agreeing to his duel with Laertes, he is still asking Horatio:

> He that hath killed my king, and whored my mother,
> Popped in between th'election and my hopes,   *r*
> Thrown out his angle for my proper life,
> And with such cozenage—is't not perfect conscience
> To quit him with this arm?

Horatio, perhaps significantly, does not answer him directly but reminds him that news of the death of Rosencrantz and Guildenstern will soon be known. Yes, he answers, "It will be short, the interim is mine." And how does he plan to use that "interim"? We never learn, for he is immediately distracted by regret for his unruly behavior toward Laertes.

Hamlet is not unaware of this propensity in himself to overintellectualize his choices. As he contemplates taking his own life, he concludes that his hesitation arises from "conscience," which "makes cowards of us all, / And thus the native hue of resolution / Is sicklied o'er with the pale cast of thought." Later, observing the armies of Fortinbras marching on Poland, he flagellates himself for lacking the resolve of the Norwegian prince, a weakness, he says, arising from

> some craven scruple
> Of thinking too precisely on th'event—
> A thought which quartered hath but one part wisdom,
> And ever three parts coward.

He is in fact impatient with himself for his delay, constantly pumping himself up to act. Before the performance of *The Murder of Gonzago*, he excoriates Claudius—"Bloody, bawdy villain! / Remorseless, treacherous, kindless villain!"—and then berates himself for resorting to words rather than acts:

> Why, what an ass am I. This is most brave,
> That I, the son of a dear father murdered,
> Prompted to my revenge by heaven and hell,
> Must like a whore unpack my heart with words,
> And fall a-cursing like a very drab.

After the performance he seems to have gained new resolve—"Now could I drink hot blood, / And do such bitter business as the day / Would quake to look on." His very next thought, however, is not of Claudius, but of his mother! And later, stung by the resolve of Fortinbras, he vows, "O, from this time forth, / My thoughts be bloody, or be nothing worth!"—this on his way to England, where his bloody thoughts would pose no threat to the King of Denmark!

Another possible explanation for Hamlet's delay is that he is simply immobilized by melancholy, a consequence of the many sorrows heaped upon him in a few short weeks, enough to reduce any young man to a state of despondency and rob him of the will to act. He hints at such a cause in his exchange with Rosencrantz and Guildenstern—"I have of late, but wherefore I know not, lost all my mirth, foregone all custom of exercise"—but of course he may be toying with them here, to put them off the scent. Later events confirm, however, that he can be decisive. He spontaneously devises a scheme to "catch the conscience of the king," a play to reenact his father's murder. He runs his sword abruptly through the draperies of his mother's bedchamber, killing Polonius. And, as he tells Horatio, he leads an assault on a pirate ship during his voyage to England, an act he admits was rash, but "praised be rashness for it." This is the key to his character perhaps—he can act if he does so without premeditation, before the consequences of his action can be "scanned."

Some interpreters suggest that Hamlet has a deep-seated moral objection to an act of violence toward another, as manifest in his obvious reluctance to undertake the vengeance demanded by his father's ghost—"O cursed spite, / That ever I was born to set it right"—and the very fact that he seems unable to act against Claudius. But again this is contradicted by his callous disregard for the lives he does take—Polonius and his two fellow students, the latter by a carefully calculated design.

In some productions it may appear that Hamlet is truly mad, a young man severely disturbed by the weight of his troubles, and that it is his unbalanced mind that continually distracts him from carrying out his vow to avenge his father's murder. It was a belief in Shakespeare's time that melancholy, if not relieved, can lead to insanity; and it must be admitted that an accumulated burden of sorrows, even in our own time, can snap the thin thread that binds the human will to reason. After Hamlet's encounter with his father's ghost, his frenzied actions amaze his friends, and he calms their fears by confiding that he may at times "put an antic disposition on," though it is not clear whether this is an effort to excuse his erratic behavior at the time or a conscious design to hide his murderous intent in the future. His later actions do often give the impression of one who has lost control of his reason—his abusive ranting at Ophelia and his mother and his assault on Laertes in the graveyard. On the other hand, his seemingly nonsensical exchanges with Polonius and the king are deliberately contrived to divert their attention, a device only partly successful, for even the fumbling Polonius detects that "though this be madness, yet there is method in't." And he takes special pains to maintain madness to cloak his intent. He adamantly insists that under no circumstances should his mother suggest to Claudius that he is "not in madness, / But mad in craft."

But Hamlet, we must conclude, is not mad, though at times he is highly irrational. His "antic disposition" is a design to deal with a practical political problem. If he kills Claudius and is discovered to have done so, and if he explains that the king's guilt was revealed to him by a ghost (the only evidence he has), doubts about the balance of his mind may indeed arise and deny him the throne. If he can persuade his Danish subjects, however, that he has been susceptible only to temporary lapses of judgment, perhaps out of sorrow for his father's death, the act may be excused. An indication that this may well be a conscious design on his part emerges in his apology to Laertes. He deeply regrets, he says, his untoward behavior toward the youth in Ophelia's grave, which he admits, "I here proclaim was madness." Hence, he protests, he was not responsible for his actions—"Hamlet does it not, Hamlet denies it. / Who does it then? His madness"—and he asks Laertes' forgiveness if in his distracted state he has "hurt his brother." Of course, if he were to make the same plea after killing Claudius, others might be no more persuaded than is Laertes; but Hamlet is a popular prince, and Denmark would not be the only kingdom in history to be ruled by a monarch given to occasional episodes of irrational behavior.

Among the more provocative explanations for Hamlet's delay in killing Claudius and his neglect to do so when the opportunity presents itself relies on Sigmund Freud's theory of early childhood development, the concept known as the Oedipus complex. Freud proposed that a young boy will often develop a strong physical attachment to his mother, one at times so intense that he sees his father as a rival and wishes him absent or even dead. This desire to eliminate the father is accompanied, according to the theory, by a parallel sense of guilt at such a thought. The normal child soon outgrows this stage, but if for any reason his emotional development is arrested, the twin imperatives—an unnatural desire for the mother and guilt at wanting to dispose of the father—sink into the subconscious and prevail into maturity. There is certainly evidence in the play of Hamlet's physical attachment to his mother—his anguish at her remarriage and his obsessive demand that she quit her husband's bed—and a performance can add emphasis to the impression by overt acts of affection between them. The parallel sense of guilt, it is said, prevents him from doing harm to a father figure, hence his inability to kill Claudius until circumstances force the act upon him. He can devise an ingenious plan to "catch the conscience of the king," but he never entertains a thought on how to "catch" the king himself.

This Hamlet is not the lover Ophelia remembers. He is still "th'observed of all observers," not, however, for his courtly charm but because of his sullen isolation and destructive behavior. He mocks or abuses everyone he encounters, except Horatio, of course. Figures up and down the social order of Elsinore, from the king himself to the dutiful Osric, feel the sting of his biting wit. He manhandles Ophelia and his mother, reducing them to tears. He kills Polonius and physically assaults the old man's son. Instead of avenging himself on one man, the source of his distemper, because of his incomprehensible delay he is responsible for the death of eight figures, himself included, three of whom die at the point of his rapier. He is a thoroughly unpleasant and, as it turns out, dangerous man to be around.

Oddly, shortly after Hamlet's tumultuous encounter with Laertes in the graveyard, he seems uncharacteristically calm, as if the physical and emotional exertion has somehow lowered the flame on his vengeful spirit. He is content, he tells Horatio, to leave the future to "providence," to "a divinity that shapes our ends." He seems to have come to terms with his own inability to act, passively surrendering his will to fate: "If it be now, 'tis not to come—if it be not to come, it will be now—if it be not now, yet it will come—the readiness is all." Is this the real Hamlet, then, the much-admired young prince whom Ophelia described as "the courtier's, soldier's, scholar's eye, tongue, sword, / The expectation and rose of the fair state"? A much more composed figure now, he confides in his friend, banters lightheartedly with Osric, agrees readily to a friendly duel with Laertes for the entertainment of the court, and graciously apologizes to the youth for his regrettable behavior in the graveyard. Ironically, if this is indeed the reemergence of the "sweet prince," as he was before countless troubles began to weigh on his spirit, it comes only moments before his sudden outburst of desperate energy during which he kills the two men who seek his life, and dies himself.

Hamlet defeats us. There are too many reasons for his behavior, and yet there are not enough. If we say simply that he is a contradictory figure, it seems almost an admission of failure on our part, but in the end that may be all we can come up with. Consider: He pledges himself passionately to avenge his father's murder and then regrets that he was "born to set it right." He tells Ophelia that he loved her, then assures her cruelly that "I loved you not," and later at her grave insists that he did so "more than forty thousand brothers." At one point he claims to have "forgone all custom of exercises," at another that he has "been in continual practice" at his swordsmanship. He vacillates in his belief in the ghost, first assuring his friends "It is an honest ghost, that let me tell you," then

"The spirit that I have seen / May be a devil," and finally, "I'll take the ghost's word for a thousand pound." He shows remorse for his intemperate behavior toward Laertes but none for killing the youth's father. He shows courageous resolve in leading the assault on the pirate ship but is paralyzed by thought when presented with an opportunity to kill the king. He can devise an ingenious plan to defeat the king's plot to have him killed but is powerless to conceive of a scheme to do away with Claudius himself. He is an enigma, both to the court of Elsinore and to us.

Perhaps in the end it may be said that Shakespeare was quite deliberate in creating a figure so profoundly contradictory. In Hamlet the playwright crafted a character who in his distraction confronts a spectrum of dilemmas that define the human condition: How should one respond to the imperatives of the supernatural? Are spiritual forces malignant or benign? Does an obligation to the dead outweigh the sanctity of the living? Can love survive the dictates of society? Is human endeavor justification in itself, even when the goal of our efforts is meaningless? Is mankind in command of its own destiny, or are we subject to the same "providence" that determines "the fall of a sparrow"? To what extend are we bound by an obligation to our parents? Is it right, or just, to take a life, one's own or another's? What is there to distinguish the prince from the jester as they gaze upon one another across the narrowing gulf that separates them? Hamlet addresses all these questions in search of a resolution to his dilemma, and in the cataclysmic conclusion of his history, as he perishes before our eyes, they all are left unanswered—"The rest is silence."

# HELENA AND BERTRAM

*"I know I love in vain, strive against hope."*

SHAKESPEARE'S LOVE MATCHES are at times puzzling. His comic heroines seem to fall for totally unsuitable young men. What in the world, for example, does Viola see in the ridiculously foppish Duke Orsino in *Twelfth Night*? And, in *Measure for Measure*, one must wonder why Mariana remains devoted for years to the straitlaced Angelo after he rejected her so harshly when she lost her dowry. Of course, a maid's choice of a man, or for that matter a man's of a maid, remains a mystery in real life, and Shakespeare, resolute in his intent simply "to hold as 'twere a mirror up to nature," makes no effort to explain the phenomenon. But some of his pairings do leave us shaking our heads.[*]

Another instance is Helena's tenacious devotion to the haughtily disdainful, philandering Bertram, Count of Rossillion, in *All's Well That Ends Well*, despite his rude rejection of her. Of course, he is a nobleman, in social rank high above the daughter of a physician who, though widely revered, was of common birth. When questioned by the sympathetic countess, Bertram's mother, she confesses her secret longing for him but concedes that "I love in vain, strive against hope." Nevertheless, consumed by her passion and undaunted by the social distance between them, Helena follows Bertram to the court of the French king where, using skills learned from her father, she cures the ailing monarch of a debilitating illness.

---

[*]Recently, an evolutionary biologist described the process in these terms: "Blindly, automatically and untaught we bond with whoever is standing nearest when the oxytocin receptors in the medial amygdala get tingled"—whatever they are. Shakespeare wisely steers clear of the inexplicable. They fall in love—so let's get on with the play.

The grateful king inquires what she will have as a reward for restoring his health, and she asks for her pick of a husband from among his courtiers. She selects Bertram, of course. He is outraged, loftily indignant at being compelled to take "a poor physician's daughter" in marriage, but he is left no choice in the matter since the king is insistent, declaring, "My honour is at the stake."

These early scenes portray Helena as a resolute and resourceful young woman, determined against all odds to capture the unwilling Bertram. She has her wish, but in her passion she fails to foresee the quite predictable resentment of a vain young man who is forced into what he considers a demeaning marriage.

Disdaining to accept Helena as his wife—"I will not bed her"— Bertram curtly directs her to return to Rossillion, and he rides off to make a name for himself in the Italian wars. Disconsolate, she does his bidding and confides in the countess that she regrets endangering his life simply because of his desire to escape her. To underscore his resentment, Bertram sends messages to his mother declaring that he will never accept Helena as his wife until she can remove a ring from his finger and show him "a child begotten" by him. In response, Helena announces that she will undertake a pilgrimage to the shrine of St. James of Compostela so that in her absence Bertram may feel free to leave the wars and return safely home.

Shakespeare conveniently relocates the shrine of St. James from Spain to Florence so that Helena may encounter Bertram in Italy, where she discovers that he is intent upon seducing a virtuous Florentine woman, Diana. Helena has been inventive in securing a husband, and she now devises a scheme that cleverly exploits Bertram's prurient desires in a design to persuade him to accept her as his wife. Promising Diana rich rewards, Helena persuades her to accept her husband's advances and to impose conditions for an assignation that will permit the two women to secretly change places without his knowledge.* So Bertram unwittingly "beds" his wife and, the wars being over, he returns to France.

---

*The success of this so-called "bed trick" is based on the presumption that the man is so consumed by passion that he is blind to the identity of woman he is bedding. Angelo is another such victim in *Measure for Measure*.

Helena continues in her pursuit of Bertram, following him from Florence to the king's court and then on to Rossillion. There matters are sorted out. She produces Bertram's ring, which she had instructed Diana to demand of him, and appears before him, obviously pregnant, thereby fulfilling both of his requirements for accepting her. A contrite Bertram promises to "love her dearly, ever, ever dearly," and all ends well. But does he in the end recognize her value? Is it possible that her ingenuity, her constancy, and her extraordinary efforts to win him have dispelled his resentment and softened his feelings toward her? Well, we may be permitted some lingering doubts as to his final sentiments on the matter.

So what is it that compels this clever, highly intelligent, resourceful, and desirable young woman to scurry back and forth across Europe in relentless pursuit of a man who is patently unworthy of her. Helena, blind to everything but her passion for Bertram, may be obliviously optimistic about her future with him, but on the whole her devotion engages our sympathy for her, and his haughty demeanor diminishes him in our eyes. As noted, Shakespeare does not presume to explore what it is that prompts a maid to fall in love. But once it happens, as it does with satisfying frequency and for whatever unaccountable reasons, its history becomes an apt subject for a playwright's pen.

# HENRY IV

*"God knows, my son,*
*By what by-paths and indirect crooked ways*
*I met this crown."*

HENRY BOLINGBROKE, Duke of Hereford, later Duke of Lancaster and King Henry IV of England, has an important role in three of Shakespeare's history plays, though he is not the chief character in any of them. In *Richard II* he is overshadowed by Richard himself, and in *Henry IV, Parts 1* and *2*, despite the appearance of his name in the titles, it is Prince Hal and Sir John Falstaff who are the center of interest.

Bolingbroke is the son of John of Gaunt, Duke of Lancaster, and the grandson of the formidable King Edward III, who humbled the French at the battles of Crécy (1346) and Poitiers (1356). On Edward's death in 1377, the crown fell to eleven-year-old Richard, whose father, the Black Prince, had died the year before. Bolingbroke, then, is close to the throne, denied it only because his father Gaunt is the younger brother of the Black Prince.

Henry Bolingbroke is an audacious man; he is also ambitious, possessed of a hidden desire to mount the throne, though of course he never voices his aspiration until the crown is firmly within his grasp. His behavior, however, speaks for itself. Richard complains of

> his courtship to the common people,
> How he did seem to dive into their hearts
> With humble and familiar courtesy. . . .
> As were our England in reversion his,
> And he our subjects' next degree in hope.

And later Bolingbroke describes to his son how at the time he

> stole all courtesy from heaven,
> And dressed myself in such humility
> That I did pluck allegiance from men's hearts,
> Loud shouts and salutations from their mouths
> Even in the presence of the crownéd king.

When we first see him in the opening scenes of *Richard II*, he challenges Thomas Mowbray, the Duke of Norfolk, accusing him of murdering another of Edward III's sons, the Duke of Gloucester. Bolingbroke's challenge is an indirect attack on the king himself, who, many are convinced, had directed Mowbray to carry out the deed. Richard, perhaps fearful that his involvement in the murder will surface, forbids the duel and, to rid himself of the threat, banishes both men from the kingdom.

After the death of his father, Bolingbroke, in a carefully calculated move, violates his exile and returns to England on the questionable legal grounds that he is now Duke of Lancaster and has come only to claim his inheritance. The nobility rally to his cause, angered by Richard's arbitrary imposition of taxes to support an extravagantly lavish court, and soon Bolingbroke is marching on Richard at the head of a formidable army. He insists throughout that he remains a loyal subject of the rightful monarch, but in effect by defying the king's sentence of exile and confronting him with an armed force he has committed an open act of treason and must depose Richard or suffer the consequences of his defiance. Still insisting on his loyalty to the crown, he does indeed take Richard into custody and eventually has him imprisoned.

In the end the king relinquishes the crown, as he knows he must, and he is finally murdered in his cell by a courtier who, according to the play, misinterprets a remark by the new king as a sanction for Richard's assassination. Historians, somewhat less kind than Shakespeare, are convinced that Bolingbroke ordered Richard's death; but the poet will go no further than his admission that, "Though I did wish him dead, / I hate the murtherer, love him murthered." The king announces that he will join a crusade to the Holy

Land in the pious hope that it will prove sufficient penance to wipe the crime from his soul and the moral stain from England itself.

Bolingbroke's audacity is breathtaking; he risks death by returning from exile to challenge a lawful king. He is shrewdly calculating in his evaluation of his country's dissatisfaction with Richard. And by posing as a loyal subject who has come solely to claim his inheritance, he provides political cover for his adherents and any others who might otherwise be reluctant to confront a sitting king. He is also lucky, catching Richard at a time when he has no royal forces at his disposal.

Several figures in *Richard II* describe the deposition of a king as a sacrilege, a disruption of a divinely ordained social and political order. An exchange between John of Gaunt and the Duke of Gloucester's widow early in the play illustrates the belief. The duchess urges Gaunt to avenge his brother's murder, but he refuses, insisting that "God's is the quarrel, for God's substitute, / His deputy anointed in His sight, / Hath caused his death [and] I may never lift / An angry arm against His minister." Others prophesy direful consequences for Bolingbroke's usurpation of the throne. The loyal Bishop of Carlisle predicts that "The blood of English shall manure the ground, / And future ages groan for this foul act." And the dying Richard himself, condemning his assassin, prophesies that his "fierce hand / Hath with the king's blood stained the king's own land."

Shakespeare's history plays confirm these prophecies, portraying the decades that follow as plagued by incessant foreign and civil wars that devastate England, during which a number of her kings suffer a fate similar to Richard's. After a short reign of fewer than a dozen years, Henry V dies of an illness during his campaigns in France. Henry VI is murdered in the Tower of London, as is young Edward V, and Richard III is killed in the battle of Bosworth Field. It was not a good time to wear the English crown.

These prophecies are borne out almost immediately, as the newly crowned king is confronted promptly with a hastily formed conspiracy to restore Richard to the throne. It is fortunately discovered and disposed of, but there are more rebellions to come. *Henry IV, Parts 1* and *2* portray a king deeply troubled in his reign, beset by constant revolts of the Scots, Welsh, and northern English nobles, the Yorks and Northumberlands. He is, further, burdened by a sense of guilt for his role in Richard's overthrow and death, as well as sorrow that his son, Prince Hal, is negligent of his public duties, preferring to spend his days in irresponsible revelry in the stews of Eastcheap with the dissolute knight Sir John Falstaff and his riotous companions.

Henry IV gives the impression of a king who, having come to power by questionable means, is especially sensitive about the prerogatives of the crown.* In an early episode in *Part 1*, he confronts young Henry Percy, known as "Hotspur," the son of the Earl of Northumberland, who has fought valiantly in his name against the invading Scots. Hotspur, however, has been dilatory in handing over to the king the prisoners he has taken, as custom requires, and the king demands heatedly that he do so promptly, threatening that should he not, "you shall hear in such kind from me / As will displease you." The king's haughty manner infuriates Hotspur and sparks the series of rebellions that ensue.

Henry at times confesses to a sense of guilt about the manner in which he has come to the throne. He begins his stormy interview with the wayward Prince Hal with the familiar complaint of an exasperated father, asking in effect: "Where have I gone wrong to deserve such a son?" The lines, however, contain an oblique reference to earlier events:

> I know not whether God will have it so
> For some displeasing service I have done,
> That, in his secret doom, out of my blood
> He'll breed revengement and a scourge for me.

Hal's behavior, he goes on, may be a mark of "hot vengeance and the rod of heaven, / To punish my mistreadings." Again, in his final exchange with Hal in *Part 2*, as the king lies on his deathbed, he admits to "what by-paths and indirect crooked ways / I met this crown" and regrets "how troublesome it sat upon my head." The theme is carried over into *Henry V*, when on the eve of the battle of Agincourt

---

*The "Bolingbroke" of *Richard II* is referred to simply as "King" in the *Henry IV* plays. We shall on occasion cite him as "Henry."

the king kneels in prayer, imploring God: "Not today, O Lord, / O, not today, think not upon the fault / My father made in compassing the crown!" Both father and son live in the hope that they have cleansed themselves and their country of the crime of deposing an anointed king; but in the context of Shakespeare's plays, the full penance will be exacted in the bloody civil wars that follow during the reign of Henry VI and in the tyrannous rule of Richard III.*

It is only in the tumultuous relationship with Prince Hal that we catch a glimpse of the private Henry IV. His son is a severe disappointment to him. In the closing scenes of *Richard II* he asks impatiently, "Can no man tell me of my unthrifty son? / 'Tis full three months since I did see him last. / If any plague hangs over us, 'tis he." When Hal finally answers his father's summons, the king goes so far as to suggest that he might even be willing to "fight against me under Percy's pay . . . to show how much thou art degenerate." Hal's ardent plea of his devotion calms his father, but not until the prince proves his allegiance by saving his father's life at the battle of Shrewsbury is the king finally persuaded of his son's constancy.

Nonetheless Henry IV is the familiar figure of a father who is never satisfied with a son who in his mind continually falls short of expectations. The father's disappointment persists in spite of Hal's efforts to please him, prevailing even to the king's deathbed in *Part 2*. Hal comes upon his father sleeping and, thinking him dead, carries off the crown, lamenting the fact that he must finally wear it. He returns to the king's chamber, indiscreetly wearing the crown, to find his father still alive, and furious. Henry is in turn incensed and saddened. He is convinced that Hal is impatient to succeed him— "I stay too long for thee, I weary thee"—and goes on at length, as if to say, "You couldn't wait, could you?" At the same time he is deeply hurt by what he perceives as his son's apparent lack of concern for a father's suffering: "Thy life did manifest thou lov'st me not, / And thou will have me die assured of it." And he deplores the fact that he must leave his kingdom to a riotous heir. He is, however, finally

---

*The three *Henry VI* plays and *Richard III* were composed before *Richard II* and *Henry IV, Parts 1* and *2*. Shakespeare seems to have adopted this theme of divine retribution in retrospect.

reconciled by his son's plea of devotion and offers advice on how to avoid the "quarrel" and "bloodshed" that has plagued his reign. Hal, he says, should "busy giddy minds / With foreign quarrels," counsel that Hal, as Henry V, follows in undertaking the invasion of France.

Shakespeare's Henry IV is an audacious, devious, and ambitious man who, having achieved the power to which he aspires, finds himself beset by the very forces of rebellion he has unleashed in gaining the crown. He is besieged by the same men who helped him to the throne, and he alienates them perhaps because of a nagging sense of insecurity, since he depended on them in his ambitious designs: what can be gained by arms, he is well aware, can also be taken away by arms. He is as well a disappointed father, distressed at an irresponsible heir who has little interest in the affairs of the kingdom, and he even goes so far as to accuse him bitterly of possible collusion with his enemies.

Henry IV is not an especially sympathetic figure. Stolid, unimaginative, and humorless, he is single-mindedly concerned with securing the crown, and he cares not that in doing so he violates the ancient English laws of succession to the throne. It has been said that he is Shakespeare's image of a new breed of power broker in English history, those who appeal to the easily swayed sentiments of the common people to further their ambitions. In any event, the poet strongly implies that the burden of Henry's high office, to which he had so long aspired, and the weight of guilt at the manner by which he acquired it, eventually break his health. In the end he becomes painfully aware that, in Richard II's eloquent lines, "within the hollow crown / That rounds the mortal temples of a king / Keeps Death his court," a nemesis that at any moment, "with a little pin / Bores through his castle wall, and farewell king!"

# HENRY V

*"This star of England."*

HAL, Harry of Monmouth, the Prince of Wales, Henry V, as he is variously called, appears prominently in three of Shakespeare's history plays, *Henry IV, Parts 1* and *2*, and *Henry V*, and he is mentioned in several others. These plays record a young man's coming of age, portraying him in three stages of his life. We see him first during his carefree Boar's Head days, when he delights in the loose gaiety of the tavern and scorns the stiff ceremony of the royal court, where grave men talk of governance, treaties, taxes, and war. In the next stage we see him as the Prince of Wales, accepting the obligations his royal birth places upon him, often in his era requiring the prince to assume a soldier's role. It is a time of conflicting allegiances for him, when he commands his father's armies to put down rebellion but responds still to the appeal of the tavern, returning there whenever his duties permit. Lastly we see him as King Henry V, a royal monarch who must finally put that early, thoughtless life behind him—not without some regret, we find—and accept his destined role as the ruler of his country.

In these plays Shakespeare structures Hal's transitions from one stage to another by hinging them upon two stormy confrontations between the prince and the king, his father.

## Hal

*". . . riot and dishonor stain the brow*
*Of my young Harry."*

In *Richard II*, Hal's father, the Duke of Lancaster, who has deposed the king and assumed the crown as Henry IV, asks his court in frustration, "Can no man tell me of my unthrifty son?" Again in *Henry IV, Part 1*, the king expresses his admiration for the prowess of the valiant Henry Percy, known as "Hotspur," who has just overcome the Scots, and laments that in contrast he sees only "riot and dishonor stain the brow / Of my young Harry."

When we first encounter Hal in *Part 1*, we learn the reason for his father's displeasure. He spends his time, it seems, in the company of a dissolute knight, Sir John Falstaff, and his common companions, a motley group including Bardolph, Nym, Peto, Gadshill, Mistress Quickly, and others. They frequent the Boar's Head Tavern in the questionable quarter of London known as Eastcheap, where Hal indulges in prankish folly, in drink, song, and the exchange of wit with the fat knight, who is the soul of irrepressible revelry.

The relationship between Prince Hal and Sir John Falstaff may seem a curious one at first. What have they in common, this youth, emerging from late adolescence into early manhood, and this irreverent libertine who admits to some sixty years of age and is unashamedly self-indulgent? We gain a taste of the bond between them when they first appear to us. Falstaff is sleeping off a night of excessive drinking, and he awakens, groggily asking the time of day. Hal scoffs at the question:

> Thou art so fat-witted with drinking of old sack, and unbuttoning thee after supper, and sleeping upon benches after noon, that thou hast forgotten to demand that truly which thou wouldst truly know. What a devil hast thou to do with the time of day?

Lest we think that Hal's remarks are a sign of scorn or disapproval, it is well to remember that the very best of friends often engage in an exchange of insults. Their words reflect, not estrangement but close affection, with each joining in the game of wit assured that the other will take no offense. Falstaff replies in the same vein: "I prithee, sweet wag, when thou art king, as God save thy grace—majesty I should say, for grace thou wilt have none." So each plays his accustomed role in this dance of friendship. They delight in the mutual exchange of ingenuity and wit as Hal chides the fat knight for his large girth, his advanced years, his love of sack (sherry), and his dissolute life, while he in turn reproves Hal as a poor example of a prince.

Hal delights in tricks, the object of which is to catch Falstaff in an outrageous lie so as to test his virtuosity in evading the truth. One such escapade is suggested by Poins, Hal's companion from court. They will agree to accompany Falstaff and his followers in a nighttime robbery of highway travelers. But, Poins explains, he and Hal will not appear until after the theft, when in disguise they will fall upon the thieves, chase them off, and secure the spoils. "The virtue of this jest," Poins concludes, "will be the incomprehensible lies that this same rogue will tell us when we meet at supper."

It is so agreed, and after Poins leaves, Hal in a brief soliloquy voices a rationalization for his errant behavior. When he does assume the crown, he says, those who are aware of his misspent youth will be amazed; he will be like the sun emerging from behind clouds, and

> My reformation, glitt'ring o'er my fault,
> Shall show more goodly, and attract more eyes,
> Than that which hath no foil to set it off.

He shows himself aware of the destiny that awaits him, but he seems callously calculating, as if to say that he is simply using others for his temporary amusement. In balance, Hal's approach to life at this stage may be compared to that of a college student in his final year who savors the last months of his carefree youth before he must leave it, too well aware that the world awaits him with its burden of responsible maturity. In the company of friends with whom he has bonded in study and sport, he picks up the pace of his merriment in celebration of their time together. No one can blame him, nor do we Hal; but, as might be expected, his father sees his behavior in an entirely different light.

The robbery takes place as planned, Hal and Poins surprise the thieves who take to their heels, and then the two retire to the Boar's Head to await Falstaff. The disgruntled knight enters, muttering about cowards and calling for a cup of sack. Hal asks him innocently what happened, and Falstaff launches into a series of "incomprehensible lies," claiming first that a hundred thieves fell upon "poor four of us." Warming to his task, he then gives an account of his own prowess in the melee, at each stage of his tale increasing the number he has personally killed, as the two listen, encouraging him with ill-concealed merriment.* Finally Hal catches him in an obvious lie, and they engage once again in an exchange of insults. Hal calls Falstaff "this sanguine coward, this bed-presser, this horseback-breaker, this huge hill of flesh," and he responds in kind: "'Sblood, you starveling, you eel-skin, you dried neat's tongue, you bull's pizzle, you stock-fish!"

Hal finally reveals the truth of the matter, as he and Poins wait expectantly to hear how Falstaff will evade this evidence of his cowardice. He proves equal to the task, insisting that he knew "by instinct" that Hal was one of the assailants, and that he retreated because it would have been improper for him to cross swords with "the true prince." He did not wish "to kill the heir-apparent," which, he implies, he most certainly would have done had he stayed to fight. The episode ends on a convivial note, all having delighted in the exchange of wit and ingenuity.†

The revelry is interrupted by a message from the court, as the real world intrudes. The kingdom is threatened by rebellions in the north and west, and the king summons his son to help meet the danger. Falstaff proposes mischievously that Hal rehearse his interview with his father, which is bound to be uncomfortable, and we are introduced to another of their entertainments, the "play extempore." In these impromptu skits they delight in satirizing figures in high places, much in the manner of TV's *Saturday Night Live*. Hal readily agrees, and Falstaff assumes the role of the king chastising his son for the low company he keeps, a disreputable group who should all be banished—except for himself, that is, "for, Harry, I see virtue in his looks." Hal insists that they exchange roles and, now in the person of the king, proceeds to warn his son about "that villainous abominable misleader of youth, Falstaff, that old, white-bearded Satan." Falstaff, as the prince, defends himself cleverly, suggesting again that all his dissolute companions should indeed be banned

---

*Their exchange in full may be found on pp. 73–74.
†Hal reveals later that he has returned the money, much to Falstaff's distress.

from his presence, with the exception once more of himself, whom to banish, he declares grandly, would be to "banish all the world." Hal suddenly steps out of his playful role and in his own person answers solemnly, "I do, I will."

"I do, I will"? We catch sight here of a side of Hal's character that casts him in a less than attractive light. His reply to Falstaff sends a chill through us, and we recall his earlier rationalization of his profligate behavior: "My reformation, glitt'ring o'er my fault, / Shall show more goodly." Does he really intend to just discard this man, whom to all appearances he loves, once he no longer serves his youthful pleasure? So it would seem.

Hal is never allowed to forget his early indiscretions. As we shall see, his father reminds him of them forcefully, and his reputation follows him in later life. In the opening scene of *Henry V*, two clerics express admiration for the young king, but as one remarks knowingly, "The courses of his youth promised it not." Having decided to invade France, Hal receives a French ambassador who bears a gift from the dauphin—a barrel of tennis balls. It is an egregious insult, implying that the frivolous youth should occupy his time not with cannon balls but with those less lethal. And later the dauphin voices his contempt for the "vain, giddy, shallow, humorous youth" who leads the English army. Shakespeare employs dramatic irony rather heavily here, of course, as the play builds toward the battle of Agincourt.

This, then, is how Hal spends his days, reveling in the company of this infectiously merry old man, conscious of the role awaiting him but pushing it from his thoughts as he loses himself in mindless youthful pranks and sparkling exchanges of wit. Meanwhile his father must contend with a conspiracy against the crown.

## The Prince

*"I shall hereafter, my thrice-gracious lord,*
*Be more myself."*

In the Middle Ages the initiation into adulthood of a young man of high birth took place more often than not on the battlefield, and England at the turn of the fifteenth century provided ample opportunity for such a rite of passage.* When Henry Bolingbroke, Duke of Lancaster, deposed Richard II and assumed the crown as Henry IV, there were many in the kingdom who deplored the deposition of an anointed king and others who resented what they saw as the usurper's high-handed manner. As a result, Henry's reign was torn by rebellions in Wales, Scotland, and among the northern English nobles, the Yorks and Northumberlands. It is in these wars that Hal assumes his destined role as a prince of the realm and acquires the scars of manhood.

This was an era when monarchs were expected to share with their soldiers the dangers of the battlefield, where strength of character was equated with strength of arm and a king's ability to rule was measured by his ability to lead his armies in conquest. Hal's forebears had been renowned warriors. His grandfather, Edward III, and his uncle, Edward the Black Prince, had won resounding victories over the French at Crécy (1346) and Poitiers (1356). His father fights at the head of his army in the battle of Shrewsbury, and it is only his growing illness that forces him later to relinquish active command to Hal and his younger brother John. It is at Shrewsbury that Hal receives his baptism of fire, when he encounters Henry Percy, known as Hotspur, the fiery son of the Earl of Northumberland. Percy has by that time acquired a reputation as a fierce warrior, having subdued the Scots in battle, and he has assumed command of the rebel forces intent upon the overthrow of the king.

In Hal's stormy session with his father, which he and Falstaff had so lightheartedly rehearsed, the king reproaches his wayward son for his irresponsible behavior, consorting with common revelers in Eastcheap and neglecting his obligations as prince. A subdued Hal replies rather lamely that he will reform: "I shall hereafter, my thrice-gracious lord, / Be more myself." The angry father warms to his subject, however, contrasting his son with the warlike Hotspur, who, to his praise, "leads ancient lords and reverend bishops on / To bloody

---

*In Shakespeare's *King John*, the young Faulconbridge is incensed that he is denied the opportunity to make his name in battle when the kings of England and France resolve their differences amicably.

battles and to bruising arms" while Hal is addicted to "such barren pleasures [and] rude society" that he is altogether discredited in the eyes of his subjects. In a final burst of outrage, the king accuses his son of disloyalty, suggesting that he might even fight "against me in Percy's pay . . . to show how much thou art degenerate."

Hal is stung into an ardent denial:

> I will redeem all this on Percy's head,
> And in the closing of some glorious day
> Be bold to tell you that I am your son.

Hotspur, he insists grandly, "is but my factor"; he will perform "glorious deeds on my behalf" only to "render every glory up" when they meet in battle. Hal's rather presumptuous claim will suggest to modern audiences legends of the lawless American frontier, where the man who outdraws "the fastest gun in the West" inherits the title of "the fastest gun in the West." The father, finally convinced of his son's sincerity, assures him that he will "have charge and sovereign trust" in the coming campaign.

Shakespeare is now confronted with the challenge of transforming the indifferent playboy into a warrior prince. He does so first in the reports of those who see him in his new role. One of Hotspur's lords tells of seeing him mount a horse, when he seemed to

> Rise from the ground like feathered Mercury
> And vaulted with such ease into his seat,
> As if an angel dropped down from the clouds,
> To turn and wind a fiery Pegasus,
> And witch the world with noble horsemanship.

And he later repeats the praise:

> But let me tell the world,
> If he outlive the envy of this day,
> England did never owe so sweet a hope,
> So much misconstrued in his wantonness.

Hotspur scoffs at the report: "I think thou art enamoured / Upon his follies." As a seasoned warrior, Hotspur is a foil to the untested Hal, a figure who in contrast or comparison highlights character traits of the chief figure. Hotspur, we find, is well named. He is headstrong

and hot-tempered, quick to take offense at the smallest slight, and
he alienates his confederates with impatient scorn. Hotspur's character is well defined in his interview with the king after his victory
in Scotland. Henry complains that he has failed to turn over the Scot
prisoners to him and demands imperiously that he do so without delay. When the king stalks off, Hotspur flies into a towering rage at
the insult to his honor, and his father and uncle attempt with little
success to calm him. This incident precipitates the rebellion against
Henry IV, causing all the later turmoil in his troubled kingdom.

This matter of prisoners deserves brief comment, since it surfaces in all three plays and reflects significantly on the character of
Henry V. In medieval conflicts a high-born soldier was worth more
alive than dead, since if taken prisoner his captors could demand a
substantial sum for his release.* Further, captives taken by forces
fighting in the king's name were by custom required to be handed
over to him, a practice Hotspur neglects to observe. In *Henry IV, Part
2*, Falstaff captures the rebel Sir John Coleville and dutifully releases
him to Prince John, anticipating that the prince will give a "good
report" of him in court. As we shall see, the matter looms larger in
*Henry V*, where the French herald, Montjoy, asks the king to name
his ransom before the battle, providing occasion for a pair of Henry's
rousing speeches. His vow not to be taken captive later becomes a
point of contention between him and a common soldier, Williams;
and in a comic scene Pistol subdues a French gentleman of some
means, whose life he spares on the promise of a ransom of two hundred crowns. Finally, in the midst of battle Henry V orders his soldiers to kill all their prisoners, an act that is said by some critics to
define the character of the figure.

Hal comes into his own as a soldier in the battle of Shrewsbury.
First he rescues his father from an attack by the sturdy Scot, Douglas; and then, finally coming face to face with the renowned Hotspur, kills him in single combat. This dramatic encounter is followed by a comic incident. Falstaff comes upon the corpse of
Hotspur, stabs it in the leg to bloody his sword, and carries it off
with the intention of claiming a reward for his conquest of the rebel.

---

*In the battle of Poitiers (1356), Edward III captured the French king, John II,
and his country felt honor-bound to pay an enormous sum to secure his return.

He soon encounters Hal, who is incredulous at the outrageous lie but agrees to support his claim: "For my part, if a lie may do thee grace, / I'll gild it with the happiest terms I have." This is a remarkable gesture on his part. He is willing to surrender credit for the victory, by means of which Hotspur was to "render every glory up"to him, in favor of his old friend, a further mark of the close bond between them.

In *Henry IV, Part 2*, we find that Hal, now secure in his father's confidence, has fully embraced his role as prince, commanding the king's forces in Wales where he subdues the rebellious province. But with a spark of his former carefree self, he is irresistibly drawn once more to his old haunt at the Boar's Head Tavern, where he and Poins again catch Falstaff in outrageous statements that he must wangle his way out of with equally outrageous lies.

But the time for any further youthful levity is drawing to a close. The king is seriously ill.

# *The King*

*"I know thee not, old man. . . .*
*Presume not that I am the thing I was."*

Hal's final transition from careless youth to King Henry V takes place, both literally and dramatically, during another stormy interview with his father in *Henry IV, Part 2*. It does not begin well. He comes upon the king and, thinking him already dead, takes up the crown, contemplating the burden it places on him: "O polished perturbation! golden care!" He that wears it, Hal muses, does not sleep so well as the homely peasant who "snores out the watch at night." It is a sentiment he later echoes, when on the night before the battle of Agincourt he observes that a king, bound by "thrice-gorgeous ceremony," cannot sleep "so soundly as the wretched slave [who] gets him to rest, crammed with distressful bread."

Hal carries the crown off to further lament his father's death, only to return and find him yet alive, and highly indignant at his presumption: "I stay too long for thee," or, that is to say, "You couldn't wait, could you!" The prince pleads his devotion, and his

father is once again satisfied, advising his son with his dying breath
on what awaits the ruler of his "poor kingdom, sick with civil
blows." His final counsel is:

> Be it thy course to busy giddy minds
> With foreign quarrels, that action, once borne out,
> May waste the memory of the former days.

And indeed this is precisely what Hal does in launching an invasion
of France.

But there is another matter that Hal has yet to address: whether
his irresponsible youth will lead his subjects to question his fitness
to rule, a question embodied in the corpulent person of Sir John Falstaff. The fat knight is a thief, a liar, a coward, an infamous consumer of sack, and, as he admits in *Part I* and demonstrates in *Part
2*, a man who exploits Hal's trust in him by accepting bribes from
potential recruits to exempt them from service in the king's armies.
Falstaff's irrepressible gaiety, wit, and warm friendship make him a
joy to know, but the new king is all too aware that he must now put
this cherished companion of his youth and all he represents behind
him if he is to deserve the love and respect of his subjects.

Falstaff is among the throng lining the ceremonial procession as
Hal emerges from his coronation, and the fat knight, fully expect-
ing royal favor, hails him: "My King! My Jove! I speak to thee, my
heart." The newly anointed king pauses to address him sternly—
"I know thee not, old man"—and orders that his friend be banished
from his presence. Hal's rejection, Shakespeare implies, is fatal to
Falstaff. In *Henry V* several figures surmise that it leads to his death.
The Hostess observes that "The King has killed his heart"; and the
subject is raised later in an exchange among his loyal captains. One
compares him to Alexander the Great in martial prowess and, further, in the fact that each of them "killed his best friend." In banishing Falstaff, Hal symbolically—and we may assume painfully—
sheds his profligate youth and accepts his public role as the emblem
of England.

To Shakespeare's contemporaries, Henry V was a figure of almost
mythic stature. He led a campaign against France and achieved a
goal that had escaped the grasp of many of his warlike ancestors: he

united the two crowns into one kingdom. The conquest was to sixteenth century Englishmen, to use a phrase applied to a later generation, "their finest hour"; and Shakespeare fashioned in him a figure of heroic proportions. His Henry V, however, is not some marble statue; as we have seen, "his youth promised it not," and his maturity is not without its flaws.

Indeed, modern response to the figure is sharply divided. Some see him as a ruthless, glory-hungry military adventurer who launches a brutal invasion of a neighboring country with callous disregard for the death and suffering it imposes on both kingdoms. To these critics he is a cold-eyed opportunist filled with hollow rhetoric about his "righteous cause," who betrays his friends and slaughters helpless victims in pursuit of power and wealth. Those of this mind cite, for example, his rejection of Falstaff, his approval of the execution of his old Boar's Head companion, Bardolph, for looting, and his order to kill all the French prisoners during the battle of Agincourt. The Irish poet William Butler Yeats, no friend of the English, characterized him as a figure who "has the gross vices, the coarse nerves of one who is to rule among violent people. . . . He is as remorseless and undistinguished as some natural force."

Laurence Olivier's film version of the play probably portrays Henry V as Shakespeare's generation imagined him. In it, produced in 1944, when Englishmen were engaged in yet another invasion of France, Henry is a sympathetic figure who forbids looting, shows compassion for the suffering of his soldiers, and leads them bravely into battle to achieve a resounding victory over vastly superior forces. He rallies his army with inspiring speeches and commands the respect, love, and devotion of all ranks.

Which is he, then, a man of "gross vices" and a "remorseless . . . force," or a heroic figure leading his soldiers courageously in a "righteous cause"?* In fact, Shakespeare allows for both responses in portraying Henry as a multifaceted character. An instance of his complexity can be observed in his order to kill the French prisoners. Contemporary chronicles leave no doubt that Henry actually issued such a command. Shakespeare could very well have left the incident

---

*As has already become abundantly evident, I prefer the latter characterization.

out of the play, but he chose to include it, and he did so not once but, according to modern editions, twice, each time attributing the decision to a different motive.

In the first instance the order is issued in the heat of battle, as a matter of tactical necessity. The English have survived two assaults, and now the king observes that "the French have reinforced their scattered men" in apparent preparation for a third. Henry has need of every soldier on the line to meet the threat. His dilemma is illustrated in an earlier comic scene in which Pistol captures a French soldier whose life he spares in promise of ransom. Pistol escorts his prisoner to the rear and, we may assume, secures him carefully in anticipation of gain. The scene, though farcical, illustrates the king's problem. Pistol is but one of any number of English soldiers who are standing guard over their investment at a time when they are needed on the line to meet the threat of a new French assault. Henry orders his men to kill their prisoners and rejoin their units, rather than leave a body of enemy soldiers to wander freely in the English rear.

He repeats the order, this time in angry reaction to an atrocity. During the battle a troop of French cavalry sack the English camp, in the process killing the boys left to guard it. The king, enraged at the senseless slaughter, orders the French prisoners killed in retaliation, in effect answering one atrocity with yet another, an act that in modern times would surely be condemned as "a crime against humanity." It is not clear which of these versions appeared on the stage of the Globe Theater; and modern directors are left to decide between them, depending on whether they wish to portray Henry V as an infamous adventurer or the model of a Christian king.*

Which is he, then? Each of us is shaped, for good or bad, by those we encounter as we mature, whether it be a schoolmate, a minister, an inspiring teacher, a public figure, or a favorite uncle. In like manner the youth of Shakespeare's Henry V is indelibly influenced by three figures—Hotspur, his father the king, and Falstaff, each of whom offers some qualities worthy of his emulation and some less attractive traits he would be wise to discard. His youth, then, is not

---

*In their film versions, both Laurence Olivier (1944) and Kenneth Branagh (1989) omitted the order.

wasted on him; those years and those figures mold his character and determine the kind of king he is to be.

Hotspur is a valiant warrior, conqueror of the Scots, in King Henry IV's words, "the theme of honor's tongue [and] sweet Fortune's minion and his pride," a youth who already "leads ancient lords and reverend bishops / To bloody war." But Hotspur has a hair-trigger temper that erupts at the slightest provocation, a fault in him that his uncle condemns as "harsh rage, / Defect of manners, want of government, / Pride, haughtiness, opinion, and disdain." His explosive arrogance alienates his allies and troubles his friends.

Hal emulates Hotspur's bravery and martial prowess, rescuing his father, and killing the high-strung Percy at the Battle of Shrewsbury. He matches Hotspur in his intensity and in the energy with which he leads his men in battle; but he displays none of his rival's abrasive temperament. This is not to say, however, that Henry V is without fire. He bursts into anger on occasion, notably when he rails at his close friend Lord Scroop for conspiring to assassinate him, again when a soldier, Williams, questions the integrity of his vow not to be ransomed, and later on discovering that the French have slaughtered the boys guarding the camp.

On at least two other occasions when he faces provocations that in all likelihood would have sent Hotspur into a rage, Henry shrewdly turns insults to his advantage. On receipt of the Dauphin's tennis balls, he maintains his composure and uses the incident to proclaim his determination to conquer France, establishing himself to his court as a resolute, defiant leader. Again, when the French herald Montjoy repeatedly asks the king to name his ransom before the battle, Henry replies only with mock exasperation—"Good God! Why should they mock poor fellows thus!" Montjoy's question is a taunt, meant to discredit the king in the eyes of his soldiers, who are well aware that a monarch is worth more to the enemy alive rather than dead and may well survive the battle while their lives are forfeit. Henry, rather than fly into a rage, seizes the occasion to issue a defiant speech identifying himself with the common soldier, both "but warriors for the working day." He ends with the promise that the French, if victorious, shall have no ransom "but these my joints."

It may well be that his association with Falstaff, with whom he regularly traded a barrage of insults, developed in the young man a toleration for taunts. At any rate, Henry embraces Hotspur's admirable qualities as a soldier and leader but rejects the stereotypical abrasive arrogance often associated with the warrior class. Further, rather than alienate his allies he forges a united army including captains from Scotland, Ireland, Wales, and England, lands that were continually at odds during his father's reign.

Henry IV is an example to his son as a man devoted to his public role. He has a clear-eyed goal as king, a determination to rid his country of the rebellious forces that torment it, and he sets about the task of preserving the integrity of the throne with dedicated resolve. That dedication, Shakespeare implies, takes its toll on his health and leads to his death under the weight of the burdens of high office upon one who is after all but a man. Henry IV, however, does not convey the image of an ideal king, nor is he a martyr to the public welfare. In his first tumultuous encounter with his son, he describes how he came to the throne. It was not, he explains, by mingling with "vulgar company" as Hal does, but by keeping his distance from the common people. "By being seldom seen," he continues, "I could not stir, / But like a comet, I was wondered at." In this way he kept his "presence fresh and clean" and was able to "pluck allegiance from men's hearts."

Henry IV, further, is like a man who, having acquired high office by questionable means, is especially sensitive to its dignities and feels the need to respond aggressively to any threat, real or imagined, posed to its privileges. Troubled by "what by-paths and indirect crooked ways / I met this crown," he reacts angrily to Hotspur's refusal to release the Scot prisoners to him, seeing it as a challenge to the royal prerogative. As we have seen, it is his imperious demand that infuriates Hotspur and precipitates the rebellions that plague his reign.

Hal adopts Henry IV's dedication to his public role, his devotion to the crown, and his desire to rid England of "civil blows." He is equally as resolute in pursuing his country's welfare and as painfully aware of the burden of the throne, having watched his father's decline in body and spirit under the weight of its responsibilities. But as Henry V he rejects the imperious air with which his father had ruled and closes the distance he had kept between the royal person and his subjects. The Chorus in *Henry V*, for example, describes the king's posture on the night before Agincourt:

> O now, who will behold
> The royal captain of this ruined band
> Walking from watch to watch, from tent to tent,
> Let him cry, "Praise and glory on his head!"
> For forth he goes, and visits all his host,
> Bids them good morrow with a modest smile,
> And calls them brothers, friends and countrymen.

He bestows on each, the Chorus concludes, " a little touch of Harry in the night."

Touring the camp in disguise, he is perfectly at ease in joining a group of common soldiers seated around a fire, where they talk of the war, the upcoming battle, and their prospects of survival. Young Williams leaves no doubt of his loyalty to the king but wonders about the fate of his immortal soul. Henry and he speculate whether each soldier will be held accountable "at the latter day" for the terrible deeds he must perform on the morrow, or if the king, whom to disobey is unthinkable, will be charged with the sins of his soldiers when he must finally face his Maker. These are deep thoughts indeed during this "little touch of Harry," as Shakespeare alludes to a moral and legal issue that troubles the conscience of nations to this day. Henry's youthful dalliance with "vulgar company," at the Boar's Head Tavern, it may be said, has endowed him with a sympathy for the plight of his common subjects and an appreciation for the strengths and weaknesses of this "band of brothers," as he calls them.

The third, and perhaps the most influential, figure in shaping the character of Henry V is Sir John Falstaff. His liberating humor, his irrepressible optimism, his sparkling wit, his delight in trickery and impromptu skits mocking the great and famous, and his unquenchable joy of life make him, as one critic put it, a man of "broad humanity." Prince Hal revels in his company and benefits from his friendship, for, as has also been said, "to love Falstaff is the equivalent of a liberal education." As we have seen, Hal's time with the fat knight and his followers has given him a sympathetic appreciation for the lot of his common subjects and has left him even-tempered in the face of affronts, which like Falstaff he cleverly turns to his advantage.

Henry V remains a trickster who delights in trapping others in their own conceits, as he had his corpulent friend, but his devices take on a darker dimension once he is king. When he learns of a plot to assassinate him, he engages the unsuspecting conspirators in amiable conversation and hands them documents implying that they are commissions. The traitors discover to their distress that they are holding their own death warrants. And after Agincourt he extricates himself from a potentially embarrassing situation brought about by his flare of temper the night before, when Williams questioned the disguised king's vow not to be captured and held for ransom. They arranged to resume their quarrel after the battle, which would have involved the king in a totally inappropriate public confrontation with one of his own soldiers. It is cruel trick he plays on Williams, but a necessary one, and it succeeds in mollifying the disgruntled man, who complains quite rightly that he had no way of knowing that he was arguing with a king.

But there is a side to Falstaff that has no place in the character of a Christian monarch. He is, as we have seen, a liar, a thief, a coward, an insatiable consumer of sack, and he betrays a public office entrusted to him. He cynically mocks those in positions of authority and then hypocritically ingratiates himself to them in hopes of gain. Henry V, knowing that he cannot allow himself to be tainted with such qualities, purges any residual stain of them from his royal person and banishes Falstaff from his presence.

Henry V, then, matches the valor of Hotspur, but not his tempestuous arrogance. He adopts his father's devotion to the crown, but not his imperious haughtiness. He embraces Falstaff's celebration of life, but rejects his intemperate excess. In the final scenes of the play he displays an iron resolve in imposing his demands on the defeated French, and he then reveals a surprising new dimension to his complex character when he woos Princess Katherine with all the eloquence of an ardent lover. Shakespeare portrays a man who represents all that his fellow Englishmen valued in a king, a figure they looked back upon with awe and affection. And his deeds were not forgotten. The legacy of his conquest survived his death for hundreds of years as English monarchs who succeeded to the crown continued to include among their many titles "King [or Queen] of England and France."

Within a year of his final triumph, Shakespeare's "star of England" was dead, the victim ingloriously of a camp sickness. He left a nine-month-old son on the throne, who during his turbulent reign lost all his warlike father had achieved in France, and in the end was forced to relinquish the crown itself. Shakespeare chronicled his history in his earliest plays, *Henry VI, Parts 1, 2,* and *3.*

# HENRY VI

*"O where is faith? O where is loyalty?"*

THE THREE PARTS of *Henry VI* dramatize half a century of English history, from the funeral of Henry V in 1422, whose death left a nine-month-old son to inherit the throne, to the murder of Henry VI in 1471. *Part 1* covers the first twenty-three years of the life of the king, *Part 2* the next ten, and *Part 3* the final sixteen. These were turbulent years for England. Shakespeare chronicles the incessant squabbling of the country's nobility during Henry's minority, which led to the loss of all the conquests his famous father had gained in France, the constant dissension within the kingdom during his maturity, and finally the devastating civil conflict between the houses of Lancaster and York, known as the War of the Roses. The trilogy ends with the ascendancy of the house of York as Edward IV resumes the throne and Henry is murdered by Richard, Duke of Gloucester (later Richard III).

During his long reign, Henry proves an inept monarch. As a child he is overshadowed by his powerful uncles, Humphrey, Duke of Gloucester, and John, Duke of Bedford, and he is little involved in managing the kingdom, a task assigned to Humphrey, who conducts affairs in his stead as Lord Protector. During his maturity, Henry is either unwilling or unable to assert royal authority, with the result that angry divisions grow unchecked within the kingdom, finally erupting into civil war. He plays no part in the conflict, a helpless pawn in the power struggle, controlled by one side and then the other while his armies are assembled and engaged by his fiery queen, Margaret of Anjou. He is a pitiable figure, a pious, ascetic man bewildered by the contentious nobles who tear at the social and political fabric of the kingdom, and he is isolated and ignored when they come to blows.

Shakespeare portrays the conflicting forces in a series of confrontations in the presence of the king. The first arises early in his reign between Humphrey and the powerful and wealthy Bishop (later Cardinal) of Winchester, Henry's uncle and great-uncle. The two engage is mutual recriminations in Parliament, which erupt into a bloody brawl between their followers. Henry pleads with them: "I would prevail, if prayers might prevail, / To join your hearts in love and amity." It is scandalous, he declares, "that two such noble peers as you should jar." The Earl of Warwick finally shames Winchester— "What, shall a child instruct you what to do?"—and the two are temporarily and, it seems clear, only superficially reconciled. They clasp hands publicly before the boy king but in private asides disavow the gesture of friendship. In later episodes Winchester orchestrates the disgrace, dismissal, and murder of the loyal and able Humphrey.

The angry animosity between the dukes of Somerset and York proves to be equally irreconcilable. In a dramatic scene entirely invented by Shakespeare, the two confront each other in the Temple Garden. York plucks a white rose from a bush and Somerset a red one, flowers that then become symbols of allegiance to the house of either York or Lancaster and provide the name for the war between them. Their feud becomes public on the day when Henry, having come of age, is crowned king in Paris. Somerset and York are present, and a servant of each appears before the king, requesting permission to fight a duel to resolve a dispute between them. The two dukes declare that their servants' quarrel is more properly their own, and they challenge one another. Henry does nothing to resolve their animosity except to direct them to desist—"Henceforth I charge you, as you love our favor, / Quite forget this quarrel and the cause"—and to remind them that their united services are needed to oppose an uprising by the French. Exeter's observation on the scene is both perceptive and prophetic:

'Tis much [difficult] when scepters are in children's hands,
But more when envy breeds unkind divisions;
There comes the ruin, there begins confusion.

The king's failure to take strong action when confronted by the "unkind division" between Somerset and York later proves devastating to the English cause. When a superior French army besieges the valiant Lord Talbot, both refuse to come to his aid, each blaming the other for their inaction, and Talbot is defeated in a battle that takes the lives of himself and his son.

Henry vacillates, allowing the social and political wounds of the kingdom to fester. When the Cardinal of Winchester and the Duke of Suffolk bring charges of treason against Humphrey, the king only protests feebly that he is confident of his innocence, a posture that prompts Humphrey's enemies to plot his death. Suffolk arranges to have him killed, and when he is charged with the murder Henry banishes him, but only when the common people, irate at the death of the popular duke, threaten to storm the palace if action is not taken against his murderer.

Henry takes comfort, and refuge, in his faith. He is a pious man—according to his queen, entirely too pious. "All his mind is bent on holiness," she complains; his habit is "to number Ave-Maries on his beads," and "his loves / Are brazen images of canonized saints." He yearns for peace and when confronted with raging adversaries seeks to reconcile them with scraps of Scripture—"For blesséd are the peacemakers on earth"—fruitless pleas to proud nobles defending their place and honor.

Henry makes some fatally bad decisions because of his youth, his weakness, or his innocent idealism. He generously restores Richard to the title and lands of the Duke of York.* Later he takes the penniless Margaret of Anjou as his queen over the objections of Humphrey, who had arranged for his marriage to the daughter of a powerful French noble. When the Duke of York returns from Ireland at the head of an army, he confronts the king, asserting his right to the throne, and two of England's most prominent nobles, Warwick and Salisbury, support him in his claim. In the face of their desertion, Henry can only exclaim plaintively, "O where is faith? O where is loyalty?" The two sides resort to arms, clashing at the battle of St. Albans, the first of many in the long civil war between York and Lancaster. The king's army is defeated, resulting in another

---

*The duke's father had been executed and his property confiscated for joining in a conspiracy to assassinate Henry V.

confrontation with the duke, this time in Parliament. York reasserts his claim, arguing that the king's grandfather, Henry IV, had usurped the crown illegally by raising a rebellion against Richard II, and in consequence that he, rather than Henry, is the rightful ruler of England. The king is defiant at first—"No: first shall war unpeople this my realm"—but inwardly he is fearful, confessing in an aside, "I know not what to say: my title's weak." Rather than stand against York, he crumbles, proposing a compromise: if he may for his "lifetime reign as king," he will confirm the duke as his heir.

The king's supporters are enraged at this submission of the "base, fearful, and despairing Henry," and they desert him. York solemnly swears agreement to the compromise, an oath he promptly breaks. But Henry's troubles have only begun. In designating York as heir to the throne he has disinherited his own son, Edward, Prince of Wales, and he soon faces an infuriated Queen Margaret, who rails at him: "Ah, wretched man!" "I shame to hear thee speak. Ah, timorous wretch!" Irate, she declares that until the decision is reversed, "I here divorce myself / Both from thy table, and thy bed," and she stalks off: "Come, son, let's away. / Our army is ready; come, we'll after them."

In these disputes Henry continually assumes the posture of conciliator, attempting to reconcile opposing forces, little realizing that his unwillingness to take strong action against one side or the other is perceived as permissive weakness. As the dying Clifford, his constant ally, later laments: "Henry, had'st thou swayed [ruled] as kings should do, / Or as thy father and his father did," ambitious spirits would not have "sprung like summer flies [and] ten thousand in this luckless realm" would not have left "mourning widows" behind.

Thus the War of the Roses begins, brought on, Shakespeare implies, by a weak, irresolute, and innocently idealistic king who cannot control his contentious nobles. In *Henry VI, Part 3* we watch the tide of conflict ebb and flow as the poet portrays the barbarism, betrayal, and horror of civil war in scenes replete with acts of savage brutality. Shakespeare packs sixteen years of carnage into one short work, tracing the shifting fortunes of the opposing sides: The house of York triumphs at the battle of St. Albans but is routed by Lancaster at Wakefield. York is victorious at Towton but suffers defeat at Warwick. In the end York closes out this dismal history with a decisive victory at Barnet. And during the course of these battles we are witness to scenes of vengeful butchery. York kills Old Clifford in battle; in retaliation his son stabs the duke's young son, Rutland. York himself is captured and killed, and in response his sons slaughter twelve-year-old Edward, the Lancaster Prince of Wales. Fathers kill sons, and sons fathers, as the conflict ravages England.

Henry VI is little involved; "the warlike Margaret" assumes command of his armies and his cause, leading the Lancaster forces in battle, securing alliances, and joining in the slaughter of York. The king is of no consequence, except as a symbol of rule. Before the battle of Towton, Clifford, who has become Margaret's chief lieutenant, advises Henry, "I would your Highness would depart the field. / The Queen hast best success when you are absent." And in a parlay between the opposing sides preceding the battle, Edward, who has succeeded his father as Duke of York and aspirant to the throne, demands of the king, "Now, perjured Henry, wilt thou kneel for grace / And set thy diadem upon my head?" But it is Margaret who answers him defiantly: "Go rate thy minions, proud insulting boy!" Henry finally demands to be heard, "I am a king, and privileged to speak," but Clifford silences him: "My liege, the wound that bred this meeting here / Cannot be cured by words. Therefore be still." And he does indeed remain silent as the feuding nobles hurl insults back and forth. Banished from the field, he sits alone upon a hill to watch the battle surge to and fro, all the time lamenting his lot. He envies the common man, he says, the simple shepherd who eats his meager meal, consumes his "thin drink," and falls asleep under a tree untouched by the "care, mistrust, and treason" that afflict a monarch.* York emerges triumphant, and the murdered duke's eldest son is crowned Edward IV. Rival kings now contest for England, already plagued by proud, factious nobles.

The battle of Towton lost, Henry flees but is soon captured and imprisoned in the Tower of London. The resourceful Margaret

---

*Compare the speech to Henry V's "Upon the king . . ." on the night before Agincourt. The sentiment is the same, but the later poetry is heightened art.

returns with new allies—the French king, the Earl of Warwick, and Edward's younger brother Clarence—who turn against the newly crowned king. They defeat Edward, rescue Henry, and restore him to the throne; but the king wants no more of ruling. He appoints Warwick and Clarence as Protectors jointly, while he, as he says, will "lead a private life, / And in devotion spend my latter days, / To sin's rebuke and my Creator's praise." His reign is short-lived, however, as Edward, aided by his brother Richard, returns, defeats Margaret at Barnet, and reascends the throne.

Henry is conveyed once more to the Tower, where he is sought out by Richard, now Duke of Gloucester, who is determined to remove once and for all the lingering threat to his brother's crown and to his own ambitions. Henry, who is well aware of Richard's intent, taunts him with allusions to his crippled body, the result, it was said, of a troubled birth that left him with a humpback, a withered arm, and a stunted leg. Richard emerged from his mother's womb, Henry scoffs, "an undigested and deforméd lump," a baby born with teeth in his head, he goes on, "to signify thou cam'st to bite the world."* This rare show of defiance is cut short, however, as Richard stabs him in mid-sentence. Henry dies with a cry of combined Christian penitence and charity: "O God forgive my sins, and pardon thee!"

Thus ends Shakespeare's dramatic chronicle of the life of Henry VI, an essentially good man but a disaster as a king. As a youth he is dominated by proud men who clash during his minority, seeking advantage from the power vacuum left by a child monarch. Arriving at maturity, he inherits a kingdom divided by ambitious nobles, accustomed to pursuing their independent ends without restraint from a strong central authority. He is a man of peace, but he is too well-meaning, too malleable, too pious to establish control over lords who, contemptuous of his docility, bristle at the slightest sign of curbs on the grasp and reach of their power. Those most devoted to him soon fall victim to a vengeful rival, as does the loyal Humphrey, or to envious adversaries, as does the brave Lord Talbot.

---

*Recent scholarship has cast doubt on reports of Richard's deformity, a fabrication, it is thought, of Tudor propagandists. Shakespeare accepts their version, however, and pursues it in *Richard III*.

Stripped of the counsel and support of such men, he seeks to maintain the peace of the realm by submitting to the demands of avaricious nobles, granting royal favors that only serve to fuel their ambition. And in the end, abandoned by his friends and imprisoned by
his enemies, he dies alone at the hands of the most avaricious of
them all, Richard, Duke of Gloucester.

# HENRY VIII

*"Would it not grieve an able man to leave*
*So sweet a bed fellow?"*

SHAKESPEARE'S HENRY VIII is not the bloated tyrant of his later years but a more youthful and engaging king at a critical juncture in his reign, during the divorce from his queen, Katherine of Aragon, and his marriage to Anne Boleyn.* The poet omits mention of his execution of Sir Thomas More and two of his six wives, one of them Anne, which came later. Shakespeare is understandably discreet in his portrayal of the father of the late, highly revered Elizabeth I and the great-uncle of the reigning English monarch at the time, James I, so we see Henry rather as a husband genuinely remorseful at divorcing his wife, as a monarch ruling over a court rife with intrigue, and as a father exultant at the birth of Elizabeth.

Henry is a sympathetic figure in the play, publicly a monarch devoted to the welfare of his kingdom and privately a troubled man, torn between his duty to the state and compassion for the wife he feels he must shed. This may not be the Henry VIII that history chronicles, but the play ends at a time when the terrors of his reign lie ahead of him, and Shakespeare is silent about later events.

Within the time frame of the play, Henry is a robust, good-hearted man in his late thirties, at times outgoing and playful. In one episode, accompanied by a group of his courtiers all disguised as simple shepherds, he bursts upon a lavish party hosted by his aus-

---

*Henry VIII* is said to be Shakespeare's last play. *The Tempest* is the last that is entirely his, while this one appears to have been composed in collaboration with John Fletcher. Scholars disagree as to which scenes should be attributed to one or the other playwright, but we shall leave the issue to them and for convenience cite Shakespeare as the author throughout.

tere lord chancellor and Archbishop of Canterbury, Cardinal Wolsey. The intrusion has obviously been prearranged, since Wolsey receives them courteously despite their homespun appearance, and once they unmask the festivities are enlivened by music and dance.* It is here, Shakespeare proposes, that the king first casts eyes on Anne Boleyn.

The plot of the play revolves around two matters chiefly, the divorce and a series of four trials, much like a modern courtroom drama, during which contentious figures vie for the king's favor. The first of these trials ends with the execution of the Duke of Buckingham after his conviction on dubious charges devised by Wolsey, who makes it a practice of disposing of anyone, other than himself, who has the king's confidence. The second is an indictment of the queen herself. Katherine had incurred the cardinal's enmity by accusing him, before the king, of filling his own treasury by imposing illegal taxes and commissions on the English people. As a consequence of this incident, Shakespeare implies, Wolsey "out of malice / To the good queen," according to a gentleman of the court, plots her downfall.

Henry's divorce is surrounded with ambiguities. On the one hand it is attributed to his fascination with Anne. As another gentleman of the court remarks, "the marriage to his brother's wife / Has crept too near his conscience," but a companion replies sardonically, "no, his conscience / Has crept to near another lady." Wolsey seizes on the king's "marriage to his brother's wife" to discredit Katherine. She had been married to Henry's brother Arthur only months before his death, and the king took her as his wife shortly thereafter, raising questions in canon law about the legitimacy of the marriage. Wolsey, intent on arranging a union between Henry and the French king's sister, raises the issue.

On the other hand it seems as if the question is raised by another party entirely. Henry gives an account of a private discussion with a French ambassador concerning a prospective bridegroom for his daughter Mary. The king relates the ambassador's doubts about the legitimacy of any of his children by Katherine since she was "some-

---

*Their entrance is announced by the discharge of ceremonial cannon, which, it is said, was responsible for the burning of the Globe Theater in 1613.

times our brother's wife." It is because of these doubts, he contends, that he has requested the pope to annul the marriage.

Shakespeare's Henry agonizes over the divorce. He deeply regrets the necessity to cast aside a loyal wife of twenty years so as to ensure the unassailable succession to the English throne. It is, however, his duty as the monarch to do so. He praises her highly:

> That man i'th'world who shall report he has
> A better wife, let him in nought be trusted,
> For speaking false in that; thou art alone . . .
> The queen of earthly queens.

And he is despondent, he says, at the need: "Would it not grieve an able man to leave / So sweet a bed fellow?" Thus the divorce is precipitated both by legal concerns over the legitimacy of the marriage and by Wolsey's enmity toward the queen. His plan to replace her with the Catholic sister of the French king goes array, however, when the king becomes fascinated with the Protestant Anne. When Katherine is brought before the king, Wolsey, and the papal legate Capuchius, she refuses to be judged by the cardinal whom she brands as "mine enemy," and after pleading her case to the king, she abruptly departs. The decision is foreordained, however; she is reduced in royal rank from queen to "princess dowager, / And widow to Prince Arthur." Letters are sent to the pope requesting approval of the divorce, and Henry promptly marries Anne.

To his credit, the king is stoutly loyal to his ministers. When Katherine accuses Wolsey of imposing commissions for the collection of onerous taxes to augment his own wealth, Henry is reserved in judgment and does no more than cancel the commissions. Later, however, he learns of Wolsey's enormous wealth, acquired at the expense of his subjects' welfare. And at the same time he is shown a letter the cardinal has sent to Rome, advising the pope to delay approval of the king's divorce. This is too much for Henry. In the third of the play's trials, Wolsey is convicted of misusing his office and stripped of all his honors. He retires to an abbey and dies shortly thereafter.

Wolsey's successor in the king's favor fares better. Archbishop Cranmer falls victim to court intrigues, and in a fourth trial envious parties accuse him of spreading "new opinions / Divers and dangerous, which are heresies." Henry, who is hidden nearby, overhears the debate and bursts upon the scene, rebuking the accusers for their disrespectful treatment of Cranmer. "I had thought I had had men of some understanding / And wisdom of my council," he says sternly, "but I find none." To confirm his unwavering faith in Cranmer, he calls upon the archbishop to baptize his newly born daughter Elizabeth and to serve as the child's godfather.

In the final scene Shakespeare selects Cranmer to deliver his eulogy to the English crown. He prophesies a glorious reign for the future queen, who, he predicts,

> now promises
> Upon this land a thousand thousand blessings,
> Which time shall bring to ripeness: she shall be . . .
> A pattern to all princes living with her,
> And all that shall succeed.

So says Cranmer, and he adds Shakespeare's bow to the sitting monarch, James I. In time Elizabeth will appoint

> another heir
> As great in admiration as herself,
> So shall she leave her blessedness to one . . .
> Who from the sacred ashes of her honour
> Shall star-like rise, as great in fame as she was.

Henry, of course, is delighted with this tribute to his daughter.

Shakespeare portrays Henry VIII as a man troubled by court intrigues but intensely loyal to his ministers. In creating a sympathetic figure who contrasts with the king that history records, the poet endows Henry with diverse motives for his actions, some of them admirable, others less so. His decision to divorce Katherine, a wife he appears devoted to, is prompted by a need to ensure the royal succession—and by his passion for Anne Boleyn. He is steadfast in his support for Wolsey until he learns of his onerous taxation—and of his opposition to the divorce. On the one hand he acts as a king dedicated to the stability of his country, on the other as a man who wants to shed one wife and marry another. Some of his qualities we can approve of, others we may deplore; but somehow Shakespeare manages to create in Henry a believable character at a crucial turning point in his life, before he embarks on his willful reign of terror. Buckingham is the only figure in the play to lose his head; both Katherine and Wolsey die natural deaths; and nothing is said of retaliation against Cranmer's accusers. But a host of others will feel the edge of an executioner's ax in the years to come, when Henry VIII will ruthlessly dispose of any that incur his displeasure.

# HOTSPUR

*"A son who is the theme of honor's tongue, . . .*
*Who is sweet Fortune's minion and her pride."*

THE EARLS OF NORTHUMBERLAND are a warlike breed. They guard the northern borders of England—the "marches" as they are called—constantly alert to marauding bands of Scots eager for their cattle and goods or an invading army intent upon conquest. The son of the present earl, young Henry Percy, called "Hotspur" by all, lives up to the reputation of his ancestors. He is a valiant warrior, fierce in battle and jealous of his honor; and as his name implies, he is quick to anger, impatient of delay, and prone to speak his mind intemperately.

We first hear of Hotspur in *Henry IV, Part 1* when the king receives news of his victory over the Scots at Holmedon. Henry is full of praise, envious, he says, that

> my Lord Northumberland
> Should be the father of so blest a son,
> A son who is the theme of honor's tongue, . . .
> Who is sweet Fortune's minion and her pride.

"It mak'st me sad," he confesses, when he hears of such a valiant young man but can see only "riot and dishonor stain the brow / Of my young Harry." Shakespeare fashions Hotspur as a foil to Prince Hal in the play, a figure whose qualities, in both similarity and contrast, lend emphasis to those of the principal character. In this opening scene Hotspur's martial prowess reflects unfavorably on the prince, who spends his time in riotous revels with the irrepressible Sir John Falstaff at the Boar's Head Tavern in London's unsavory Eastcheap. Later, in a stormy interview with his son, the king contrasts the two. While Hal is irresponsibly pursuing his "inordinate and low desires [in] rude society," Hotspur, a "Mars in swathling clothes," gains honor by leading "ancient lords and reverend bishops on / To bloody battles and to bruising arms."

Much that we learn of Hotspur is revealed in what others say about or to him, and at one point we gain an impression of him from Hal's perspective. Well aware that he is compared unfavorably to Percy, he describes him with satiric wit as a thickheaded warrior, all brawn and no brain:

> I am not yet of Percy's mind, the Hotspur of the north, he that kills me some six or seven dozen of Scots at a breakfast, washes his hands, and says to his wife, "Fie upon this quiet life! I want work." "O my sweet Harry," says she, "how many hast thou killed to-day?" "Give my roan horse a drench," says he, and answers, "Some fourteen," an hour after; "a trifle, a trifle."

Hal's wit may be tainted with a touch of envy, but it surely colors our response to Hotspur as we encounter him in later scenes. By the end of the play, Hal has matched him in valor but not in some of his less agreeable qualities, such as his quick temper and habit of intemperate outbursts.

Hotspur's temper is immediately evident in his first appearance when he is confronted by an angry Henry IV. It was the accepted practice of the time that prisoners taken by the king's forces were to be turned over to the monarch. This was no small matter since highborn captives were customarily ransomed for handsome sums, adding to the coffers of the royal exchequer. Hotspur, it appears, has been dilatory in delivering his captives, and Henry demands an explanation. Hotspur insists that he has not denied him the prisoners and gives an account of an incident that caused the delay. While recovering from the battle, he explains, "dry with rage and extreme toil, / Breathless and faint, leaning on my sword," he was approached by "a certain lord, neat and trimly dressed, / Fresh as a bridegroom," who as an agent of the king demanded the prisoners.

We never see this "certain lord," but Hotspur's picture of him is Shakespeare's most complete description of a stock character of the theater, the "court fop." This figure is skilled in courtly manners but little else. He generally appears outlandishly attired in garments trimmed liberally with lace and an ornamented hat, which he sweeps off flamboyantly in executing exaggerated bows. Shakespeare's fops are for the most part dim-witted, effete individuals who are uncomprehending targets for the wit of principal characters, who talk rings around them.*

Hotspur describes the fop in scornful detail:

> He was perfumed like a milliner,
> And 'twixt his finger and his thumb he held
> A pouncet-box,† which ever and anon
> He gave his nose and took't away again. . . .
> And as the soldiers bore dead bodies by,
> He called them untaught knaves, unmannerly,
> To bring a slovenly unhandsome corpse
> Betwixt the wind and his nobility.

He was so exhausted, Hotspur goes on, "all smarting with my wounds being cold," that it angered him to see the lord "shine so brisk, and smell so sweet, / And talk so like a waiting-gentlewoman / Of guns, and drums, and wounds." Especially galling was his condescending remark that "but for these vile guns / He would himself have been a soldier," and in response, Hotspur explains, he "answered neglectingly I know not what" and dismissed him.

The king is unimpressed: "Why, yet he doth deny his prisoners." Send them, he warns ominously, "or you shall hear in such a kind from me / As will displease you." And he stalks out, Hotspur flies into a rage at this affront to his honor, and he launches into a stormy tirade, citing at length his many grievances against Henry, as his companions attempt to calm him. He concludes with a fiery

---

*Others are *Hamlet's* Osric and Le Beau in *As You Like It*. Still other figures are "foppish," those such as Sir Andrew Aguecheek in *Twelfth Night* and Alexander Slender in *The Merry Wives of Windsor*, but they are not attached to a court.

†The box contains aromatic herbs with which the bearer wards off unpleasant odors. A modern fop will be seen waving a perfumed handkerchief about.

vow: "All studies here I solemnly defy, / Save how to gall and pinch" the king—and his playboy son as well, whom he would have "poisoned with a pot of ale." This heated exchange, in Shakespeare's account, ignites the rebellions that plague the king during his reign, as chronicled in the two parts of *Henry IV*.

In another episode Shakespeare portrays Hotspur's intemperate tongue and quarrelsome spirit. He has forged a formidable alliance with which to challenge the king: his father the Earl of Northumberland, his uncle the Earl of Worcester, his brother-in-law the Earl of March, the Scots under Douglas, and the Welsh led by Owen Glendower. They meet in Wales to finalize the plan of campaign, where, it appears, Glendower singles out Hotspur to relate in excruciating detail his many exploits and the extraordinary events in the heavens and on earth that accompanied his birth—signs, he insists, of his future greatness. Hotspur scoffs at the notion: "Why, so it would have done at the same season, if your mother's cat had but kittened, though yourself had never been born." The exchange becomes bitter, as Glendower continues to insist on his uniqueness and Hotspur to heap scorn on it.

They almost come to blows but are distracted by a more critical matter, the division of the spoils, an agreement to carve up the kingdom among them once they defeat the king. Here Hotspur proves unexpectedly quarrelsome, complaining that the border between his anticipated lands and Glendower's is inequitable. He insists that it be redrawn, and the smoldering Welshman adamantly refuses:

> *Hotspur.* I'll have it so, a little change will do it.
> *Glendower.* I'll not have it altered.
> *Hotspur.*                                    Will not you?
> *Glendower.* No, nor you shall not.
> *Hotspur.*                                    Who shall say me nay?
> *Glendower.* Why, that I will.

The tension between the two mounts until Hotspur abruptly relents, calling the difference inconsequential. He tosses the matter aside with the offhand admission that

> I do not care, I'll give thrice so much land
> To a well-deserving friend:

But in the way of bargain, mark ye me,
I'll cavil on the ninth part of a hair.

Thus Hotspur needlessly alienates his friends and allies. When
Worcester and March reprove him for riling Glendower, he defends
himself by describing him as a man who is "as tedious / As a tired
horse," and he complains that the Welshman had kept him awake
"last night at least nine hours" with accounts of the supernatural
signs of his destined renown. Worcester's reproof is a catalogue of
Hotspur's qualities: "You are too wilful blame,"* he counsels, and

You must needs learn, lord, to amend this fault.
Though sometimes it show greatness, courage, blood,
Yet oftentimes it doth present harsh rage,
Defect of manners, want of government,
Pride, haughtiness, opinion, and disdain.

Thus Henry Percy, in the words of one who knows him well. He
shrugs off the advice: "Well, I am schooled—good manners be your
speed!" Later, on the eve of the battle of Shrewsbury, Glendower
fails to join the rebel forces, a defection fatal to their cause; and,
though Shakespeare does not say as much, we are left with the implication that the Welshman absents himself because of pique at
Hotspur's taunts.

   In the end Hal slays Hotspur, and in contrast to his earlier
ridicule he pays tribute to the fallen warrior: "Fare thee well, great
heart!" By this time Hal has shown himself Hotspur's match in
valor, though he has yet to demonstrate his inspiring leadership. In
time he embraces some of Percy's qualities and shuns others. As
Henry V he emulates the dead man's courage, dedication, daring,
and leadership, but not his penchant for "wilful blame" nor his vol-
canic temper.† He manages to control his tongue when provoked,

---

*The phrase is variously interpreted, but in the context it most likely means
"too ready to find fault." But since, as Worcester says, it also shows "greatness,
courage, blood," it has the added meaning of "decisive" or "quick to act."
   †He becomes enraged only at the treachery of Lord Scroop, the challenge to his
integrity by the soldier Williams, and the French slaughter of the boys in the English camp. He is, after all, human.

even turns the occasion to advantage, as he does before the battle of Agincourt when he answers a French herald's repeated request that he name his ransom. And he demonstrates his skill in uniting rather than dividing his allies, winning the loyalty of the Welsh, Irish, Scot, and English captains.*

*See "Henry V," pp. 118–119.

# IAGO

*"I hate the Moor."*

IAGO'S MOTIVES are a mystery. What could have possessed him to orchestrate "the tragic loading of this bed" in the final scene, the lifeless bodies of his wife Emilia, Othello, and Desdemona—for surely, as Lodovico says to him, "this is thy work"? In this, the most tightly plotted of Shakespeare's plays, the chain of events leading to that "tragic loading" can be clearly traced. The reason for it is more uncertain.

We learn little of Iago's background. Apparently he has long been Othello's loyal subordinate, an aide in whom the general places absolute trust—he is "honest, honest Iago." In the opening scene of the play, however, we find that he is something else entirely. Othello has appointed Cassio to the position of his lieutenant, leaving Iago in the less important military rank of "ancient," and Iago is incensed at what he sees as a betrayal of his long and faithful service. Is it this alone, the disappointment at being passed over for promotion, that causes him to seethe with envy and so "hate the Moor," as he confesses?

Shakespeare keeps us abreast of Iago's inner thoughts and plots throughout by means of his asides, his soliloquies, and the confidences he shares with his companion, Roderigo. This ineffectual dupe, it appears, has hopes of winning the lovely Desdemona, daughter of a wealthy Venetian senator, and has been using Iago as a go-between to deliver expensive gifts to her on his behalf—gifts, we become aware, that never reach her hand. Roderigo remains blind to his duplicity, even when Iago confides in him that "I am not what I am"—not, that is, the honest, dedicated, loyal, trustworthy ancient to Othello. With all these revelations and confidences, however, we remain uncertain why he "hates the Moor" so intensely. In time he voices the suspicion that Othello has seduced his wife, that "'twixt my sheets / He's done my office." But he suspects the same of Cassio, and the accusation sounds contrived, as if in justification of an already deeply embedded enmity. None of these motives, however, can adequately explain his determination to be avenged on them both.

Iago's first exercise of that hatred occurs in the opening scene when he incites Desdemona's father with the news that his daughter has secretly married Othello. This attempt to foment trouble for the Moor fails, however, when the matter is peacefully resolved in the court of the duke, who then sends Othello on a military mission to meet the threat of a Turkish invasion of the distant Venetian colony in Cyprus. The general is accompanied by his staff, including Cassio and Iago, and by his bride.

Iago's malice grows and widens as we watch his progress from small to larger iniquity. In Venice his chief concern, he says, is to discredit Cassio so as "to get his place," and he conceives of a scheme "to abuse Othello's ear / That he is too familiar with his wife." The arrival of the party in Cyprus, however, proves a watershed event for Iago, one in which his malice takes on new dimensions. When Desdemona comes ashore, Cassio greets her with a courtly gesture, taking her "by the palm," as Iago observes in a muttered aside. And further: "With as little a web as this will I ensnare as great a fly as Cassio" in order to strip him "out of his lieutenancy." Immediately after, he witnesses the passionate reunion between Othello and Desdemona and, stung by the scene, his malignancy rises to embrace them as well: "O, you are well tuned now! But I'll set down the pegs that make this music, as honest as I am."

There is no evidence that he intends the death of anyone up to this point. But after witnessing that joyful reunion his malice mounts. No longer content to simply "abuse Othello's ear" about Cassio, the focus of his anger has shifted to the happy couple themselves, and he decides to "put the Moor / At least into a jealousy so strong / That judgment cannot cure" it. His scheme is still a work in progress, however, "'tis here, but yet confused," one that will evolve in time. The opportunity soon presents itself. Pursuing his vendetta against Cassio, he plies the lieutenant with wine, and Cassio proves to be an aggressive drunk, easily enraged by the former governor, Montano, whom he wounds in a fight. Othello enters to prevent further bloodshed, and on hearing Iago's account of the brawl, dismisses Cassio.

So far, so good. The ancient is now in line to succeed the disgraced lieutenant, but Iago is no longer satisfied with that simple outcome. When a distraught Cassio confides in "honest Iago," he advises the lieutenant to enlist Desdemona's aid, asking her to plead his case with her husband so that he may be restored to the general's good graces. The intrigue has reached a new level now, a design to discredit her as well. He will contrive an occasion for the Moor to witness Cassio and Desdemona deep in intimate conversation, after which he can "pour this pestilence into his ear / That she repeals [pleads for] him for her body's lust." In this way, he says, he will "turn her virtue into pitch" and "out of her own goodness, make the net / That shall enmesh them all."

In the long central scene of the play, Iago is able to transform Othello from a loving husband into a man consumed by jealousy, intent upon the death of his wife. This episode deserves close attention for a number of reasons. Prominently, the success of a performance depends on whether that transformation is convincing, that is, whether we accept Shakespeare's proposition that a man's faith in his wife could dissolve in such a short space of time. Then too, the scene is a dramatic portrayal of the depth of Iago's hatred and the scope of his iniquity. His achievement is stunning. It is not his relatively simple task to nourish a seed of discontent in an already suspicious husband; his challenge is to arouse jealous rage where before there had been only profound love. His progress is, further, a vivid illustration of a theme that threads its way through many of Shakespeare's plays: Evil leads on to larger evil.*

How does he do it? His success depends, of course, on Othello's unquestioned trust in "honest, honest Iago." Lest we think that the Moor is too gullible for belief, we are told that everyone in the play is convinced of the ancient's integrity, each at one time or another

---

*Notably in the career of Macbeth. He kills a king to gain a crown and soon finds that he must take more lives to keep it, until, as he discovers, "I am in blood / Stepped in so far, that should I wade no more, / Returning were as tedious as go o'er."

expressing a conviction that he is "kind" and "honest," a man of absolute "trust." His devices are familiar, a series of subtle hints and insinuations, culminating in outright fabrications. His first approach is quite direct. In persuading Cassio to enlist the aid of Desdemona, he promises to divert Othello so that the two might confer more freely. Instead he ushers the Moor into the very room where they can be seen together. Cassio slips away, too embarrassed to face his general, and Iago mutters, "Ha! I like not that," explaining "I cannot think it, / That he would steal away so guilty-like, / Seeing you coming." Desdemona disarms the insinuation, however, by acknowledging openly that she had indeed been speaking with Cassio, and then proceeds to plead his case. Othello finally agrees to hear him out, and she leaves satisfied.

A different approach is now called for, and Iago begins to accuse Cassio by indirection. He asks Othello if the lieutenant knew about his courtship of Desdemona. Yes, Othello replies, and adds that in fact he "went between us very oft." Iago responds with a significant "Indeed!" and then adopts the manner of a man who has some hidden knowledge that he is unwilling to share with a friend. Othello, suspecting that there is "some monster in [his] thought / Too hideous to be shown," is maneuvered into a position where he has to pry the truth out of his loyal ancient.

Again by indirection, Iago plants the seed of jealousy by cautioning against it: "O beware, my lord, of jealousy; / It is the green-eyed monster, which doth mock / The meat it feeds on"; but, he adds, how terrible it must be for one "who dotes, yet doubts, suspects, yet fondly loves!" The hook is in—now to set it securely! "Look to your wife," he advises, "observe her with Cassio," and then he dwells on the Moor's lack of sophistication, his inexperience with Venetian women, who, he confides, "do let heaven see the pranks / They dare not show their husbands." As for Desdemona herself, he reminds Othello that "She did deceive her father in marrying you; / And when she seemed to shake and fear your looks, / She loved them most."

Iago then backs off, advising Othello to interpret his remarks to no "longer reach / Than to suspicion," but at the same time to take notice if Desdemona should plead for Cassio "with any strong or vehement importunity"—which, of course, she has already and will soon again. "Much will be seen in that," he adds knowingly. Iago leaves on that note but returns to confront a dangerously distraught Othello torn between love for his wife and rage at the thought of her infidelity. Iago is taken aback by his success. Listening to him rave about his loss—"Farewell! Othello's occupation's gone!"—he is stunned: "Is't possible, my lord?" But then Othello turns his wrath on the accuser, seizing him by the throat and threatening: "Villain, be sure you prove my love a whore . . . [or] thou hadst better have been born a dog / Than answer my waked wrath!" Astonished at the intensity of Othello's passion—"Is't come to this?"—Iago adopts the stance of an unjustly maligned friend: "Take note, take note, O world, / To be direct and honest is not safe."

Othello demands, "I'll have some proof," and the situation obviously calls for a more direct device. Iago concocts the fiction of an occasion when he occupied the same bed with Cassio, who, he says, uttered endearments in his sleep, "sweet Desdemona" and "sweet creature," and, still asleep, kissed him repeatedly. Othello is now firmly convinced and begins to utter violent oaths against his wife. At this point, however, Iago's scheming has entered a new phase, one in which he must suppress the truth to avoid endangering himself; and only the grave can ensure silence.

Again by indirection, he seals Desdemona's fate. "Let her live," he advises, prompting Othello to devise "some swift means of death for the fair devil." Meanwhile the Moor's loyal ancient is to carry out another task: "Within these three days let me hear you say / That Cassio's not alive." Oh, and by the way, "Now art thou my lieutenant." Thus, Iago, who begins with the relatively modest goal of replacing Cassio, arrives at a stage where to save himself he must secure the death of those he has ensnared in his web of deceit. Evil has led inexorably on to larger evil.

For the balance of the play, Iago improvises measures to cement Othello's conviction and prevent disclosure of their murderous intent, and the chief means of prevention is to eliminate those who might stumble on the truth. He persuades Roderigo to ambush Cassio, but the inept dupe succeeds only in wounding him and ends up being killed himself by Iago. Meanwhile Othello has indeed murdered Desdemona; and when Emilia insists that she was an innocent victim of Iago's duplicity, her husband stabs her as well. He silences her too late, however, for the truth is known; and when Othello demands of Iago why he has "ensnared my body and soul," he vows that henceforth he "never will speak word."

Iago, then, is villainous from the outset, but the play suggests motives that would seem insufficient to justify his hatred of the Moor. It may well be that in plays like *Othello* and *Richard III* Shakespeare is simply not concerned with attributing motives to obviously evil characters, any more than he is with explaining why men and women fall in love in any of his plays. In the poet's dramatic cosmos, evil simply exists—for who can deny its presence—and when unleashed it takes on a life and momentum of its own.

Shakespeare's vision of evil may owe something to the biblical account of its origin and nature. This tale, told so majestically in John Milton's epic poem *Paradise Lost*, begins with a war in Heaven, where Satan leads a rebellion against the Almighty. Failing, he and his rebel hoards are condemned to suffer the eternal fires of Hell. They are free to roam the cosmos outside of Heaven, however, and Satan undertakes a perilous voyage to Eden, where he encounters Adam and Eve. For him and, it is said, for all the fallen angels ever after, the sight of joy, or beauty, or love among humans is a painful reminder of the bliss they have lost, filling them with anguish and an uncontrollable urge to destroy all signs of goodness in mankind.

Read from this perspective, Iago's motives are irrelevant. Shakespeare offers an image of naked evil that cannot abide the spectacle of happiness and seeks to obliterate it so as to be relieved of the painful memory of happiness lost. The love between Othello and Desdemona is an affront to Iago, and he justifies his anger at the sight of it by heaping scorn on their devotion. "It is merely a lust of the blood and a permission of the will," he assures Roderigo, a consequence of "our raging motions, our carnal stings, our unbitted lusts." Further, Iago becomes obsessed with the sight of an innocent Desdemona. Witnessing her joyful reunion with her husband, he is incensed—"O, you are well tuned now!"—and plots to "turn her virtue into pitch" and "out of her own goodness" to destroy her. He hates Cassio as well, because of his promotion, of course, but also because he is a handsome, courtly gentleman, schooled in social graces, possessed of "a daily beauty in his life / That makes me ugly."* Iago, it may be said, bears a resemblance to Milton's devils; he seethes at the sight of Othello's nobility, Cassio's beauty, and Desdemona's virtue, is enraged by the display of love between the Moor and his wife, and is compelled to despoil all that is good in them.

In a brief episode during the closing scene of the play, Shakespeare draws the curtain aside momentarily to give us a glimpse of this tradition. Facing Iago, a distraught Othello exclaims, "I look down towards his feet: but that's a fable; / If that thou be'st a devil, I cannot kill thee." The lines conjure up the image of medieval depictions of Satan as half man, half goat, a cloven-hoofed satyr with hairy shanks and a horned brow. A "fable" it may well be, but when Othello, who is armed, attempts to kill this "demi-devil," as he calls him, it is perhaps significant that he finds he cannot.

Othello's question, then, "why he hath ensnared my soul and body," is never answered. Today we strive to reduce evil to a subject for clinical analysis. Its causes are to be found, it is said, in social ills, poverty, childhood abuse, parental neglect, or it is attributed to physical and psychological disorders, schizophrenia, attention deficit, retardation, or to religious mania. But to Shakespeare the devil was a devious and destructive presence in human affairs, eager for human souls, at times concealed behind a mask of respectability, at others openly displayed in all its ugliness.

It is difficult, despite Iago's iniquity, not to admire his ingenuity. If at any time during a performance we may pause and ask, "Why is he doing this to them?" the only answer, however unsatisfactory, is because Iago is who he is. When asked his reasons at the end of the play, he refuses to answer, and it may well be that he doesn't know himself. To Shakespeare, then, evil simply exists, and those who may wonder what it looks like with a human face need look no further than the motiveless malice of Iago.

---

*There is a hint here also of class animosity. In some productions Cassio is played as a gentleman and Iago as a commoner, identified as such by his speech patterns and demeanor.

# JAQUES

*"All the world's a stage."*

AS A MEMBER of Duke Senior's banished court in *As You Like It*, "the melancholy Jaques" provides diversion for the lords in their Forest of Arden exile. Unlike the cheerfully optimistic duke, who "Finds tongues in trees, books in running brooks, / Sermons in stones, and good in every thing," Jaques looks upon nature with mournful sympathy. The even-spirited duke regrets the necessity to kill a deer for their sustenance, but for Jaques the depredation of forest creatures is a cause for sorrow. One of the duke's lords reports watching him reduced to tears at the sight of a wounded stag and hearing him philosophize on the spectacle. The suffering animal provided occasion for him to indict the entire "body of court, city, court, / Yea, and of this our life" for killing a creature in its "native dwelling-place."

Jaques has a sharply sardonic sense of humor. On one occasion the lords pass an idle hour listening to one of their number sing a ballad that has in it the refrain, "come hither, come hither, come hither." Jaques adds a stanza substituting "ducdame, ducdame, ducdame," and when asked the meaning of the word by the group assembled about him, he replies that it is "a Greek convocation, to call fools in a circle." At one time or another Jaques exchanges wit with most of the cast, in one episode with the lovesick Orlando. The two have not warmed to one another, and they parry with what the jester Touchstone later describes as the "Retort Courteous":

> *Jaques.* I thank you for your company, but good faith, I had as lief have been myself alone.
> *Orlando.* And so had I: but yet for fashion sake I thank you too, for your society.

*Jaques.* God buy you, let's meet as little as we can.
*Orlando.* I do desire we may be better strangers.

Jaques detects a kindred spirit in Touchstone, whom he met, he tells the duke, by chance in the forest. The jester consulted his watch, Jaques relates, and commented gloomily on the passage of time: "And so from hour to hour, we ripe, and ripe, / And then from hour to hour, we rot, and rot, / And thereby hangs a tale." The comic art of the jester includes a talent for accommodating his wit to suit his audience, and, apparently sensing Jaques's melancholy temperament, he addressed him in that spirit. Jaques is elated to find a companion so closely attuned to his own sentiments, and so, he goes on, "I did laugh, sans [without] intermission, / An hour." In view of the fact that we never see so much as a single smile crack his dour visage, this account may be an exaggeration, but there is no discounting his delight in the jester: "O noble fool! / O worthy fool! Motley's the only wear."

Later in the scene Jaques elaborates on Touchstone's theme—"we ripe, and ripe, / And then . . . we rot, and rot"—in what are his most memorable lines. Beginning with one of Shakespeare's familiar analogies between life and art—"All the world's a stage"—he goes on to describe the seven ages of man as so many acts in a pointless play:

- "The infant / Mewling and puking in the nurse's arms."
- "The whining school boy . . . creeping like snail / Unwillingly to school."
- "The lover . . . with a woeful ballad / Made to his mistress' eyebrow."
- "A soldier . . . seeking the bubble reputation / Even in the cannon's mouth."
- "The justice . . . full of wise saws, and modern instances."
- "The lean and slippered pantaloon . . . [with] his shrunk shank, and his big manly voice / Turning again to childish treble."
- And finally, "second childishness and mere oblivion / Sans teeth, sans eyes, sans taste, sans every thing."

Life then, to "the melancholy Jaques," ends where it has begun, and all in between is a succession of predetermined scenes empty of apparent meaning.

Jaques's commentary on passing events and life in general casts him at times in the role of a chorus, and nowhere so conspicuously as in the closing lines of the play. Following the marriage of the four couples, he bids each farewell with a parting prophecy of their lives to come. He addresses the men, beginning with a generous prediction for Orlando—"You to a love that your true faith doth merit"— and another for Oliver with a hint of the prosperity awaiting a man wedded to the daughter of a duke—"You to your land and love and great allies."

His prophecy for Silvius, "You to a long and well-deserved bed," has a subtle sting, implying that all his chivalric pleas to Phebe in which he pledged his faith, duty, service, purity, and humility are but a thin veneer to his true intent, to "bed" her. There is nothing subtle about his prediction for Touchstone, however. The sophisticated jester has pursued the simple goatherd Audrey with but one goal in mind, and that once achieved, Jacques forecasts, they will fall to "wrangling, for thy loving voyage / Is but for two months victualled." As for himself, he declines the invitation to return to court, now restored to Duke Senior by his brother, who, having met "an old religious man," has been converted "from the world." Jaques will remain in the forest to converse with the brother, for as he explains, "Out of these convertites, / There is much matter to be heard and learned."

For Jaques, then, the glass of humanity is always half empty, and life itself seems a cruel joke. He likes nothing better than to sit, as he puts it, and "rail against our mistress the world and all our misery." And like many who deplore the sorry state of the human race, he idealizes the rest of nature, weeping over a wounded deer (though later he is perfectly at ease joining in a meal of the hunter's game). In balance, his melancholy fits provide entertainment for the banished lords, and his mournful wit is not without its share of wisdom. And in a larger sense, his somber presence forms a realistic backdrop to Shakespeare's romantic tale of love in the Forest of Arden.

# THE JESTERS

THE JESTER was a familiar figure in the courts of medieval Europe, entertaining the lords and ladies of the nobility during an era when entertainment was hard to come by. With his antic pranks, his songs, his acrobatic wit, and his sharp intelligence, he offered them distraction from the harsh realities of the time. Perhaps Shakespeare's most graphic evocation of the jester's appealing mischief is the description of a dead one, *Hamlet*'s Yorick. The gravedigger, tossing a skull to the prince, identifies it as the remains of the former king's fool and recalls one of his pranks: "A pestilence on him for a mad rogue! 'a poured a flagon of Rhenish on my head once." Hamlet remembers him fondly from his childhood: "Alas, poor Yorick! I knew him, Horatio—a fellow of infinite jest, of most excellent fancy. He hath borne me on his back a thousand times." And addressing the skull, he asks dolefully: "Where be your gibes now? your gambols, your songs, your flashes of merriment, that were wont to set the table on a roar?"

Shakespeare's jesters exercise their art in the plays principally, though by no means exclusively, in three ways. First, they entertain with comic episodes at otherwise tense moments in the action. Then, with their riddles, songs, and displays of wit, they lay bare the truth of events. Finally, in consequence they often fill the role of a chorus, voicing the themes of a play, though often in such arch, ironic terms that their meaning seems to escape the grasp of their troubled patrons. These three functions, then—the comic, the perceptive, and the choric—largely characterize the dramatic function of Shakespeare's fools.

There are other characters who serve in similar roles, of course— Enobarbus in *Antony and Cleopatra*, Thersites (bitterly) in *Troilus and Cressida*, Puck in *A Midsummer Night's Dream*, and Pompey in *Measure for Measure*, among many—all of whom offer those same comic, perceptive, or choric observations on unfolding events, but they are not in the strict sense jesters, our concern here. Among those specifically identified as such are Lear's Fool, Feste in *Twelfth Night*, and Touchstone in *As You Like It*.* Each, however, appears as a distinct character in himself, as Shakespeare fashions multiple variations on the figure.

The appeal of the jester lies in his wit, and the only way to convey the essence of that wit is to quote it at some length. Hence these character sketches will cite specific lines somewhat more often than is the practice elsewhere in these pages.

## Lear's Fool

*"Truth's a dog must to kennel."*

King Lear divides his kingdom between his two eldest daughters and disowns his youngest, Cordelia, when she refuses to put her love for him on public display. We sense that both acts are sheer lunacy and wonder if his advanced age has addled his wits. It is his Fool who voices our sentiments with his mocking jests and riddles, as he attempts to convince the king of his folly.

One of the jester's comic devices is the mockery of court members, which he is at liberty to do up to a point. He must be circumspect in his satiric thrusts, however, for should he exceed his license he may well suffer for it; as Lear warns his Fool at one point, "Take heed, sirrah—the whip."[†] The principal target of the Fool's mockery is Lear himself, though he at times directs his "gibes" at both Kent and Goneril; and the chief theme of his incisive jests is the king's folly in dividing his kingdom between his daughters. It is Lear, not his jester, he insists repeatedly, who is the fool.

In his opening salvo the Fool address the subject with sharp irony: "Why, this fellow has banished two on's daughters and did

---

*Lavatch, the "Clown" in *All's Well That Ends Well*, is another, though he is of less interest than these others. In *The Tempest*, Trinculo is also a jester, but we do not see him in his courtly role.

[†]Operagoers will recall that Rigoletto so infuriates the Duke of Mantua's courtiers with his insults that in retaliation they aid the duke in his scheme to seduce the jester's daughter, Gilda.

the third a blessing against his will." He dwells on the theme that Lear is the real fool since "all thy other titles thou hast given away; that thou wast born with." He continues in this vein:

Thou mad'st thy daughters thy mothers—for thou gav'st them the rod and putt'st down thine own breeches.

And:

Thou hast pared thy wit o' both sides and left nothing in'th'middle.

He sings songs, ridiculing the daughters:

Then they for sudden joy did weep,
        And I for sorrow sung,
That such a king should play bo-peep,*
And go the fools among.

He proposes riddles:

*Fool.* Canst tell how an oyster makes his shell?
*Lear.* No.
*Fool.* Nor I neither; but I can tell why a snail has a house.
*Lear.* Why?
*Fool.* Why to put's head in; not give it away to his daughters, and
    leave his horns without a case.

And he voices a theme of the play: "Thou should'st not have been old till thou hadst been wise."

It is notable that the Fool's effort to force the truth of his rashness on Lear avoids the subject of the banishment of Cordelia. He mentions it only once, when in his opening sally he remarks that Lear has done "the third a blessing against his will." It is this allusion that draws the king's warning about "the whip," to which the Fool replies with mock resignation that "Truth's a dog must to kennel," that is, must not be allowed to roam free, rather must be caged. Lear's treatment of Cordelia is too sore a subject for him to hear it parodied with ironic levity; it is too close to the bone of his sorrow, so the Fool judiciously steers clear of that painful folly thereafter.

*That is, act childishly.

The Fool is faithfully loyal to Lear, sharing his master's distress as he wanders over the heath, raging at the pitiless elements. He pleads with the king to seek shelter, urging wittily, and reasonably, that "'tis a naughty night to swim in." He recites doggerel verse and sings songs:

> He that has a little tiny wit—
>> With heigh-ho, the wind and the rain—
> Must make content with his fortunes fit,
>> Though the rain it raineth every day.*

He remains at the king's side after he goes mad, and when Lear is finally persuaded to rest, he lies beside him. In lines that reflect the sense that the natural order of their lives has been overturned, Lear mutters, "we'll go to supper in i'th'morning," to which the Fool replies, "and I'll go to bed at noon." This is the last we see or hear of him. Shakespeare simply drops him from the play, perhaps because, as some have suggested, Lear finally gains wisdom in his madness and no longer has need of his wise Fool's counsel.†

# Feste

*"Nothing that is so is so."*

In *Twelfth Night*, Feste, called simply "Clown" in the text, is an altogether different jester. Indeed he seems more of a troubadour, moving from court to court, seeking profit for his services wherever it may be found. Olivia leaves the impression that he is a member of her household, however, and when he returns tardily she expresses her displeasure at his absence, dismissing him curtly: "I'll no more of you. Besides you grow dishonest." Attempting to regain her favor with his wit, he employs a common device of Shakespeare's jesters,

---

*See also Feste's epilogue to *Twelfth Night*, p. 157.

†In the closing scene Lear remarks that "my poor fool is hanged," but, as has been suggested, the word "fool" here is a term of endearment, and he is referring to Cordelia. This seems reasonable; Lear has no room for thoughts other than the loss of his daughter.

a question followed by a circuitous line of reasoning, to show, as the Fool does Lear, that she is the true fool:

> *Clown.* Good madonna, why mourn'st thou?
> *Olivia.* Good fool, for my brother's death.
> *Clown.* I think his soul is in hell, madonna.
> *Olivia.* I know his soul is in heaven, fool.
> *Clown.* The more fool, madonna, to mourn for your brother's soul, being in heaven. Take away the fool, gentlemen.

Feste later appears in Duke Orsino's court, where he entertains him with a song appropriate to his melancholy distress over Olivia's rejection:

> Come away, come away, death,
>     And in sad cypress let me be laid,
> Fly away, fly away, breath;
>     I am slain by a fair cruel maid.

He expects to be well rewarded for his performances, here accepting payment from the duke for his song. On other occasions he cleverly solicits a higher fee. When Viola gives him a coin for his witty discourse, he asks hopefully, "Would not a pair of these have bred, sir?" And when Orsino later does the same, he replies, "but that it would be double-dealing, sir, I would that you could make it another"— and then he asks for a third, which he says "pays for all."

Feste plays the more traditional jester's role in replying to various figures who address him in expectation of a witty response, and he does not disappoint:

> *Olivia.* What's a drunken man like, fool?
> *Clown.* Like a drowned man, a fool, and a madman. One draft above heat [too many] makes him a fool, the second mads him, and the third drowns him.

And later:

> *Viola.* Save thee, friend, and thy music. Dost thou live by thy tabor?*
> *Clown.* No, sir, I live by the church.

*That is, make a living with his music.

*Viola*. Art thou a churchman?

*Clown*. No such matter, sir, I do live by the church; for I do live at my house, and my house doth stand by the church.

Still later, he banters with Orsino:

*Duke*. I know thee well. How dost thou, my good fellow?

*Clown*. Truly, sir, the better for my foes, and the worse for my friends.

*Duke*. Just the contrary: the better for thy friends.

*Clown*. No, sir, the worse.

*Duke*. How can that be?

*Clown*. Marry, sir, they praise me and make an ass of me. Now my foes tell me plainly I am an ass; so that by my foes, sir, I profit in the knowledge of myself, and by my friends I am abused.

Feste is not just the arch observer, however, one who stands off and comments on events from a distance. He is closely involved in the action, carousing with Sir Toby Belch and Sir Andrew Aguecheek as they drink, dance, and sing into small hours of the morning, and he participates in the humiliation of Malvolio. The steward is imprisoned in "a dark room," the customary therapy for his supposed madness, and Feste assumes the role of "Sir Topas the curate" to insist that he is possessed by the devil, widely believed to be the cause of it: "Out hyperbolic fiend! How vexest thou this man!" "Fie, thou dishonest Satan!"

In his role as a chorus, Feste also voices the themes of the play. As Shakespeare constantly reminds us, especially in the comedies, nothing is what it seems. In *Twelfth Night*, Viola disguises herself as Orsino's page Cesario; Olivia is in mourning for her brother's death but unveils herself to Cesario; the twins, Sebastian and Viola, are mistaken for one another; and Feste, as we have seen, assumes the identity of the parson Sir Topas. In this sense it is he who tells us: "Nothing that is so is so." And when Malvolio demands of Olivia why she has permitted him to be subjected to such rough treatment, Feste is delighted that he has been repaid for his earlier insults: "And thus the whirligig of time brings in his revenges." It is he as well who sings the puzzling epilogue to the play, beginning with the stanza:

When that I was a little tiny boy,
    With hey, ho, the wind and the rain,
A foolish thing was but a toy,
    For the rain it raineth every day.*

Why, we may ask, this melancholy note here at the close of a comedy: "The rain it raineth every day"?

## Touchstone

*"Ay, now I am in Arden, the more fool I."*

The fool of *As You Like It*, Touchstone, plays two roles chiefly—he is at times a jester, at others a lecher. He displays all the traditional qualities of the first of these figures, except that he does not sing, a talent left to others in this tuneful play. He is seen initially in the company of Rosalind and Celia, with whom he exchanges witty banter. When they are invited to join the court of Duke Frederick to witness a wrestling match, he remarks sardonically that "It is the first time that ever I heard breaking of ribs was sport for ladies."

Frederick has deposed Rosalind's father, the former duke, called simply "Senior," but allows her to remain at court because of her close friendship with his daughter Celia. He has a sudden change of mind, however, and banishes Rosalind as well. Celia is so attached to her friend that she decides to join her in exile, and the two conspire to join Duke Senior in his refuge in the Forest of Arden. They persuade Touchstone to join them in their flight and he agrees to do so, though with some reluctance.

The rustic life is not congenial to Touchstone, who is very much a creature of the court. In a comic confrontation between court and country, he finds himself completely out of his element, with no one in this pastoral setting to appreciate his sophisticated wit. In an

*Again, see the Fool's song from *King Lear*, p. 154.

exchange with the simple shepherd Corin, he has recourse to the jester's customary device of a question followed by a circuitous chain of logic:

> *Touch*. Wast ever in court, shepherd?
> *Corin*. No truly.
> *Touch*. Then thou art damned.
> *Corin*. Nay, I hope.
> *Touch*. Truly thou art damned, like an ill-roasted egg, all on one side.
> *Corin*. For not being at court? Your reason.
> *Touch*. Why if thou never wast at court, thou never saw'st good manners; if thou never saw'st good manners, then thy manners are wicked, and wickedness is sin, and sin is damnation. Thou art in a parlous state, shepherd.

The good-natured Corin takes no offense, however, and replies only that "You have too courtly a wit for me. I'll rest." The jester, desperate now for a response, accuses him in plainer terms of yet another sin, profiting from "the copulation of cattle," for which he is surely "damned"; but Corin still refuses to rise to the bait. Touchstone is no more successful with the goatherd Audrey, whom he attempts to seduce with witty advances, only to find that she has no idea what he's talking about. As he says in frustration, "When a man's verses cannot be understood, nor a man's good wit seconded with the forward child, understanding, it strikes a man more dead that a great reckoning in a little room."

The only exception to this vexing pattern, though we only hear of it, is a chance encounter with the melancholy Jaques, one of several courtiers who have joined Duke Senior in his exile. Jacques is elated over his meeting with the "motley," yet another term for the jester, based on the traditional multicolored costume he wears. In an account of their exchange, he praises Touchstone—"O noble fool! / A worthy fool! Motley's the only wear"—extolling his doleful philosophy of time and life. Jaques quotes him at some length, delighting in his conclusion that "from hour to hour, we ripe, and ripe, / And then from hour to hour, we rot, and rot." It is a sentiment so attuned to Jaques's own melancholy temperament that shortly thereafter, inspired by Touchstone's remark, he expands on this theme of dissolution in his famous speech on the "seven ages" of man. Opening with the familiar, "all the world's a stage," the lines conclude with the final age, an echo of "we rot, and rot":

> Last scene of all,
> That ends this strange eventful history,
> Is second childishness and mere oblivion,
> Sans teeth, sans eyes, sans taste, sans everything.

It is with obvious relief that Touchstone eventually joins the company of Duke Senior and his courtiers, who serve as a more appreciative audience for his talents. Finding the group receptively sophisticated, he entertains them with a lengthy description of the various levels of insult that could precipitate a duel of honor, ranging from the innocuous "Retort Courteous" to the inflammatory "Lie Direct." The performance is warmly applauded, much to his satisfaction. He is finally back among his own people.

In Touchstone's pursuit of the simple goatherd Audrey, he has only one thing in mind. His problem, as mentioned, is that his wit is completely lost on her. She misunderstands or misinterprets everything he says, picking up on only those words that are familiar to her:

*Touch*: Truly, I would that the gods had made thee poetical.

*Aud.* I do not know what "poetical" is. Is it honest in deed and word? Is it a true thing?

*Touch.* No truly; for the truest poetry is the most feigning, and lovers are given to poetry; and what they swear in poetry may be said as lovers they do feign.

*Aud.* Do you wish then that the gods had made me poetical?

*Touch.* I do truly. For thou swear'st to me thou art honest. Now if thou wert a poet, I might have some hope thou didst feign.

*Aud.* Would you not have me honest?

*Touch.* No truly, unless thou wert hard-favoured [ugly]; for honesty coupled to beauty is to have honey a sauce to sugar.

*Aud.* Well, I am not fair, and therefore I pray the gods make me honest.

*Touch.* Truly, and to cast away honesty upon a foul slut were to put
good meat into an unclean dish.

*Aud.* I am not a slut, though I thank the gods I am foul [ugly].

*Touch.* Well, praised be the gods for thy foulness; sluttishness may
come hereafter.

Audrey is not so dense, however, as to be ignorant of Touchstone's
lecherous intentions; and she remains resolutely virtuous until he
agrees to marriage. Forced into this necessity, however, Touchstone
resorts to deception, engaging a country vicar, Sir Oliver Martext, a
cleric of questionable credentials. Jaques, who has watched them in
hiding, comes forth and rebukes the jester for planning to "be married under a bush like a beggar." Go to a church, he urges, and do it
properly. Touchstone replies in confidence that he prefers Sir Oliver,
"for he is not like to marry me well; and not being well married, it
will be a good excuse for me hereafter to leave my wife." Jaques prevails, however, and they set off to join the other couples.

They come upon the happy pairs, Rosalind and Orlando, Phebe
and Silvius, Celia and Oliver, all preparing to be wed, and Touchstone greets them wittily in terms that reflect his own perspective
on marriage. They are to him "country copulatives," and he will join
them in a ceremony that in his eyes is no more than a formality that
legitimizes lust. He presents Audrey, and, perhaps embarrassed by
the knowing looks of the assembled courtiers, he attempts to justify
his choice with a bit of witty bluster. She is, he says dismissively, "a
poor virgin sir, an ill-favored thing sir, but mine own; a poor humour of mine sir, to take that that no man else will." Once the rites
are over, Jacques has words for each of the couples—kindly for the
most part, except for those to Touchstone, whose "happy voyage," he
predicts, "is but two months victualled." And so it seems.

It has been suggested that Touchstone fills the role of "the scapegoat of Arden" in the play. The other marriages, it is said, are idyl-
lic romances. Rosalind and Orlando fall in love at first sight, as do
Celia and Oliver; and Silvius describes his love for Phebe as "all made
of faith and service . . . all adoration, duty, and observance [respect]
. . . all purity, all trial." There is nothing untoward in the play to
sully this idealistic vision of the attraction between man and woman;

and so Shakespeare provides Touchstone to complete the picture. Physical desire, which hovers just beneath the surface of these images of "adoration" and "purity," cannot be ignored; so the poet in his exploration of the theme of love gives us Touchstone's lust for Audrey. He is a "scapegoat" in the sense that anything lecherous or otherwise demeaning about these other attractions is attributed to him so that they may remain undefiled. He is realistically cynical and highly entertaining in his observations on love, and through him Shakespeare is able to portray it in all its contradictory dimensions.

Thus Shakespeare's jesters all employ similar devices designed to entertain, while at the same time they voice timeless themes that define the human condition. They play on words, pose riddles, toy with meaning, engage in pranks, sometimes sing and dance, and distract with witty chains of logic; and even as they "set the table on a roar," they explore common human failings. Lear's Fool is loyal to the king while urging him to accept the folly of his acts. Feste finds the mourning of his mistress a façade and Malvolio's pretensions a parody of respectability. And Touchstone exposes the primal urge beneath the fanciful veneer of romantic and courtly love. We hear truth and wisdom in the voices of these fools who, like Hamlet's players, "are the abstracts and brief chronicles of the time."

# JOAN PUCELLE

*"Assigned am I to be the English scourge."*

JOAN OF ARC, the Maid of Orleans, is a figure of international renown, revered by the Western world as a symbol of spotless virtue combined with martial prowess.* She rallied the French, cowering in the south after Henry V's victories, defeated the English, and persuaded the Dauphin to enter Rheims, there to be crowned King Charles VII. She accomplished all this in a single year, inspiring resistance that in time would sweep English armies from French soil, save only for their foothold in Calais. And, as is well known, she was captured by the English, condemned as a witch, and burned at the stake.

In Shakespeare's time, 150 years after her death, England still did not look upon Joan with favor, and indeed would not for another two centuries.† In *Henry VI, Part 1*, the poet gives Joan her just due as an inspirational figure and able warrior, but he persists in the English belief that her powers derived from collusion with the underworld. The eighteen-year-old daughter of a simple shepherd, she has received a miraculous vision of the Virgin Mary, she reports to the Dauphin, by whom she was "assigned . . . to be the English scourge." "This night," she announces, "the siege [of Orleans] assuredly I'll raise." The French, inspired by her unshakable confidence in her vision, rally and do indeed raise the siege, defeating the English led by the fearsome Lord Talbot.

Shakespeare's Joan is a formidable warrior. When she first appears before a skeptical Dauphin, he proposes that they engage in a

---

*In my native Philadelphia her gilded equestrian statue stands opposite the Museum of Art at the entrance to Franklin Boulevard.

†I am indebted to Dr. Kevin Harty for this insight. It was the Romantics at the beginning of the nineteenth century who revised the English image of Joan.

duel to test her prowess. She agrees and in the brief bout "overcomes" him, confirming in his eyes the validity of her prophetic mission. In the struggle for Orleans she encounters the famed Talbot in single combat and forces him to retire. Later she relates her challenge to Talbot's son on the field of battle, where he had arrogantly refused to fight what he called a mere "gigot [wanton] wench." Joan, moreover, is resourceful. In a clever ruse, she enters Rouen in disguise and signals to the waiting French the location of the most thinly guarded walls, leading to the fall of the city. Later in an inspirational speech she persuades the Duke of Burgundy to abandon his alliance with the English and join in the defense of France.[*]

Thus Shakespeare gives us a courageous, skillful, devout, and resolute young woman, but at the same time he diminishes the figure. For one thing she is not called the traditional, honorific "Joan of Arc" in the play; rather, she is referred to plainly throughout as "Pucelle," which can be translated either as "virgin" or "little flea."[†] And in the end she is unmasked as an agent of the underworld. Deserted by the French and trapped outside the walls of Angiers, she calls upon the forces of darkness to rescue her; and it is they, it appears, not the Virgin Mary, who are the source of her powers:

Now help, ye charming spells and periapts [talismans],
And ye choice spirits that admonish [inform] me
And give me signs of future accidents.
You speedy helpers, that are substitutes
Under the lordly monarch of the north,
Appear and aid me in this enterprise.

In reply, a procession of "fiends" appears. They do not speak, but the stage directions describe their reaction to her pleas: "They hang

---

[*]Shakespeare, here and elsewhere, is cavalier with history. Burgundy did not renounce his alliance until three years after Joan's death. In another instance, of many, *Part 1* portrays the death of Talbot, who in fact was killed some twenty years later. No matter. His death makes for a very moving scene, some say the most effective in the play.

[†]In the First Folio (1623) she is variously "Puzel," "Ioane Puzel," "Ioane de Puzel," or simply "Ioane." On one occasion she is called (contemptuously) "virtuous Iaone of Acre," on another (by herself) "Ione of Aire." It was not until the Rowe edition (1709) that she is referred to as "*la* Pucelle."

their heads." "They shake their heads." In a final desperate cry she offers, "Then take my soul; my body, soul and all" in return for their aid, but to no avail: "They depart." And the English capture her.

Shakespeare, to enhance the dramatic effect, greatly simplifies Joan's trial, which was protracted and complex.* She is confronted by the relentless Duke of York and Earl of Warwick, and in her defense she resorts to outright falsehoods. Faced with her humble father, who has come to give his final blessing, she renounces him, claiming that she is high-born: "Not me begotten of a shepherd swain / But issued from the progeny of kings." Of course, if this were true she would be worth more alive than dead and in all likelihood held prisoner in anticipation of a substantial ransom. She defies the English lords, denying collusion with "wicked spirits" and declaring, "Joan of Aire hath been / A virgin from her tender infancy."

The lords are unmoved: "Away with her to execution!" Desperate now, Joan resorts to another device, denying her virginity. "I am with child," she claims, defying them to "murder not" the unborn "fruit within my womb." She further identifies the father as the Duke of Alençon and then changes her story, insisting that it was "Reignier, king of Naples, that prevailed." The lords are scornful of her claim and again order her to be taken off to execution. She is defiant to the end, cursing England, which, she predicts, will be deprived of sunlight: "Darkness and the gloomy shade of death / Environ you, till mischief and despair / Drive you to break your necks or hang yourselves!" Shakespeare endows her with prophetic sight here, foreshadowing the War of the Roses, during which both York and Warwick lose their lives.

So Shakespeare portrays Joan with all the martial and saintly qualities that legend attributes to her. But he then demeans that image by attributing her military success to allegiance with underworld "fiends" and compromising her virtue with the lies she invents in an effort to save her life. She is not what one would call an ambiguous character; there is too stark a difference between the fig-

---

*Joan of Arc was imprisoned for a year after her capture. She was tried by an ecclesiastical court, found guilty of witchcraft, and turned over to English civil authorities for execution.

ure we see at the opening and closing of the play. The poet, here in one of his earliest works, portrays a Joan whom we at first admire and in the end contemn. She does not trouble us as a figure who elicits a mixed response, that is, both sympathy and repulsion at once, as do those figures Shakespeare fashioned in later years—a Lear, a Shylock, or a Richard II—characters that leave us at times unsettled and divided in our reaction to them.

# KING LEAR

*"Who is it that can tell me who I am?"*

WE ENCOUNTER Lear in many guises, and we respond differently to each change in him as his trials play upon his character. Initially he is an irascible old monarch, aged but robust and commanding, quick to anger and, when aroused, harsh in judgment. Later he is a pathetically helpless father bartering shamelessly for the love of his children, and when they reject him, a majestic figure, raging at the heavens, demanding justice for their betrayal. His grief drives him to madness, his imagination warped, his utterance incoherent; and then, recovering his senses, he is a subdued penitent, "old and foolish" by his own admission. Next he is a joyous father reunited with a daughter he had wronged and thought forever lost to him. In the end, when he finally does lose her, he is for a moment once again the awesome monarch, and then, bowing under the weight of his sorrows and his years, he dies.

At the closing curtain an audience may justifiably feel that their sensibilities have been pummeled by the play. Shakespeare has taken our emotions on a roller-coaster ride in following Lear as he falls and rises and falls again. We have responded to him successively with disgust, dismay, awe, joy, and finally a profound pity, and we often experience a complex mixture of these emotions. Late in the play, an unnamed gentleman describes Cordelia's reaction to the news of her father's suffering: "You have seen / Sunshine and rain at once; her smiles and tears / Were like." In similar words, Edgar describes the death of his father, Gloucester: "His flawed heart / 'Twixt two extremes of joy and grief, / Burst smilingly." In such lines Shakespeare seems to be guiding our own response to Lear, one of conflicting "smiles and tears," of simultaneous "joy and grief."

Lear, "fourscore and upward" years old by his own admission, decides, in his words, to "shake all cares and business from our age." He intends to divide his kingdom among his three daughters, but to keep "the name and th'addition of a king." Lear is an autocratic old monarch, accustomed during his long rule to absolute obedience from subjects who defer to his every wish. He expects his three daughters to engage in a public display of their affection for him, in gratitude for his generous gift. The two eldest, Goneril and Regan, satisfy him with extravagant protestations of their love, but Cordelia, his youngest and his favorite, refuses. Apparently the only one of the three who truly loves him, she is adamant that she will not debase her affection in honeyed words forced from her before the assembled court. Her refusal infuriates Lear. It is a defiance of his royal rule, which he has been accustomed for so long to impose with unquestioned authority, as well as a bitter disappointment to a father at what he sees as a betrayal by his most favored child. In an irrational rage, he disowns Cordelia—"We / Have no such daughter"—and releases her to the French king, who gallantly takes her as his queen even though she comes without the customary dowry.

It is sheer folly, we sense, for Lear to believe that he can surrender the titles and revenues of his land, as well as the authority that accompanies such possession, and still keep the respect and deference they entail. Lesser figures in the play often echo our own response to events, and it is the Fool who confirms our fears. "Thou mad'st thy daughters thy mothers," he tells Lear, "for thou gav'st them the rod and putt'st down thine own breeches," and "thou hast pared thy wit o'both sides and left nothing i'th'middle." Again:

*Fool.* I can tell why a snail has a house.
*Lear.* Why?
*Fool.* Why, to put's head in; not to give it away to his daughters, and leave his horns without a case.

And finally: "Thou shouldst not have been old till thou hadst been wise." As for Lear's intemperate anger at Cordelia, which we watch with dismay, it is the Earl of Kent who voices our disgust at his blindness: "I'll tell thee thou dost evil."

We certainly do not warm to Goneril and Regan, but they prove perceptive. In a private exchange at the close of this troubling scene, they share confidences:

> *Goneril.* He always loved our sister most, and with what poor judgement he hath now cast her off appears too grossly.
>
> *Regan.* 'Tis the infirmity of his age; yet he hath ever but slenderly known himself.
>
> *Goneril.* The best and soundest of his time hath been but rash.

In this brief but critical exchange, the sisters define their father's character, introducing those qualities that will be played out in events to come: He is old. He is rash. And he does not know himself.

Lear's rashness is already evident, but subsequent scenes find him in an even higher rage. He imagines his remaining years as a long holiday during which, though relieved of the responsibilities of the crown, he will be able to retain the deference due it. As a provision of his abdication he will retain a retinue of a hundred knights with whom he will alternate monthly visits with his two daughters. He will spend his days hunting, feasting, and enjoying the antics of his Fool while his knights will preserve the fiction that he still rules over a royal court.

Lear encounters resistance to the arrangement almost immediately. Goneril soon tires of accommodating such a large body of men in her home castle and confronts her father, complaining that his knights are "men so disorderly, so debauched and bold" that her court "shows like a riotous inn." She demands that he "disquantify [his] train," and in response he erupts into a towering rage, hurling terrible curses on his daughter. He calls on the "dear goddess," nature, to punish her: "Into her womb convey sterility; / Dry up in her the organs of increase," but "if she must teem, / Create her child of spleen" so that "she may feel / How sharper than a serpent's tooth it is / To have a thankless child!" This from a father! He'll no longer trouble her, he concludes, calling his train to prepare for departure, and he dashes out to seek shelter with Regan: "I have another daughter," who, he says confidently, is sure to be "kind and comfortable."

Warned by Goneril, however, Regan and her husband, the Duke of Cornwall, pay a visit to the Earl of Gloucester in an effort to avoid her father, but they encounter him outside the earl's castle. Goneril joins her sister, and between them they reduce Lear to a pathetic remnant of his former regal self. Seeing Goneril approach, he continues his invective, branding her "a boil, / A plague-sore, an embossed carbuncle / In my corrupted blood." But Regan agrees with her sister that he should reduce his train to fifty knights, and then on second thought that he should need no more than twenty-five. At this Lear turns back to Goneril, whom he had only just reviled as "a boil" and "plague-sore", in the belief that since her offer of fifty is "double five and twenty," it is evidence of "twice [Regan's] love." But then Goneril reduces the number further and finally agrees with her sister: "What need one?" In response Lear turns on them both savagely—"You unnatural hags"—and sputtering in helpless fury he promises obscure vengeance: "I will do such things— / What they are, yet I know not, but they shall be / The terrors of the earth!" He dashes away to vent his grief and anger in the tumult of a violent storm, with no regard for the assault of crashing thunder, wind, and rain, and Regan closes the gates of the castle on him with an air of grim satisfaction.

Up to this point in the play, we have wasted little sympathy on Lear. Accustomed to unquestioned obedience to his royal will, he strikes out rashly at any who dare challenge him. He disowns Cordelia and then banishes the Earl of Kent when he dares to confront him with his folly. When his other daughters make it clear that he no longer wields the power of the throne, he lashes out at them with a torrent of curses. It is clear that he has no idea of love's meaning, measuring it by a contest of flattering speeches in a royal court and later by the number of knights he is allowed to keep.

We are appalled at his folly in dividing his kingdom and his harsh treatment of Cordelia; but at the same time we are embarrassed to watch a once regal figure reduced to obsequious fawning before his unfeeling daughters, who refuse to permit him even a tattered remnant of his former dignity. Though the two sisters are far from sympathetic figures themselves, their treatment of their father seems not entirely unjustified as they endure his imperious bearing and intemperate rage, which, we may assume, they have done all their lives. Our response to Lear is decidedly mixed here, between a sympathy for his distress and a conviction that it is his own unrelenting rashness that has brought this suffering upon him.

We become aware, on the other hand, that however irascible and precipitous Lear is, he has qualities that have won him the loyalty and affection of his subjects, who forgive his sometimes irrational behavior. The Earl of Kent is so devoted to him that he violates his banishment and, at the risk of his life, returns in disguise to rejoin Lear's service. The Earl of Gloucester defies his lord, the Duke of Cornwall, and comes to the old king's aid in his distress, an act of loyalty that costs the earl his eyes. His Fool clings to him, and Cordelia, despite her father's harsh rejection, remains unreservedly devoted to him. Lear is a man whom Kent—and it would appear many others—"would fain call master."

It is in the stunning storm scene that we become fully aware of Lear's age, his "fourscore and upward" years. The spectacle of this old man at the mercy of the roaring elements excites a sense of profound pity, mixed with awe at his fierce indictment of nature's abuse, which he identifies with his daughters' neglect. We may have felt his former distress a consequence of his own folly, but surely this is more suffering than a man of his years deserves, abandoned by his heartless daughters to the assault of the wind, the rain, and the thunder above. "Here I stand, / A poor, infirm, weak, and despised old man," he declares, challenging the justice of the abuse being hurled upon "a head / So old and white as this." And in a final defiant cry, he calls upon "the great gods" that have raised the storm to deal justly with "a man / More sinned against than sinning."

Lear has been "sinned against" surely, but here he acknowledges that he has "sinned" as well. The admission calms him abruptly, and we witness yet another change in him: in his distracted state he seems to gain an understanding and compassion that his long reign has denied him, and in his own suffering he becomes sensible to the suffering of others. His Fool has been at his side all during the storm, and Lear attempts to comfort him: "Come on, my boy. How dost, my boy? Art cold? . . . Poor fool and knave, I have one part of my heart / That's sorry yet for thee." Shortly thereafter Lear kneels to pray, meditating on the "poor naked wretches" whose "houseless heads and unfed sides" must endure all such "pitiless storm[s]." And he concludes, "O, I have ta'en / Too little care of this!"

Here is a new Lear indeed! We recall Regan's remark that "he hath but slenderly known himself," and his ignorance of who he is has surfaced from time to time to this point in the play. When Goneril first challenges her father, he looks about him incredulously, asking, "Does any here know me?" and "Who is it that can tell me who I am?" He asks ironically, of course, since everyone knows who he is, and his questions imply that his daughter seems to have forgotten. The irony is double-edged, however, since he still thinks he is a king and, as the Fool tells him, that is a title "thou hast given away." Now, battered by the storm like those "poor, naked wretches," he realizes that he is something less, that he is but a man, and an old one at that.

And then he goes mad. The play is sometimes said to portray "the education of Lear," and its theme may indeed be described as the growth of wisdom through suffering as he learns the true meaning of love and becomes aware of who he is. But that wisdom comes at a heavy price. Wracked by grief and guilt, he rails at the storm, the gods, and his ungrateful daughters until, overcome by the assault upon his sanity of the roaring elements and human cruelty, he finally loses control of his reason. The harsh truth thrust upon him proves too heavy a burden for his sanity to bear. Although we may have responded to Lear with exasperation at his blind folly and a sense that he has brought these indignities on himself, yet our reproach has been tempered throughout by the realization that he is man sinking slowly into madness under the weight of his sorrows. His growing distraction may be of his own doing, brought on by a combination of his stubborn refusal to accept his new state of dependence, the dawning conviction that he has done Cordelia an injustice, and his elder daughters' callous ingratitude, which we suspect he has well earned; but we cannot help but feel compassion for a man we watch losing his mind. Shakespeare foreshadows Lear's gradual decline by the king's own repeated allusions to it, his awareness of what is happening to him and his struggle to resist it: "O, let me not be mad, not mad, sweet heaven!" "O, Fool, I shall go mad!" "O that way madness lies; let me shun that!" Again, his plight excites mixed emotions—disgust at his behavior, sympathy for his suffering, and fear at the sight of a man on the verge of insanity.

In a brilliant theatrical effect, Shakespeare has Lear lose his reason at the sight of madness itself. Edgar, the legitimate son of the

Earl of Gloucester, has assumed the disguise of "Tom o'Bedlam"* to escape the wrath of his father, who suspects him of a design on his life. Edgar appears suddenly before Lear, a raving lunatic, in some productions clad only in a loincloth and bespattered with mud, raving about the "foul fiend" pursuing him. Lear, seeing in him perhaps one of the "poor, naked wretches" for whom he had only just found sympathy, immediately identifies with "poor Tom" and irrationally insists that he is "a learned Theban," "a good Athenian," and a "noble philosopher" with whom he would talk further. In his distraction he recognizes the pathetic figure as "the thing itself. Unaccommodated man is no more but such a poor, bare, forked animal as thou art." The revelation inspires in him an urge to join in the naked squalor of the "poor, bare, forked" Edgar, and he tears at his clothes: "Off, off, you lendings! Come, unbutton here!"

Lear, in brief, finally learns who he is. But there are added effects. Deprived of his reason, he seems to gain a sensitivity to the natural world—"Look, look, a mouse! Peace, peace: this piece of cheese will do't" and "O, well flown, bird." As king he often acted in a legal role as a judge, conferring punishments and rewards on his subjects, and in his demented state he voices a new appreciation for the meaning of justice. It is not right, he declares, to condemn a man for adultery, for after all, "The wren goes to't, and the small gilded fly." In a later scene he denounces the "rascal beadle" for whipping a whore, since he "hotly lusts to use her in that kind" for which he punishes her; and he perceives that the "robes and furred gowns" of the rich and powerful hide "great vices." To recall the Fool's insightful wit, Lear, now "old," has in his madness finally grown "wise."

Lear is rescued by Cordelia who has invaded England with a French army to come to his aid. And here again is yet another Lear. He awakens as she hovers by his side, no longer the intemperate monarch or the incoherent madman. He seems to have recovered his senses. At the sight of her he is pitifully repentant: "Pray you now, forget and forgive; I am old and foolish." He now has our entire sym-

---

*So named for inmates of St. Mary of Bethlehem, London's hospital for the insane.

pathy. Having followed him through his trials, which, we sense, have been sufficient penance for his sins, we are only too willing to "forget and forgive" them.

The reunion between Lear and Cordelia is short-lived, however. The French are defeated by English forces under the command of the treacherous Edmund, now Earl of Gloucester after his father's disgrace, and they are taken prisoner. So elated is the father at having his lost daughter restored to him that he is oblivious to their danger. When Edmund orders that they be held in captivity, Lear accepts the sentence joyfully, comforting Cordelia:

> Come, let's away to prison:
> We two alone will sing like birds i'th'cage;
> When thou dost ask me blessing, I'll kneel down
> And ask of thee forgiveness.

It is not to be, however, for Edmund orders them put to death. Later, suffering a fatal wound in a duel with Edgar, his half brother, Edmund reveals with his dying breath that he has ordered their execution. The distraught English rush off to prevent the deed—too late, as it happens, for Cordelia has already been hanged.

Shakespeare, having endowed Lear with those "fourscore and upward" years, is faced with the challenge of engaging our sympathy for the old king so that at the end the spectacle of his death arouses in us a sense of the tragic. We do not customarily think of the passing of an aged person as a tragedy, especially in the case of one who has lived a full, rich life and finally goes to the destined end of all God's creatures. Shakespeare achieves the effect in the final scene by momentarily restoring the image of a man who, though advanced in age, still retains the vigor and promise of one who has many vital years before him—the image of Lear, in brief, that we see at the opening of the play. We are reminded of him as the robust king who dominates his court and returns from the hunt, reveling in life, not as a man, ancient of years, slipping into his grave. The Lear of the final scene does not go quietly to his end but displays all the strength and resolve of his earlier self; and Shakespeare fills the episode with brief echoes of what we have learned of him, his rashness, his age, and the self-knowledge he has gained in his suffering. He comes upon his stunned followers sturdily bearing Cordelia's body in his arms and rages at them for their apparent lack of grief—"A plague upon you, murderers, traitors all!" He is for a moment his old imperious self—"I killed the knave that was a-hanging" her—but then reflects, "I am old now." And then in a final dramatic gesture, he recalls who he is, Tom o' Bedlam's "unaccommodated man," and asks, "pray you, undo this button." Lear dies convinced that the love so recently restored to him still lives—"Look on her! Look—her lips! / Look there, look there!"

*King Lear* is an assault on the sensibilities of any audience. We scarcely have time to entertain one emotion when another is thrust upon us. When we first see Lear, we are at first appalled at his folly and blindness to Cordelia's love, and repulsed by his intemperate outbursts against his own daughters. We watch in dismay, even embarrassment, as he is reduced to bartering with them to retain his retinue. All sympathy is wasted, it seems to us, on a father who measures his daughters' devotion by their stilted speeches and the number of knights they will permit him. But sympathy arises when the old man is abandoned to wander without cover in the teeth of a wild tempest. We sit in pity and awe at the intensity of his grief and rage as he challenges the elements and demands justice from the gods who submit him to this suffering. Then he goes mad, and we watch with the mixed emotions—fear, pity, and aversion—of anyone confronted with the spectacle of insanity.

But there is more to come. When he awakens from his madness, he is a pathetic old man, repentant, resigned, and then exalted by his reunion with Cordelia, a joy we share, even knowing, as we do, how brief it will be. The final scene brings all these emotions to bear— awe at his rage and grief, pity for a man who has miraculously recovered a love only to have it snatched from him, and anguish as he hovers between hope that Cordelia lives and despair that she is gone. We depart with a deep sense of the tragic at the loss of a spirit who suffers so profoundly because of a failing so common to the human race, a blindness to love. Having been submitted to this range of emotional responses to the figure, we may well leave the theater exhausted.

# LADY MACBETH

*". . . unsex me here."*

WHEN WE FIRST ENCOUNTER Lady Macbeth, she is a resolute woman, a forceful influence on her husband, shaming him into carrying out their plan to murder King Duncan. When we last see her, she is a pitifully troubled woman who walks in her sleep, muttering all the while a rambling recital of her husband's crimes. When we last hear of her, she is afflicted, according to her doctor, "with thick-coming fancies, / That keep her from her rest"—and shortly thereafter she is dead. What could have reduced this dauntless woman to a demented shadow of herself?

There is distressingly little to go on. Lady Macbeth appears in only a third of the scenes in this, Shakespeare's shortest play, so evidence for an evaluation of her character must be drawn at times from single lines and isolated actions as well as the response of others to her. We watch the progress of her deterioration in three episodes and are told of her death in a fourth. In the first of these, Macbeth writes to his wife informing her of the witches' prophecies and King Duncan's impending visit. She is exultant. This fateful combination of events, she is confident, offers an opportunity for her husband to achieve greatness if he can be persuaded to seize the occasion. There is a problem, as she concedes, since he may prove unwilling to do so. He is a man, in her words, "too full o'th'milk of human kindness," one with ambition, certainly, but "without the illness should attend it."

Lady Macbeth will have to supply that "illness," and to prepare herself for the task she intones a frightening prayer. Calling on the forces of darkness, "you murd'ring ministers," she entreats them to "unsex me here," to "come to my woman's breasts, / And take my milk for gall." She asks in effect that they drain her of all the qualities said traditionally to be natural to a woman, the instinctive desire to nurture, comfort, and protect human life, so that she may urge her husband to perform a single night's demonic work. This is a plea not so much that she take on the character of a male but that she may shed the attributes that the age bestowed on women. In Shakespeare's time, wives and daughters were valued, aside from emotional personal ties, as security for the future of a clan or family, and in practice they were insulated from the harsh realities of the contentious world in which their husbands and fathers lived.

Lady Macbeth asks to be released from this restricted role, to be "unsexed," freed from all maternal instincts of compassion and reverence for life; but in consequence she surrenders the cultural shield that customarily protected wives from the wars, intrigues, and harsh punishments of their husbands' world.* In doing so, her spirit becomes vulnerable in the end to forces it cannot long endure. In one sense, by addressing the "murd'ring ministers" of darkness she becomes identified with the androgynous witches, of whom Banquo observes, "you should be women, / And yet your beards forbid me to interpret / That you are."

Macbeth, as she expected, proves reluctant, deciding that "We will proceed no further in this business," and she must marshal all her weapons to overcome his timidity. She unleashes a verbal assault on his manhood, accusing this renowned warrior of cowardice, and closes with a terrible oath, confirming her wish to be released from the confines, and the protection, of maternity: "I have given suck," she raves, but would have "plucked my nipple from [the baby's] boneless gums, / And dashed the brains out, had I so sworn as you / Have done to this." He fears failure, but she reassures him with a plan that will divert the blame from him. She will ply the king's sentinel grooms with wine so that he can enter the king's chamber undetected; then he will smear the grooms with blood to make them

---

*It is a status rejected in modern society certainly, but more the norm in Shakespeare's time. Other instances include Hotspur's admonition of his wife in *Henry IV, Part 1*—"I must not have you henceforth question me / Whither I go, nor reason whereabout. / Whither I must, I must."—and the reluctance of Brutus to tell Portia of the conspiracy to kill Julius Caesar.

appear guilty of the crime. Finally persuaded, he is in awe at her resolve: "Bring forth men-children only! / For thy undaunted mettle
should compose / Nothing but males."

Lady Macbeth reduces the grooms to a drunken stupor and
leaves daggers at the scene for her husband's use, displaying at the
time, as she admits later, a touch of humanity, suggesting that she
has not been entirely "unsexed": "Had [the king] not resembled /
My father as he slept, I had done't." Macbeth returns, having killed
the king, but he is unnerved by what he has done, unaware that he
still has the incriminating daggers in his hands. Horror-stricken, he
refuses to return to the scene of the murder; and it is she, demanding in exasperation, "Infirm of purpose! / Give me the daggers,"
who must go back and place them by the sleeping grooms. Macbeth
is distraught, lamenting, "Will all great Neptune's ocean wash this
blood / Clean from my hand?" and his wife, in full control of her
will, attempts to calm him—"A little water clears us of this deed; /
How easy is it then!" As they hear a knocking at the castle gate, she
leads her husband off to prepare for discovery of the dead king, urging him to "Get on your nightgown" and "Be not lost / So poorly in
your thoughts."

We next see Lady Macbeth after her husband's coronation, and
we find her much changed. She is noticeably subdued, no longer the
fiery advocate of murder: "Naught's had, all's spent," she laments,
"when our desire is got without content." She recovers, however, as
her husband enters; and we find that he has changed as well. Sullen
now and vexed, he complains that "we eat our meals in fear, and
sleep / In the affliction of these terrible dreams / That shake us
nightly." She attempts to console him with practical advice: "Things
without remedy / Should be without regard: what's done, is done."
She is as yet unaware, however, that he has in fact "done" something.
The witches' prophecy that the heirs of Banquo, his friend and comrade-in-arms, will be kings of Scotland preys on his mind. In his
words, their prediction has placed on his head "a fruitless crown, /
and put a barren sceptre in my gripe"; and he has only just come
from a meeting with men he has engaged to kill Banquo and his son.
He chooses not to tell his wife of his plan, however: "Be innocent of
the knowledge, dearest chuck, / Till thou applaud the deed."

To this point she has been an active partner in her husband's affairs, indeed the dominant figure of the two in securing the crown, but now it seems she is to be excluded from his close counsels, henceforth to be informed of his intentions, it would appear, only after the fact. It cannot be said that Macbeth mistrusts his wife—he remains devoted to her throughout the play—but he has become isolated from all about him, and she must feel that his secrecy has opened a distance between them. She has been relegated to the traditional woman's role, but having renounced all claim to it, is now adrift in a cultural and emotional limbo. In the conviction that her husband could "be great," she has devoted her life and spirit to his welfare, and we can only surmise the effect his growing reticence has upon her.

In an effort to raise her husband's spirits, Lady Macbeth encourages him to be "bright and jovial among your guests to-night." They are to have a celebratory feast with all the Scottish thanes in attendance—all but one, that is, since it is Macbeth's hope and belief that Banquo will be absent. At the feast he is seized, suddenly and unaccountably, by a fit of wild agitation. The cause is the appearance at the table of the murdered Banquo's bloody ghost, but the apparition is visible to him alone, and his behavior is inexplicable to all present. Lady Macbeth assumes the role she played in persuading him to kill the king. She impugns his courage—"Are you a man?"—and brands his exclamations as no better than those of "a woman's story at a winter's fire, / Authorized by her grandam. Shame itself." The ghost disappears, and Macbeth recovers his composure, but, sensing that the evening is in ruins, his wife dismisses the guests. Macbeth is still distraught, however, muttering, "It will have blood, they say, blood will have blood," and she, still ignorant of the cause of his distemper, attempts to comfort him. "You lack the season of all natures, sleep," she counsels, and they retire to bed.

They retire in vain, however, for sleep continues to evade them; and in our final view of Lady Macbeth we observe the effect of their history upon her—she has taken to sleepwalking, denied physical as well as emotional solace. Under the watchful eye of her doctor and gentlewoman, she frantically rubs her hands, exclaiming in frustration, "Out, damned spot! out, I say!" In her distracted mind she relives Macbeth's many crimes in a litany that moves from one to another of them in abrupt, chaotic leaps. And, as if attempting to erase them from her memory, all the while she is rubbing, rubbing, at first in frustration—"Yet who would have thought the old man to have had so much blood in him"—and then in despair—"All the perfumes of Arabia will not sweeten this little hand." Her utterances bring to mind Macbeth's distress on the night of Duncan's murder, when he doubts that all the waters in the ocean can "wash this blood / Clean from my hand?" and his wife's reply that "A little water clears us of this deed."

In her sleep-induced ramblings, Lady Macbeth reflects the concern of a wife attempting to encourage her husband or to comfort his troubled spirit:

- First she recalls the night of the king's murder, where she had to calm his anxiety and urge him to the deed: "One: two: why, then 'tis time to do it. Hell is murky! Fie, my lord, fie! A soldier, and afeard? What need we fear who knows it, when none can call our power to accompt?"
- Next her mind turns to the murder of Lady Macduff, and she recalls the crime with a nursery-rhyme jingle, as if to dismiss the incident as inconsequential: "The Thane of Fife had a wife: where is she now?" Her disdain is a heartless response to the brutal murder of Macduff's wife and child, to be sure, but it is yet another instance of her loyalty to her husband.
- Now she switches abruptly to his erratic behavior at the feast on the night of Banquo's murder: "No more o'that, my lord, no more o'that: you mar all with this starting." Her mind then flashes back to their first crime—"Put on your nightgown, look not so pale"—and then forward once more: "I tell you yet again, Banquo's buried; he cannot come out on's grave."
- Finally she returns to Duncan's murder: "To bed, to bed: there's knocking at the gate: come, come, come, come, give me your hand: what's done cannot be undone: to bed, to bed, to bed."

This recital of all her efforts to counsel and console her husband is pathetic in that as he grows more distant and secret in his designs, she no longer plays the central role in his life that she once had. She learns of his actions, certainly, but again—as with the plot to murder Banquo—only after the fact. He now goes his own way, and she is left with but a vivid memory of their close union. Her gestures, ineffectual it appears, to wipe the blood from her hands and her litany of crimes leaves the impression of a spirit burdened with a subconscious guilt—she is after all asleep—but there is no indication elsewhere in the play that she regrets any of their actions. Indeed, her scornful "The Thane of Fife had a wife" would seem to indicate satisfaction with a senseless slaughter. Shakespeare leaves us uncertain as to what causes her growing distemper. We have only the observation of a practical-minded doctor who, watching her in her sleep, remarks vaguely, choruslike, that "unnatural deeds / Do breed unnatural troubles" and "More she needs the divine than the physician." He is more circumspect, however, in reporting her illness to Macbeth: she is "not so sick, my lord, / As she is troubled with thick-coming fancies, / That keep her from her rest."

This the last we see of Lady Macbeth. We hear of her illness and death in the final scenes, leaving open the question of what it is that has reduced this resolute woman to a pitiful sleepwalker plagued with dreams of her husband's crimes and fatally denied rest by reliving them nightly. At every step she has been a loyal wife, indeed the only person who has stood by Macbeth during his troubled reign, but the crown has wrought a fearful change in him. Encrusted by his crimes, he has become a savage tyrant, dead to any normal human sentiment. On hearing an anguished cry of the women caring for his wife, he mutters to himself, "I have almost forgot the taste of fears"; and now, he says, having "supped full with horrors; / Direness, familiar to my slaughterous thoughts, / Cannot once start me." On receiving word of her death, he is incapable of mourning the loss; all he can muster is the sour reflection that life is meaningless, "a tale / Told by an idiot, full of sound and fury, / Signifying nothing."

Shakespeare leaves the cause of Lady Macbeth's derangement tantalizingly undefined. But, this examination of her character, based admittedly on scattered evidence, suggests some of the causes for her demise. First, her early prayers and oaths reflect a desire to be released from the role of a woman as it was conceived at the time; but her wish, apparently granted, has the effect of depriving her spirit of the protection and solace that role affords. She is set adrift between two worlds, without the strength or authority that allows men to survive in theirs nor the security traditionally assured females in theirs. In the end, it may be said, nature takes its toll, and her spirit, now empty of that which has sustained it, cannot survive in that brutish world.

Second—and this we can only surmise—she is depressed by the change in her husband. Her concern throughout has been for his welfare, but in time he grows more distant and distracted, obsessed with imagined threats to his crown. He confides in her less and less, shredding the close bond that had united them as a couple. His fears render him callous, a sullen, angry man, incapable of a reasoned response to events or a normal human reaction to others. Cut off from him, she withers.

Third, perhaps the most suggestive possibility, her spirit is ravaged by guilt. As we have seen, Shakespeare fills the lines with images of a conscience under siege—"these terrible dreams," sleepwalking, and that obsessive rubbing of the hands. But if this is the case, the assault of guilt on her spirit is entirely subconscious, for she voices no word of remorse for her acts or for those of her husband.

Thus Lady Macbeth is a woman who denies her humanity, becomes estranged from her husband, to whom she is devoted, and suffers from a stricken conscience. Is this enough to afflict her with the "thick-coming fancies" that bring her to her death? Perhaps.

Despite her unfaltering devotion to her husband, it is difficult for us to summon any sympathy for Lady Macbeth. Those early scenes in the play, wherein she seems the incarnation of evil, a devil in a gown, have left too indelible an impression for us to entertain what might be called mixed feelings about her decline and death. The best we can say of her is that in her final days she may have come to regret her fervent appeal to those "murd'ring ministers" to "unsex me here." Her impious prayer brings to mind an ancient adage: Be careful what you wish for—it may be granted to you.

# MACBETH

*"I am in blood*
*Stepped in so far that, should I wade no more,*
*Returning were as tedious as go o'er."*

SHAKESPEARE'S *Macbeth* is the portrait of a good man gone wrong. It is true that we actually witness little of the good in him, but in the early scenes we hear much of it from others. As the play opens he is a loyal thane* to the Scottish king, Duncan, and we receive reports of his prowess in his country's wars. A wounded captain returns from the battlefront to report on the martial deeds of the valiant Macbeth and his comrade-in-arms Banquo, who have fought, he tells the king, like eagles among sparrows and lions among hares. Leading the king's forces, Macbeth has put down an inner rebellion and beat back an invasion by Norway, which was aided by the traitorous Thane of Cawdor. To Duncan he is the "noble Macbeth," and as a reward for his valor the king announces that he shall inherit the title and lands of the turncoat Cawdor.

Some of Shakespeare's villains, like *Othello's* Iago and Aaron the Moor in *Coriolanus*, are wicked from the outset. They are evil incarnate, scheming to wreck lives, and for motives that seem to fall far short of justifying the scope of their iniquity. Macbeth is not one of these, however. The play records a man's decline into evil, displaying both change and constancy in his character; hence the most revealing approach to the figure is to trace the means and manner of that decline as he is reduced from an initially valorous nobleman to a manic tyrant.

---

*"Thane" was a heraldic title in Scotland, like duke or viscount. In the closing scene Malcolm raises all his loyal thanes to the rank of earl.

Macbeth is not without ambition, but at the outset no more so perhaps than anyone in his time or our own who aspires to wealth, fame, or higher office. The first two of these common aspirations he achieves in reward for his triumphs in battle, and his success, it seems, encourages thoughts of the third. Shakespeare implies that this final ambition would have remained dormant in Macbeth, a secret seed of unrealized desire, had it not been nurtured by supernatural forces.

We first meet Macbeth when he is returning from the wars in the company of his friend Banquo. Trudging across the desolate heath, they are suddenly confronted by three witches, who greet them with surprising predictions. Hailing Macbeth as Thane of Glamis, his title at the time, they go on to say that he will be the Thane of Cawdor and, most startling of all, "king hereafter." The source of the witches' knowledge is left undefined—such creatures were said to have otherworldly powers—as is their motive for singling out Macbeth to torment with their prophecies.* Banquo must be satisfied with their promise that he will "get kings, though thou be none." And then they abruptly disappear.

When Macbeth learns from a messenger that the king has indeed awarded him the title of Thane of Cawdor, that small seed of ambition bursts into flourishing growth, and he begins to contemplate the prospect that the witches' predictions might be valid, that he might indeed be "king hereafter." The news comes as a shock, like an electric surge that energizes a thought until then quietly latent in his consciousness. Why, he asks himself, does it "unfix my hair / And make my seated heart knock at my ribs / Against the use of nature?" But he calms himself with the thought that "If chance will have me king, why, chance may crown me, / Without my stir." Macbeth responds, in brief, as a loyal thane to the Scottish king, but the prospect unnerves him.

It is Lady Macbeth who provides the most complete description of the honorable Thane of Glamis. He is, she regrets "too full o'th'milk of human kindness / To catch the nearest way," a man who is "not without ambition, but without / The illness should attend

*See pp. 68–69.

it." It is she who brings that flourishing plant to flower, persuading her husband to murder the king and seize the crown. Macbeth wavers at first between his desire for the throne and fear of failure in the attempt, and he decides to abandon the plot. Shamed by his wife, who questions his courage, he renews his resolve and carries out the deed. But he is horrified by what he has done, and, rejoining her, he is startled to find that he still holds the incriminating daggers in his hands. Overcome by fear, he refuses to return them to the murdered man's chamber, and it is she who must place the weapons by the king's sleeping grooms and smear them with his blood to establish their guilt. Macbeth is quick to recover from his fit of terror, however, and, returning to the scene of the murder, he kills the grooms to prevent them from denying the charge. At the close of this traumatic scene, we receive a final glimpse of the man he was, as, startled by a knocking at the castle gate, he is swept by a surge of remorse: "Wake Duncan with thy knocking! I would thou couldst!"

The next stage in Macbeth's decline from nobility to tyranny is apparent once he is on the throne. He is obsessed with the thought that, since the witches' prophecies for him have been fulfilled, their prediction that Banquo will "get kings" may be as well. "Upon my head they placed a fruitless crown," he complains, "and put a barren sceptre in my gripe." To allay his anxiety, he arranges for the murder of Banquo and his son Fleance, but the plan goes array and the son escapes. "Then comes my fit again," he mutters, "I had else been perfect . . . now I am cabined, cribbed, confined, bound / In saucy doubts and fears."

This trail of blood has a degrading effect on Macbeth, evident in his wife's lament that "Nought's had, all's spent, / When our desire is got without content," and his complaint that "we eat our meal in fear, and sleep / In the affliction of these terrible dreams / That shake us nightly." Although outwardly Macbeth voices no remorse for his crimes, sleeplessness and nightmares are traditional signs of a conscience wracked with guilt, and his decline into "saucy doubts and fears" produces a marked change in him. He has murdered his king and mounted the throne, then has rid himself of a potential threat to the crown—events not unknown in the turbulent early history of Scotland—but his success has left him plagued with anxiety.

It may be said that his crimes haunt Macbeth, and nowhere so dramatically as in the appearance of Banquo's bloodied ghost when it suddenly materializes in the midst of a royal feast, where it remains invisible to all but him. He shrinks in horror at the sight, with an incriminating cry, "Thou canst not say I did it," while his guests look on dismayed. Lady Macbeth attempts to shame him into his senses— "Are you a man?"—and once the ghost has vanished, he recovers his composure: "[It] being gone, / I am a man again." In response to the encounter, he resolves to seek out the witches and demand of them an unequivocal answer to the question of Banquo's heirs.

Macbeth's "doubts and fears" arise from a conviction that since he has murdered a king, all about him are as treacherous as he and scheme to do the same. He mistrusts his subjects, and as a precaution against treason he tells his wife, "There's not a one of them but in his house / I keep a servant feed." As his crimes mount, so does his fear that there will be a reckoning in time: "It will have blood, they say," he mutters grimly, "blood will have blood." His anxiety compels him to engage in acts of mounting cruelty, as evil leads inexorably on to greater evil. He rationalizes his brutal career as forced upon him by necessity and, finally, justified by precedent: "I am in blood / Stepped in so far that, should I wade no more, / Returning were as tedious as go o'er."

Macbeth's actions become more erratic and extreme as he consults the witches in a frenzy of uncertainty. They answer his demands with a series of ghostly apparitions arising from a boiling cauldron, who intone a warning and a pair of cryptic assurances. He is first cautioned to "beware Macduff," then told that "none of woman born / Shall harm Macbeth," and finally that he cannot be vanquished until "great Birnam wood to high Dunsinane hill / Shall come against him." His last demand is to know if Banquo's heirs will indeed sit on Scotland's throne, and in answer he is taunted by a ghostly procession of crowned kings, all descendants of the murdered man, followed by Banquo himself, who, eyeing Macbeth, points mockingly at them.

Infuriated by the vision, and helpless to do any further harm to Banquo, Macbeth turns his wrath irrationally on the family of Macduff, whom he orders murdered. We witness the slaughter of Lady

Macduff and her young son, a scene in which Shakespeare places before us grim evidence of the inhumanity to which Macbeth has sunk. He has gone beyond reason now, venting his frustrated anger on innocent women and children, and we learn that this is not an isolated incident. He has imposed a reign of terror on Scotland until, as Macduff laments, "New widows howl, new orphans cry, new sorrows / Strike heaven on the face."

When we see him next, Macbeth has again changed markedly. He is a man warped by his crimes, transformed from the noble figure we first encountered into a manic despot. In the final scenes he exemplifies the corrosive effect of evil on the human spirit, corrupting whatever good might have dwelt there. He has become an abusive tyrant, drained to the last drop of the "milk of human kindness" that his wife had complained of. Preparing for battle at his castle Dunsinane, he awaits an approaching army led by Macduff and Duncan's heir, Malcolm, who are marching on Scotland to rid it of the despot. As his servants and soldiers bring him reports of the advancing enemy, he responds with rough abuse, calling one a "cream-faced loon" and "lily-livered boy," and raging mindlessly at the "liar and slave" who brings the news that Birnam Wood is indeed on the move.

In the final scenes Shakespeare portrays a man who has become callously incapable of any normal human response, a spirit encrusted by his crimes in a hard shell that denies him the ability to react to suffering. Hearing a cry of the women tending his sick wife, he is empty of feeling: "I have almost forgot the taste of fears: / The time has been, my senses would have cooled / To hear a night-shriek," but no more, "I have supped full with horror." Brought news of her death, he cannot even register regret at the loss of his only companion, whose loyalty has comforted him during the dark days of his reign: "She should have died hereafter / There would have been time for such a word [as death]." All that his scarred spirit can muster is a sullen observation that life is futile; it is "but a walking shadow . . . a tale / Told by an idiot, full of sound and fury, / Signifying nothing." He looks back on his own life with sour regret: "That which should accompany old age, / As honour, love, obedience, troops of friends, / I must not look to have." And he seems totally ignorant of why he has come to this end, or why his country is so tragically torn.

When told of his wife's illness, he chides the doctor, challenging him to "cast / The water of my land, find her disease, / And purge it to a sound and pristine health," blind to the fact that it is all his doing.

It has been observed that Macbeth is a victim of his own vivid imagination. Here is a man who follows a dancing dagger to the king's chamber, who hears voices that condemn his brutal act— "Sleep no more! / Macbeth does murder sleep"—who sees a ghost invisible to others, and who consorts with witches that plague him with grizzly apparitions. He suffers from nightmares and imagines conspiracies against his life, seeing treachery at every turn. We detect the force of Macbeth's imagination in what he says as well as what he sees and hears and suspects. Shakespeare has endowed his most terrifying villain with some of his most powerful poetry, filled with striking images and memorable lines. Consider, for example, his secret thoughts as he awaits news of Banquo's death:

> Come, seeling night,
> Scarf up the tender eye of pitiful day,
> And with thy bloody and invisible hand
> Cancel and tear to pieces that great bond
> Which keeps me pale! Light thickens, and the crow
> Makes wing to the rooky wood;
> Good things of day begin to droop and drowse,
> Whiles night's black agents to their prey do rouse.

Or his famous grim response to word of his wife's death:

> To-morrow, and to-morrow, and to-morrow
> Creeps in this petty pace from day to day,
> To the last syllable of recorded time;
> And all our yesterdays have lighted fools
> The way to dusty death. Out, out, brief candle!

Thus Macbeth's incessant doubts and fears, it may be said, arise from his own overwrought imagination.

Shakespeare is confronted with the challenge of portraying the death of this villain, which we may consider only just, as a tragic event. He does so in these closing scenes by reminding us in brief flashes of the figure Macbeth was at the outset, a valiant warrior possessed "of human kindness," and by emphasizing how far he has fallen. He confronts his fate defiantly: "I'll fight, till from my bones my flesh be hacked." To be sure, the witches have filled him with a false sense of his invincibility, but it is shaken when he learns that Birnam Wood is indeed coming to Dunsinane. His first response is to "pall in resolution," but he recovers quickly to rally his soldiers with renewed energy: "Blow, wind! Come, wrack! / At least we'll die with harness on our back."

Macbeth swings back and forth abruptly between debilitating despair and bold defiance, and he does so nowhere so dramatically as in his confrontation with Macduff. When they finally meet, Macbeth at first refuses to answer his challenge. Confident in his invulnerability to any "of woman born," he is momentarily moved by a touch of remorse, declaring himself reluctant to do Macduff further harm: "Get thee back, my soul is too much charged / With blood of thine already." When Macduff reveals that he is not born "of woman" but was "from his mother's womb / Untimely ripped," Macbeth is taken aback, admitting that the revelation "hath cowed my better part of man," and he declares, "I'll not fight with thee." But he promptly recovers to confront his all but certain death. Shakespeare revives the image of the dauntless soldier, who here accepts the challenge of the vengeful Macduff, urging a duel that he knows he can only lose: "Yet I will try the last. . . . Lay on, Macduff, / And damned be him that first cries 'Hold, enough.'" That final cry, however, is as much a challenge to the forces of darkness embodied in the witches, "these juggling fiends . . . that palter with us in a double sense" as it is to his opponent, who here at the end seems to Macbeth but an instrument of their malice.

Macbeth constantly wavers between fear and resolution, between terror at the thoughts and sights that afflict him and a determination to challenge them in a manner reminiscent of "the brave Macbeth," with whom the play opens. He plots to kill Duncan but is then beset by doubts of success. His resolve renewed by his wife, he performs the deed and then is horrified by it, but he quickly recovers and returns to kill the grooms. He is terrified by the sight of Banquo's ghost but reclaims his manhood when it disappears, and he is determined to compel the truth from the witches. Unnerved by

Macduff's revelation, he refuses at first to fight him but then rises to accept the challenge.

As a result we react to Macbeth with conflicting emotions, wavering between abhorrence and awe, a paradoxical response that arises from two effects. First, he is undeniably a consummate villain and unrepentant tyrant who imposes a reign of terror on his country, thoughtless of the suffering he causes. Second, he is a soul in turmoil, on the one hand wracked by fear and guilt, on the other defiantly resolved at the end to confront the forces that seek to destroy him; and there is a certain majesty in that resolve.

We deplore his crimes, then, but are awed by his defiance. And we recognize in him the embodiment of ambition, a familiar human passion carried in his case to excess, and a vision of what the spirit may shed of virtue and compassion in climbing steps to fame, or wealth, or office. Macbeth is a victim of his own aspirations and fears magnified by his heated imagination. And that indeed is tragic.

# MALVOLIO AND
# SIR TOBY BELCH

*"Is there no respect of place, persons, nor time in you?"*

*"Dost thou think, because thou art virtuous, there shall
be no more cakes and ale?"*

*Twelfth Night* is a play about identical twins, the brother and sister
Sebastian and Viola, who are shipwrecked in Illyria, each of whom
believes that the other has been drowned. It is perhaps better
known, however, for its subplot, in which two opposing concepts of
human conduct, indeed of humanity itself, come into contention.
These conflicting approaches to social behavior are embodied in the
persons of Malvolio, the austere steward to Lady Olivia, and Sir Toby
Belch, her irresponsible, high-spirited uncle. Shakespeare presents
neither of them as an especially admirable or exemplary figure.
Malvolio is a grim-faced, unbending authority figure, Toby a ro-
tund, ruddy-featured, exuberant libertine who, as his niece observes,
is customarily "half drunk"—a character who has much in common
with Sir John Falstaff.

The contrast between the two is vivid. Malvolio is admittedly responsible for the orderly management of Lady Olivia's household, but
he seems to disapprove of anything that disturbs the settled decorum
of the estate, even the faintest hint of frivolity or disregard for sober
behavior. When we first meet him, he interrupts the witty banter between Olivia and Feste with a haughty dismissal of the "Clown": "I
marvel your ladyship takes delight in such a barren rascal."* Olivia

*Feste is called "Clown" in the play, though he is otherwise known as "Fool." He
is the traditional jester, employed to entertain the court with wit, pranks, and songs.

replies sharply: "O, you are sick of self-love, Malvolio, and taste with a distempered appetite." It is apparent that she values her steward highly, but at the same time she is acutely aware of his temperament.

Olivia suffers the presence of Sir Toby Belch, since he is a close relative, but he is a disruptive influence in the household, given to uproarious antics, engaging in dance, drink, and song at all hours in the company of his dim-witted friend, Sir Andrew Aguecheek. In our first encounter with Toby, he is rebuked by Olivia's maidservant, Maria, for his boisterous behavior: "You must confine yourself within the modest limits of order." Toby responds indignantly: "Confine? I'll confine myself no finer than I am." He identifies himself immediately as one who resents any restraint on his pursuit of pleasure, his freedom to do "what you will," in the words of the play's subtitle.

These representatives of two apparently irreconcilable philosophies of life clash when Toby, Andrew, and Feste are engaged in late night revels, joking, drinking, and singing noisily. Maria enters, vainly attempting again to quiet them, followed quickly by Malvolio, who demands imperiously: "My masters, are you mad? Or what are you? Have you no wit, manner, nor honesty, but to gabble like tinkers at this time of night? . . . Is there no respect for place, persons, nor time in you?" Toby and Feste ignore him, singing snatches of songs and perhaps dancing to their own tunes in a deliberate mockery of his pretensions while he looks on with mounting indignation. In a sudden change of tone, however, an incensed Toby turns on Malvolio: "Art any more than a steward? Dost thou think, because thou art virtuous, there shall be no more cakes and ale?" Malvolio, somewhat disconcerted by the knight's rebuke, takes his displeasure out on Maria, accusing her of contributing to "this uncivil rule," and stalks off to inform Olivia of their insolence.

Maria, who has been doing her best to quiet the revelers, is now identified with them in Malvolio's mind as guilty by association, and she does not take kindly to the role. It is she who gives us what is perhaps the most acute description of the steward:

The devil a Puritan that he is, or anything constantly but a time-pleaser; an affectioned ass, that cons state without book and utters it by great swaths; the best persuaded of himself, so crammed, as he thinks, with excellencies that it is his grounds of faith that all that look upon him love him; and on that vice in him will my revenge find notable cause to work.

In effect the line is now drawn between the two contentious opposites, and it is Maria, seething over Malvolio's unjust rebuke, who devises a plan to humiliate him. Playing on his conviction "that all that look on him love him," she writes a letter, imitating Olivia's hand, designed to persuade Malvolio that his mistress is in love with him. Maria places the letter where the steward will come upon it, and, as Toby and Andrew look on from concealment, he reads it as confirmation of his secret aspiration to be "Count Malvolio." The letter asks him to signal his return of Olivia's love by appearing before her in garish apparel, wearing yellow stockings with his legs "cross-gartered," fashions Maria assures Toby that her mistress abhors, and, what is more, that he "smile" a lot, an expression entirely unsuited to her present mood and comically unnatural to his customarily stern features.

Malvolio's appearance before Olivia proves to be all the revelers could have wished. He is ridiculous, and she is bewildered by his behavior; convinced that he has taken leave of his senses, she entrusts his care to Toby. The knight adopts the stance that Malvolio has been possessed by the devil, an accepted diagnosis for madness in Shakespeare's time, and that in consequence he must be imprisoned in "a dark room," an accepted therapy for the affliction. Once he is imprisoned, Toby and Feste toy ruthlessly with the distraught steward, continuing with the fiction that he is possessed while he insists plaintively that he is not mad. Finally, tiring of the jest, they permit him to write a letter to Olivia, complaining of his treatment.

Thus the spirit of revelry triumphs over the stern demand for order, sobriety, and decorum—for the moment, at any rate. Sir Toby's irrepressible pursuit of fun, however, eventually leads to his discomfort. He persuades Viola, who is in disguise as Duke Orsino's page Cesario, and the simpleminded Sir Andrew Aguecheek to fight a duel, meanwhile informing each that his opponent is a skilled swordsman responsible for the death of many who have dared to answer his challenge. The result is a ludicrous scene in which the two face one another, each desperate to avoid a fight. They are mercifully interrupted by the intrusion of Duke Orsino, but matters are complicated by the arrival in Illyria of Viola's twin brother Sebastian, who has also survived the shipwreck. Later, we hear, Andrew and Toby, encountering Sebastian and thinking him the unwarlike Cesario, challenge him to a duel. As Andrew explains, "We took him for a coward, but he is the very devil incardinate [incarnate]." The result is that each of them ends up with a battered head, calling for a doctor. Andrew commiserates with his friend, but Toby turns on him harshly: "Will you help? As ass-head, and a coxcomb and a knave, a thin-faced knave, a gull?" Their revels now over, the revelers fall into discord.

As for Malvolio, once released from his "dark room," he confronts Olivia, demanding to know why she has made him "the most notorious geek and gull [dupe] / That e're invention played upon. Tell me why." Maria's trick is explained to him, and Feste takes pleasure in his disgrace. Recalling the steward's earlier taunt that he is a "barren rascal," the clown concludes gleefully that "thus the whirligig of time brings in his revenges." Malvolio turns angrily on them all, promising, "I'll be revenged on the whole pack of you!" And he stalks out.*

Thus the contending forces within society, and in the human spirit, both come to a bad end in the play. The revelers, Toby and Andrew, suffer lacerated heads and fall to angry wrangling; and Malvolio, the paragon of rectitude, is brought low because of his presumption that "virtue" lies in social order and mirthless sobriety, which must therefore be enforced. Shakespeare plays no favorites, though Toby is certainly the more entertaining of the two, and we delight in his devices. These extremes in human behavior, the poet

---

*Shakespeare is unconsciously prophetic here. Some forty years after the first appearance of *Twelfth Night*, "Puritan" forces seized control of Parliament and closed all the theaters in England. They were not allowed to reopen until after the Restoration of Charles II in 1660.

implies—Toby's irresponsible self-indulgence and Malvolio's haughty self-regard—are both at fault, equally self-destructive. The play concludes with a scene of reconciliation, not between these two but among the other figures involved, whose unions confirm that the power of love can prevail over the conflicting opposites that contend for supremacy in the human spirit.

# MARGARET OF ANJOU

*"A tiger's heart wrapped in a woman's hide."*

MARGARET OF ANJOU appears in four of Shakespeare's history plays, *Henry VI, Parts 1, 2,* and *3,* and *Richard III.* She is the daughter of an impoverished French nobleman who fancies himself King of Naples, Sicily, and Jerusalem, which at the time are firmly in the hands of Spain and the Turks. We see her in succession as an enchanting young woman, and later, once married to Henry VI, as a passionate force in the power struggles within the king's divisive court. She then assumes the role of the "warlike Queen" leading the Lancaster forces in the War of the Roses, and finally the vindictive harridan of *Richard III,* prophesying the fall of the house of York and reveling in the sorrow of her enemies. Shakespeare captures her beauty, shrewdness, fire, cruelty, and fierce resolve in the *Henry VI* plays, and her vengeful rage in *Richard III.*

Margaret first appears at the end of *Part 1,* where she comes to the attention of the Duke of Suffolk, who is captivated by her. Struck by her charms, he addresses her as a "fairest beauty" and "nature's miracle," and in a series of asides contemplates gaining her as a "paramour." What's to be done? Why not, he decides, marry her to King Henry! He returns to England and describes Margaret in such glowing terms that the young, impressionable king agrees to the match. He does so, however, over the objections of his Lord Protector, Humphrey, Duke of Gloucester, who has been negotiating a marriage between the king and a daughter of a powerful French noble in a design to cement a peace between the two kingdoms. Suffolk prevails and, confident of Margaret's affections, he is not unmindful of the advantage to himself: she "will be queen, and rule the king; / But I will rule both her, the king, and realm."

Henry and Margaret do indeed marry, and in time she reveals another side of her chimerical character. She produces an heir to the throne, Edward, Prince of Wales, but the devout king proves an inattentive husband. "All his mind is bent on holiness," she complains to Suffolk, "to number Ave-Maries on his beads." She comforts herself with the duke, however, and the two are soon enmeshed in the conspiracies that plague Henry's factious court. The lords contend for control of the ineffectual king, who, though he has arrived at manhood, still relies on his uncle Humphrey as Lord Protector to rule the land.

Margaret and Suffolk ally themselves with Humphrey's sworn enemy, the Bishop of Winchester, in a scheme to discredit the duke and enhance their sway over the king. When Henry, in a rare show of resolve, refuses to accept the charges against his uncle, the conspirators agree that the duke must die. Suffolk arranges for his murder, but his role becomes known and Henry banishes him from the kingdom. At his departure he and Margaret engage in a long, plaintive farewell, lamenting their separation. She: "Give me thy hand, / That I may dew it with my mournful tears . . . I am banishéd myself: / And banishéd I am, if but from thee." And he: "Where thou art, there is the world itself . . . and where thou art not, desolation." Suffolk is eventually killed on his voyage to exile, but his death seems only to animate Margaret's passion and resolve as she is left the dominant influence over the weak-willed king.

Thus far we have seen Margaret as the flirtatious young beauty who captivates Suffolk and as the scheming conspirator, vying for power among wrangling lords. In *Henry VI, Part 3*, she appears in another role entirely, the "warlike Queen" who leads Lancaster armies to battle the York faction in the War of the Roses. When Henry's forces suffer defeat at St. Albans, the first engagement of the war, the king meekly agrees to appoint the Duke of York his heir. Coming on the scene, Margaret berates her "timorous wretch" of a husband for disinheriting his son Edward, and she stalks out, calling the boy after her: "Come, son, let's away. / Our army is ready; come, we'll after them."

The two sides in the war line up over who should wear the crown, the Duke of York claiming that it is rightfully his. Margaret, defending her son as heir to the throne, routs the York forces at Wakefield, where two episodes illustrate the brutality of the conflict. Lord Clifford, the queen's close adviser now that Suffolk is gone, captures and kills York's young son Rutland in vengeance for his father's death at the duke's hand.* Of more significance, York himself is taken prisoner and Margaret taunts him, placing a paper crown on his head in ridicule, prompting his defiant charge that she has "a tiger's heart wrapped in a woman's hide." Angered, she stabs him and orders his head placed above the city gates, remarking sardonically that now "York may overlook the town of York."

The duke's eldest son Edward inherits his father's title and claim to the throne. In the bloody advances and retreats of the war, Margaret is defeated at Towton and the king captured, forcing her to seek refuge in France, where she pleads with the king for support. As it happens, Edward, now crowned Edward IV, makes a sudden, injudicious marriage to the widowed Elizabeth Grey. In so doing he angers his brother Clarence and the powerful Earl of Warwick, who commit themselves to Margaret's cause and persuade the French king to join them. As a result Margaret returns to England at the head of a formidable army and scatters the York forces at Warwick. Edward escapes, however, and with his brother Richard, Duke of Gloucester (later Richard III), finds an ally in the Duke of Burgundy. Returning, they inflict a crushing defeat on Margaret at Barnet, taking her prisoner with her young son, the Lancaster Prince of Wales. In brutal reprisal for Clifford's murder of young Rutland, the York brothers slaughter the prince before his mother's eyes. She rages at them—"Butchers and villains! Bloody cannibals"—and pleads to be killed as well; but Edward forbids it, sending her instead to her native France in exile.

Thus ends the martial career of the "warlike Queen," but Margaret has one more role to play: the prophetic witch of *Richard III*.†

---

*Rutland was actually York's second son, older by some years than his brothers Clarence and Richard, but Shakespeare portrays him as a boy to accentuate the pathos of his death.

†Shakespeare again alters history. Margaret died in 1482, before the time frame of events in the play, and she never left her exile in France. The poet resurrected her to enact her prophetic role in the play.

She makes an appearance only twice in the play, which is concerned for the most part with Richard's relentless elimination of all who stand between him and the throne. But in these scenes she plays the critical role of a demonic chorus, prophesying the destruction of the house of York and hurling curses at those who have deprived her of her family and crown.

The death of Edward IV widens the breach between the two factions within the monarchy, the York nobility and Queen Elizabeth's family, a brother and two grown sons by her first husband, who have enjoyed preferment as a result of her marriage to the king. Elizabeth has the temporary advantage, however, as the mother of the dead king's two young sons, Edward, heir to the throne, and his brother Richard, Duke of York. The contending parties are immediately embroiled in acrimonious dispute, and Margaret comes upon them, undetected at first, to overhear Richard and Elizabeth exchange abusive charges. She bursts upon them—"Hear me, you wrangling pirates, that fall out / In sharing that which you have pilled [pillaged] from me"—and curses each in turn. Accusations fly back and forth as the only recently squabbling factions unite in denunciation of her, drawing her scornful reply: "What? Were you snarling all before I came . . . And turn you all your hatred now on me?"

In a prophetic mode she predicts that, like her son Edward, Elizabeth's Edward will "die in his youth, by like untimely violence," and that Elizabeth, like herself, will "die neither mother, wife, nor England's queen." But Margaret reserves her most vituperative curses for Richard, whom she brands as an "elvish-marked, abortive, rooting hog," a "bottled spider," and a "poisonous bunch-backed toad." She predicts that conscience will "begnaw thy soul" and that he will in time look upon all his friends as traitors. Pursuing that prophecy, she turns to the Duke of Buckingham, Richard's closest ally, and warns him to "take heed of yonder dog! / Look when he fawns, he bites," and his teeth are venomous. She leaves them stunned by her curses, predicting that some day they will "say, poor Margaret was a prophetess."

Margaret's second appearance comes in the wake of Richard's success in disposing of all those who blocked his path to the crown—his brother Clarence, Elizabeth's older relatives, and her young sons, the famous "Princes in the Tower." He is now king, and Elizabeth, as Margaret prophesied, is "neither mother, wife, not England's queen." He has also executed two loyal supporters, the innocently trusting Lord Chamberlain Hastings as well as his indispensable aide in gaining the crown, the Duke of Buckingham, who failed to heed Margaret's warning that Richard would in time suspect his friends of treason.

On this occasion Margaret comes upon Richard's mother, the Duchess of York, and Elizabeth, who are joined in sorrow over their tragic losses. Undetected, she listens to their laments for a time before addressing them, which she does with an air of grim satisfaction. It is a striking image, the three widows dressed in mourning and sunk to the ground, sharing their grief. Margaret assumes a choric role here, summing up the carnage of the War of the Roses and Richard's trail of blood. She confronts Elizabeth with parallels that evoke the rhythm of ritual incantation:

> I had an Edward, till a Richard killed him;
> I had a husband, till a Richard killed him:
> Thou hadst an Edward, till a Richard killed him;
> Thou hadst a Richard, till a Richard killed him.

Margaret has lost a son and a husband and Elizabeth her two young princes, all by Richard's hand. The duchess picks up on the solemn parallels to indict Margaret in turn:

> I had a Richard too, and thou did'st kill him;
> I had a Rutland too: thou holp'st to kill him.*

And she replies:

> Thou had'st a Clarence too, and Richard killed him.

In a few lines, then, the women recall the brutal history of the war and strike a central theme of the play: in Shakespeare's vision, all the

---

*Not precisely true. Clifford killed Rutland, though Margaret's victory at Wakefield may be said to have "helped" him. The "Richard," of course, is the Duke of York whom, as we have seen, Margaret captured and slaughtered in the same battle.

sins of the time are embodied in the person of Richard, and only his death will cleanse the land.

Margaret is an arresting character, one shaped by Shakespeare's early pen. In these four plays he follows her, a figure never far from the heart of events, through England's convoluted forty-year history of political intrigue, devastating civil war, and suffering under a tyrannical king. And in the end he introduces her as a choric voice that places the entire time in stark perspective. We see her first as a seductive young woman, then as a passionate conspirator in a contentious court, later as a queen matched with an irresolute king, compelled by his weakness to assume command of his armies, and finally as the voice of vengeful retribution, gloating over the justice that fate has visited upon her enemies. She could well have been the subject of a fascinating play of her own, but Margaret is unique in the Shakespeare canon: never again would a single female figure have so central a role in so many of his plays.* The poet, it seems, found it necessary at this juncture of his budding career to turn his attention to works more appealing to his London audience, composing in swift succession his first comedy, *The Comedy of Errors,* and his first tragedy, *Titus Andronicus*.

---

*In the so-called "second Henriad," *Richard II, Henry IV, Parts 1* and *2,* and *Henry V*, women appear in only marginal roles.

# MARK ANTONY

*"Let Rome in Tiber melt . . ."*

SHAKESPEARE chronicles the life of Mark Antony in *Julius Caesar* and *Antony and Cleopatra*, two plays that span some fifteen years in Roman history, which the poet condensed into five or six hours on the stage. When we first see Antony, he is Caesar's devoted follower, vowing vengeance on the great man's assassins, the collective body of Roman senators. A charismatic figure, he delivers an inspired speech to the citizens, transforming them from a docile assembly that at first accepts, even applauds, the justice of the murder into a raging mob that roars off in a mindless frenzy to kill the murderers. Later, in concert with Caesar's heir, the young Octavius, and Lepidus, the third member of the so-called Second Triumvirate ruling Rome, Antony plots the destruction of the Senate.* In a brief, chilling scene, the three compile a list of senators and their families whom they condemn to death in a campaign to eliminate the power of that body once and for all. At the end of the play he crushes the last remaining hope of the Senate by defeating the forces of Brutus and Cassius at the crucial battle of Philippi.

In *Julius Caesar* we learn that Antony is a man of passion whose love for Caesar inspires in him an iron determination to avenge the great man's death, irrespective of the cost to Rome. He is also a skilled leader of men, a general who inspires courage and confidence in his soldiers. Shakespeare omits an episode in the civil wars that followed the assassination of Caesar, before the formation of the Triumvirate. Antony raised an army against the Senate but suffered a crushing defeat at Modena, an event referred to briefly in *Antony and*

---

*The First Triumvirate was Caesar, Pompey, and Crassus.

*Cleopatra*, where Octavius, lamenting the change in Antony, remarks on his courage and resolve at the time. During his army's retreat, Antony shared the hardships of his shattered legions, Octavius recalls, drinking "the stale of horses" and eating "the roughest of berries on the rudest hedge" and "strange flesh / Which some did die to look on." "All this," he goes on, "was borne so like a soldier, that thy cheek / So much as lanked not." Antony, needless to say, survived the defeat and lived to fight again.

Antony is also an acute politician in unrelenting pursuit of power. He dominates the youthful, inexperienced Octavius, with perhaps a touch of resentment that Caesar chose the young man as his heir rather than himself. And he is contemptuous of Lepidus, "a slight unmeritable man, / Meet to be sent on errands," though a temporarily useful partner in their enterprise. There is, then, an unattractive strain of arrogance in Antony, a haughty air that, however justified, leaves an audience with mixed feelings about the figure. We may sympathize with his devotion to, and grief at the death of, Caesar; but we may also be repelled by his ruthlessness.

As *Antony and Cleopatra* opens, the Roman Empire has been divided into three parts, with Antony ruling the East, Caesar Italy and the West,* and Lepidus some lesser kingdoms in Africa (Lepidus is disposed of later in the play, after he has served his purpose). Antony, however, is enthralled with Cleopatra, so much so that he has neglected his imperial duties. While the Parthians overrun Asia Minor and Pompey's son threatens Rome, Antony remains in Alexandria, bestowing on Cleopatra the same passion that marked his devotion to Julius Caesar. "Let Rome in Tiber melt," he exclaims, "and the wide arch / Of the ranged empire fall! Here is my space."

We see another side of Antony here, one only hinted at in the earlier play. He is a voluptuary, given to riotous living, a man in uninhibited pursuit of sensuous pleasure; and now, as emperor of the opulent East, he can liberally license his appetites. Caesar, anxiously awaiting Antony's return to help him subdue the forces ranged against Rome, is impatient at his indifference to the threats: "He fishes, drinks, and wastes / The lamp of night in revel," he com-

*Octavius is called Caesar in the play.

plains, and "reel[s] the streets at noon."* "Antony," he pleads with his absent ally, "leave thy lascivious wassails."

But Antony has become captivated by Cleopatra, who plays upon his sensual nature to enhance her hold over him. They feast and drink and love into the small hours of the day while the empire is threatened on all sides. Cleopatra employs all her wiles to keep him from returning to Rome: she attempts to provoke him with remarks about his subservience to his wife, Fulvia, and "the scarce-bearded Caesar"; she adopts an air of sullen discontent when she detects that "a Roman thought hath struck him"; and then she promises yet more rapturous pleasures to distract him from departure. Lest these provocative poses lead us to think otherwise, there seems little doubt that she loves him. When in the end duty prevails over love, when it is finally clear to Cleopatra that Antony is determined to return to Rome, she is suddenly solemn and plaintively sincere, powerless to describe her distress: "O! my oblivion is a very Antony, / And I am all forgotten." Nor should we doubt that Antony loves her. Her very perversity, he finds, only enhances her appeal: "Fie, wrangling queen! / Whom every thing becomes, to chide, to laugh, / To weep." He is all too conscious of his bondage, however—"These strong Egyptian fetters I must break, / Or lose myself in dotage"—and he finally succeeds in leaving her.

Unlike in Alexandria, where the talk is all of food and wine and the pursuit of delight, in Rome grave men discourse on war, alliance, and the affairs of empire. We see a different Antony here as the three emperors meet. He is all business—the soldier, statesman, and politician; and he reacts with acid disdain to any reference, however oblique, to his dalliance in Egypt. With Lepidus as mediator, the two emperors arrive at a tenuous accord, and it is suggested that to cement their reconciliation Antony will marry Caesar's sister, Octavia. He agrees to the arrangement, but as his knowing companion, Enobarbus, observes, it cannot last: "He will to his Egyptian dish again."

And in time he does, precipitating a confrontation between the armies of East and West at Actium, two emperors contending for

---

*It is striking that Caesar characterizes both Antony's courage and his decadence in terms of drinking and eating.

control of "the ranged empire." Here we see another Antony, the skilled and dauntless soldier, but one diminished, Shakespeare implies, by his enthrallment with Cleopatra. As one of his captains laments, "our leader's led, / And we are women's men." On three separate occasions in the balance of the play, Antony suspects her of treachery, of collusion with Caesar to betray him, each episode portrayed by Shakespeare in terms so ambiguous as to raise a question about her continued allegiance.

At Actium the Egyptian fleet raises sail and deserts in the middle of the battle. Antony follows Cleopatra impulsively, leaving his forces to certain defeat. Later, as Caesar lays siege to Alexandria, he sends an envoy to Cleopatra, offering her inducements to abandon her husband; and Antony, bursting on the scene, concludes that she has agreed to the terms. Still later, in the final battle, the Egyptian fleet surrenders to Caesar, effectively ending Antony's reign as emperor. In response to the first two episodes, Antony rages at her, accusing her of betraying their love; and on both occasions, in response to her entreaties, he forgives her: "Give me a kiss; / Even this repays me" and "I am satisfied." When the Egyptian fleet defects, however, he becomes convinced of her betrayal, and, enraged at the treachery of the "triple turned whore," he vows to kill her. Hearing of his anger and seeking to deflect it, Cleopatra sends word that she has taken her own life, news that reduces him to despair. Faced now with the loss of his love as well as his empire, he attempts to kill himself by falling on his sword. The wound is fatal, but he survives long enough to be reunited with Cleopatra, and the two declare their eternal love as he dies.

This, then, is Mark Antony, devoted servant to Julius Caesar, ruthless politician, consummate soldier, profligate libertine, passionate lover. He is a figure much like others we find elsewhere in Shakespeare—Julius Caesar, Macbeth, Richard III, Claudius—who are raised up by courage, treachery, ingenuity, and resolve, or like Richard II by birth, only to be brought low by an improvident appetite for power or pleasure. He is, to be sure, not the central tragic figure of these plays. In Julius Caesar it is the noble Brutus who engages our sympathies, a man who falls victim to his own virtues in a climate of violence, deception, and treachery, from which he stands apart as one who acts only out of devotion to an impossible ideal. In the later play it is Cleopatra's tragic end that is most moving, as she bares her breast to the poisonous asp and affirms her love for Antony: "Husband, I come! / Now to that name my courage prove my title!"

In some ways, however, Antony strikes a familiar chord of sympathy as we watch his heedless flight to destruction. I'm confident that such a figure hovers in the memory of each of us—a handsome, impetuous, magnetic companion who seems inordinately alive, easily attracting a devoted circle of admiring friends by the sheer intensity of his spirit, the wild energy he exudes unmindful of the toll. This same passion, however, this obsessive pursuit of all that life offers, comes at a price. We sense that such a profligate expense of spirit will burn itself out in a tragically short time, consuming the one it has enflamed. Such a figure, at any rate, seems Shakespeare's Mark Antony, a man who, torn between the conflicting demands of love and duty, chooses the former and loses an empire.

# MOTHERS

IN SHAKESPEARE'S PORTRAYAL of the patriarchal societies of medieval and Renaissance Europe, mothers appear only infrequently. Fathers abound, but the maternal presence is apparent in only a dozen or so of his thirty-eight plays. Married women are both wives and mothers, of course, but even when children are present the poet dwells predominantly on his female figures as wives. In the earliest of his history plays, the so-called "first Henriad," mothers play no part in *Henry VI, Parts 1* and *2*, but have important roles in *Part 3* and *Richard III*. In the latter two we encounter successively Margaret of Anjou fiercely defending her son Edward's position as heir to the throne, and the three grieving widows lamenting the death of their sons.* In the later "second Henriad," *Richard II, Henry IV, Parts 1* and *2,* and *Henry V*, mothers are entirely absent, save for a brief appearance by the French queen in the final scene of the last work. It is as if Shakespeare, satisfied that he has pretty much exhausted the subject for the moment, turned his attention to other matters. In *King John*, Lady Constance is the fiery champion of her son Arthur's claim to the English throne, but in *Henry VIII*, though Queen Katherine in one speech pleads with her husband to care for her daughter Mary, she is primarily a wife the king wants to divorce.

In the comedies we find mothers only in *The Winter's Tale, The Merry Wives of Windsor, All's Well That Ends Well,* and *Cymbeline*. Thaisa appears at the end of *Pericles* and the Abbess in the closing scene of *The Comedy of Errors*, but again the emphasis is on the happy reunion of husband and wife. In the tragedies, mothers appear only in *Romeo and Juliet, Hamlet, Macbeth,* and *Coriolanus*. When they do have a prominent part in a play, Shakespeare's mothers are cast pri-

*See "Margaret of Anjou" pp. 195–200.

marily in two roles: they are fierce advocates of their children, as with the aforementioned Margaret and Constance, and grief-stricken mourners at their death, as in the case again of the three widows in *Richard III*, each of whom has lost one or more sons during the war and Richard's rise to power.

All is not stereotype, however, for Shakespeare endows his mothers with qualities that emphasize their individuality. A glance at three of them will illustrate the poet's variety in characterization: Cymbeline's Queen and Volumnia in *Coriolanus*, both of them intent upon enhancing their sons' prospects, and *Hamlet's* Gertrude, who has a troubled relationship with hers.

## Cymbeline's Queen

*"She being down, I have the placing of the English crown."*

Shakespeare's plays frequently portray mothers who are ambitious for their children, but the consort of King Cymbeline of Britain, identified simply as the "Queen" in the text, is perhaps unique in resorting to treacherous measures to advance her unsavory son Cloten. He is her offspring from a previous marriage, and she schemes to ensure his ascent to the throne by matching him with the king's daughter Imogen. That path is blocked when Imogen secretly marries "a poor but worthy gentleman," Posthumus, angering her father, who banishes the young man from the kingdom.

The resourceful Queen now turns her attention to Imogen, whose death, she concludes, will leave Cloten as the sole successor to the throne: "She being down, I have the placing of the English crown." Pretending sympathy for the separated couple, she secures a potion of "most poisonous compounds" from a doctor, but he, mistrusting her intentions, substitutes a harmless mixture that will only temporarily produce the appearance of death. The Queen gives the potion to Imogen's faithful servant Pisano, claiming that it is a restorative medicine that has "five times reduced the king from death," and suggesting that he offer it to her should she become ill. In the end Imogen survives, Cloten is killed, Posthumus returns, and all are reconciled. The doctor reveals that the Queen had plotted the king's death as well "to work / Her son into th'adoption of the crown," but her plans having failed, she

> Grew shameless desperate; opened, in despite
> Of heaven and men, her purposes; repented
> The evils she hatched were not effected; so
> Despairing, died.

Cymbeline's Queen, then, embodies the dark side of a mother's passion to advance the prospects of her son. But though she resorts to iniquity to gain her ends, she is no less determined than are Constance in *King John*, who attempts to foment a war between England and France to enforce her son's claim to the English throne, or Queen Margaret in *Henry VI, Part 3*, who engages in a bloody conflict to ensure that hers will inherit the crown.

## Volumnia

*"O, he is wounded, I thank the gods for that."*

We have encountered Volumnia in the chapter on Coriolanus, but it will be rewarding to revisit the figure in the context of this consideration of mothers and their children.[*] She has raised her son to be a warrior and has been "pleased," she says, "to let him seek danger where he is like to find fame." In his early manhood, she continues proudly, "to a cruel war I sent him, from whence he returned" with honor. Actually, her child-rearing methods are not without a practical design. In the time frame of the play, early pre-Augustan Rome, the republic was surrounded by enemies, and those who distinguished themselves in battle were richly rewarded, often with high office. We gain some notion of Coriolanus's upbringing in Volumnia's account of an incident involving his young son, still a toddler. The boy was chasing a butterfly, she recalls, and fell down in the pursuit. Rising in anger, he caught the insect and tore it to pieces, proving himself in her eyes a chip off the old block: "Indeed la, 'tis a noble child."

[*]See pp. 47–54.

Early in the play we see Coriolanus in a "cruel war" against the neighboring Volcians. He returns highly acclaimed for his valor and suffering from wounds received in battle, news of which delights his mother: "O, he is wounded, I thank the gods for that." She rejoices that he will have more scars to show the people as evidence of his worthiness "when he shall stand for his place." Volumnia collects his scars, keeping a careful count of them—twenty-seven so far, she reports with satisfaction—much as a modern mother might display a son's sports trophies or academic honors.

The Senate elects Coriolanus consul, the highest honor in the Roman republic, but he balks at the traditional ceremony required of all candidates for the office, a public appearance before the common citizens to secure their approval. It was customary on such occasions for candidates to display their scars as evidence of their service to Rome, and Coriolanus disdainfully refuses to demean that service by using it as a bid for office. Volumnia rebukes him for his reluctance: "Thy valiantness was mine, thou suck'st it from me, / But owe [own] thy pride thyself." She is blind to the fact that in persuading him of his unique destiny she has at the same time imbued him with a contempt for those who have less than his lofty sense of duty. He "suck'st" from her not only his martial valor but a belief in his moral superiority as well. He recalls her ridicule of the common people, calling "them woolen vassals, things created / To buy and sell groats,"* who will only "yawn, be still, and wonder," in effect stand slack-jawed in the presence of great men. She is responsible, in brief, for both his valor and his pride.

She finally persuades her son to submit to the ceremony, and she does so with a familiar maternal appeal. "Do as you list [please]," she says dismissively, and turns to leave, clearly conveying her disappointment at his ingratitude for her lifetime of devotion to his welfare. Coriolanus reluctantly agrees, but he is unable to muster the expected measure of humility before the people and angers them with his haughty manner. He is banished for his arrogance and, seeking revenge for his humiliation, allies himself with the enemy

---

*A groat is a menial coin, worth four pence. Volumnia is voicing the soldier's discontent with the commercial class, who are concerned only with profit, or "commodity" as *King John's* Faulconbridge calls it.

Volcians. He returns at the head of an army, determined to level the city, now apparently defenseless, having exiled its greatest soldier.

He is confronted once again by his mother, this time accompanied by his wife and young son, who plead with him to spare the city. Volumnia marshals an array of maternal complaints: he threatens to tread upon her "womb / That brought thee to this world" and is guilty of disrespect and ingratitude, "Thou hast never in thy life / Showed thy dear mother any courtesy." Coriolanus remains adamant, and in a final desperate gesture she, his wife, and his son kneel before him—"Down ladies! Let us shame him with our knees"—but even that fails to deter him. Finally, after all her appeals have proven fruitless, she turns to go, but not without a parting shot: "So, we will home to Rome, / And die among our neighbours." Coriolanus, disarmed by this onslaught of maternal pleas, finally relents, though he knows what submission will cost him: "O, mother, mother! / What have you done?" He dismisses his soldiers and is slain by the Volcians for his betrayal.

Volumnia's ambition for her son disables him for any career other than a soldier. She has encouraged his vision of himself as one destined for greatness, but at the same time she has instilled in him a contempt for the common citizens of Rome, the "woolen vassals" who pursue their ordinary lives uninspired by aspirations of fame. The very qualities she urged upon him—sacrifice, courage, strength, devotion to duty—leave him vulnerable to a debilitating pride that leads to his downfall. After a lifetime dominated by his mother's lofty ambition, he is powerless to resist her fatal influence.

## Gertrude

*"O Hamlet, thou hast cleft my heart in twain."*

In the early scenes of *Hamlet*, Queen Gertrude seems a contented wife to Claudius, her late husband's brother, and he seems equally fond of her, a lady, he remarks later, who is "conjunctive to my life and soul." It is an easy matter for players to give the impression of genuine affection between the two, a matter simply of an exchange of affectionate glances or subtle touch of hands, all of which justify Hamlet's indignation at the sight. Gertrude is deeply disturbed by her son's melancholy, however, which she assumes has been brought on by sorrow at his father's death. She counsels him to set aside his black looks and dress and accept the fact that "all that lives must die," advice that only darkens his mood. He is clearly grieved at the loss of a father, but it is the royal couple's obvious attachment that most incenses him, especially his mother's failure to observe the customary period of mourning following the death of a husband. She has remarried, he rages inwardly, though his father is "but two months dead, nay not so much, not two," and it is "within a month . . . a little month" of his funeral that she has hastened "with such dexterity to incestuous sheets."

We have discussed elsewhere the suggestion by Freudian scholars of an unnaturally close physical relationship between the mother and son in the play, one that could also be implied by the players' gestures or embraces, and we need not rehearse the matter here.[*] Suffice it to say that Gertrude obviously dotes on her son, so much so, Claudius later observes, that she "lives almost by his looks," and Hamlet's anger at her hasty remarriage may indeed arise from a sense of desertion or betrayal.

Matters between them come to a head in the explosive "Closet Scene" when Hamlet confronts his mother. He has orchestrated the performance of a play, *The Murder of Gonzago*, for the entertainment of the court, one that reenacts his father's treacherous murder, at the sight of which the guilty king rises abruptly and rushes from the room. Gertrude has summoned her son for reprimand, but he quickly reverses their postures:

*Queen*. Hamlet, thou hast thy father much offended.
*Hamlet*. Mother, you have my father much offended.

Two things seem to trouble Hamlet deeply: first, his fear that Gertrude has been complicit in his father's death, and second, his fierce resentment that she shares her bed with Claudius. The first he

[*]See "Hamlet," p. 94.

addresses as he lifts the wall hanging to reveal the body of Polonius to his horrified mother:

> *Queen.* O what a rash and bloody deed is this!
> *Hamlet.* A bloody deed—almost as bad, good mother,
>     As kill a king and marry his brother.
> *Queen.* As kill a king!
> *Hamlet.*                    Ay, lady, it was my word. . . .

Her shocked response to the accusation apparently satisfies him of her innocence, for the subject is not raised again.

But the second matter festers in his spirit. He draws attention to portraits of her two husbands. To his father's: "See what a grace was seated on this brow, / Hyperion's curls, the front of Jove himself, / An eye like Mars to threaten and command." And then to Claudius's: "Here is your husband, like a mildewed ear, / Blasting his wholesome brother." His anger mounting, he then unleashes a torrent of abuse upon the king, "a murderer and a villain, / A slave that is not twentieth part of tithe / Of you precedent lord, a vice of kings, / a cutpurse of the empire." Gertrude in response is overcome with remorse: "O speak to me no more, / These words like daggers enter in mine ears, / No more, sweet Hamlet."

Hamlet's diatribe is interrupted by the entrance of the ghost, who is visible to him alone, and Gertrude is stunned by the spectacle of her son addressing empty space, all the time insisting that his father stands before them. The ghost departs, and, calmer now, Hamlet exploits her anguish: "Confess yourself to heaven, / Repent what's past, avoid what is to come." She must "avoid" two things, he insists: first, advising her cruelly to "assume a virtue, if you have it not," he demands that she abandon her husband's bed; second, she must not in any way reveal to Claudius that their son is "not in madness, / But mad in craft." She agrees meekly to both and he leaves, as she is forced to endure the wrenching sight of her son dragging the corpse of Polonius from her chamber to "lug the guts into a neighbour room."

We can only imagine Gertrude's state of mind at the close of this tumultuous encounter with her son. She seems genuinely contrite— "O Hamlet, thou hast cleft my heart in twain"—but also sorrowful

at the breach between them, shamed that she has so unwittingly for-
feited his love and respect, and fearful of what will come of it all. On
the other hand, her ready submission to his demands may arise from
a simple desire to be rid of her raving son, who is so quick with his
rapier and talks to the walls. Nothing in the play indicates that she
abandons her husband's bed—at least Claudius makes no mention of
it—and the relationship between them seems to show no sign of
strain. But she apparently does not confide in him that her son is
"mad in craft"; Claudius detects Hamlet's deception on his own.

Gertrude makes brief appearances in the balance of the play,
poignantly describing Ophelia's death and laying flowers on her
grave with moving regret: "I hoped thou shouldst have been my
Hamlet's wife." In the final scene she drinks impulsively from the
poisoned cup the king intends for her son; and she dies, a sight that
compels him into action at last. He kills the king and himself falls
victim to Laertes' "envenomed" sword with a last curt farewell to his
mother: "Wretched queen, adieu!"

Mothers in Shakespeare's histories and tragedies are for the most
part suffering survivors of their sons and husbands, victims left to
mourn the loss of loved ones in a brutally contentious man's world.
They suffer as well in the comedies, but, again for the most part, they
remain virtuously constant and in the end are happily reunited with
their children and spouses. At the same time, however, Shakespeare
varies these patterns, creating figures with unique qualities. Both
Cymbeline's Queen and Volumnia, like many others in the plays, are
ambitious for their sons. The Queen, however, is a treacherous vil-
lainess who schemes to poison those who stand in Cloten's way to the
throne, while Volumnia, who has raised her son as a fearsome warrior
to ensure his fame, proves willing to sacrifice him to save herself and
Rome. Gertrude, in another variation, may be a victim of her own desires, and she falls a casualty of passions beyond her control, having
come between what Hamlet calls "the pass and fell incenséd points /
Of mighty opposites," her vengeful son and murderous husband.

# OTHELLO

*"No, to be once in doubt / Is once resolved."*

THE LONG THIRD SCENE of Act Three in the play opens on an Othello devoted to, indeed doting on, his young bride, Desdemona. At its close, a victim of Iago's lies and insinuations, he calls for her death. The success of the play depends upon the effectiveness of this scene, upon the actor's ability to convince an audience that so dramatic a transformation could take place in such a short passage of time. In preparing us to accept as credible Othello's vulnerability to Iago's subtle hints and fabrications, Shakespeare provides in earlier scenes some critical insights into the character of the figure. Othello, we have learned, is a soldier, a husband some years older than his wife, and a Moor.

Othello's life as a soldier has been arduous. In describing the course of his courtship to the Duke of Venice, he reveals that he had often accepted the invitation of the rich merchant Brabantio to give an account of his adventures, of "the battles, sieges, fortunes, / That I had passed." It is a tale, he says, "of moving accidents by flood and field, / Of hair-breadth scapes i'th'imminent breach," and of suffering as a prisoner of war, reduced to slave labor. Othello has survived these years of danger and toil, however, and risen in the ranks of his profession until Venice placed him in command of the city's armed forces, a *condottiere,* or mercenary soldier, one of many employed by the city-states in medieval and Renaissance Italy to protect their lands or encroach on a neighbor's.

The years of experience as a soldier and commander have left Othello with a single-minded view of life and his fellow humans. As a leader of men in battle, he found it necessary to make quick judgments of an enemy's strengths and weaknesses, often on the basis of scant information, depending on an instinct born of many campaigns and an intuitive grasp of the critical moment and place that determines the difference between victory and defeat. On such occasions, when the battle hangs in the balance and delay can end in disaster, he does not have the luxury of pondering alternatives, of contemplating, Hamlet-like, the fall of a sparrow. There are no shades of grey in battlefield decisions to advance or retreat, to attack or defend, to maneuver right or left, or to commit forces held in reserve. Othello's life has been shaped by such decisions, when a momentary hesitation can spell defeat.

Early in the play Iago attempts to incite a brawl between the followers of Othello and Brabantio when they come upon one another around a darkened corner by a Venetian canal. He fails, however, when Othello abruptly commands, "Keep up your bright swords, for the dew will rust them." He senses quickly that this is neither the time nor the place for an armed encounter and without hesitation acts to prevent one.

In Cyprus, Iago attempts once again to incite a brawl, this time successfully, between Othello's lieutenant, Cassio, and the former governor, Montano. Othello appears and commands, "Hold, for your lives!" though not before Montano is wounded. After hearing Iago's account of the altercation, in which he omits his own role in fomenting it, Othello unhesitatingly dismisses his lieutenant, "Cassio, I love thee; / But never more be officer of mine."

The actor in the role of Othello is called upon to convey a commanding presence, a manner and voice that demand obedience along with the implied threat of fearful consequences for those who fail to instantly obey. When he prevents the brawl in Venice with the command, "Keep up your bright swords," both sides freeze in response to the tone and bearing of a man accustomed to immediate compliance. The threat to those who fail to obey is more overt in Cyprus: "My blood begins my safer guides to rule," he thunders; and

> If I once stir,
> Or do but lift this arm, the best of you
> Shall sink in my rebuke.

And then, ominously, "He that stirs next . . . holds his soul light; he dies upon his motion."

The soldier's life, then, encourages a certain habit of mind that calls for quick judgments between stark opposites—advance or retreat, bravery or cowardice, ally or enemy. It leaves him uncomfortable with indecision, with the legal profession's ponderous weighing of evidence or the politician's slow approach to compromise, measures which if employed on a battlefield would jeopardize victory. Othello cannot live with uncertainty. He says as much as Iago plants the seeds of doubt that later flourish in his conviction that Desdemona has been unfaithful to him with Cassio: "No, to be once in doubt / Is once resolved." And he goes on:

I'll see before I doubt; when I doubt, prove;
And on the proof, there is no more but this,
Away at once with love or jealousy!

It is simply not in Othello's nature to remain in a state of indecision. The matter must be quickly resolved one way or another; and once determined, action must follow hard upon.

Another quality of the soldier's life leads to Othello's fatal decision. He has spent his professional life in rough encampments, on long, exhausting marches, and locked in fierce struggle on scarred battlefields. This background has left him more comfortable on the robust tented field than in the elegantly appointed drawing rooms of a sophisticated Venetian society. Iago dwells on his social naiveté in building the image of a promiscuous Desdemona, and Othello acknowledges him to be an astute insider, one who "knows all qualities, with a learned spirit, / Of human dealings," while he himself, he admits, has "not those soft parts of conversation / That chamberers have."

An audience may justifiably wonder why Othello fails to see through Iago, to catch a glimpse of his hatred and recognize him not as a friend but an enemy. It is perhaps that soldier's habit of mind, the tendency to interpret reality in terms of severe opposites, that renders Othello blind to Iago's true nature. Battle presents the stark spectacle of the difference between life and death, when there is no lingering twilight or first faint blush of dawn, only the light and the darkness of victory or defeat. It is so with men in battle, and the commander quickly observes, often on evidence of a single act, the sharp distinction between the brave and cowardly, the loyal and treacherous, the resolute and fainthearted, the disciplined and disorderly. We learn nothing of Iago's background except that he has been the general's "ancient," a subordinate rank in medieval armies, but he has obviously proven himself a loyal and dedicated comrade-in-arms, and once Othello has judged him worthy, he resolutely rejects any suggestion to the contrary. Until the very end he is "honest, honest Iago," a man "of honesty and trust." "This honest creature," Othello is convinced, "doubtless / Sees and knows more, much more, than he unfolds."

In defense of Othello's seemingly flawed judgment, Iago in fact deceives everyone in the play. To Desdemona he is "an honest fellow," and Cassio declares that he has never known "a Florentine more kind and honest." His wife, Emilia, who should know better, is also deceived by him. Learning of Cassio's predicament, she assures him that "it grieves my husband / As if the case were his." It doesn't even occur to the ridiculous Roderigo, to whom Iago confides, "I am not what I am," that he might be untrustworthy, that the valuable gifts he has entrusted to him for delivery to Desdemona may never have reached her. In the end, of those who trust him, four—Othello, Desdemona, Emilia, Roderigo—are dead, and Cassio has suffered a severe wound. Othello is surely deceived, but he is not alone in trusting "honest, honest Iago."

Another factor contributing to Othello's insecurity is the age disparity between him and his wife. He mentions it only twice in the play, on the first occasion when he requests that Desdemona accompany him to Cyprus. He assures the duke, rather disingenuously, that he is past the age of youthful passion and so does not ask "to please the palate of my appetite / Nor to comply with heat,—the young effects / In me defunct." Later, as he searches his mind to understand her betrayal, he acknowledges that he is "declined / Into the vale of years." While it may be only a minor consideration to either of them—Desdemona makes no mention of it—Iago dwells on the difference in persuading Roderigo to continue his suit: "She must change for youth: when she is sated with his body, she will find the error of her choice."

Of more importance than age disparity in contributing to Othello's insecurity is the fact that he is a Moor. In Venice he is a highly respected Moor, to be sure, one who has enhanced his assimilation by becoming a Christian; but he is a Moor nonetheless, whose essential difference is emphasized visually by the color of his skin. Iago is not so indiscreet as to refer to his racial background to him personally, but it is prominent in his inflammatory report of the marriage to Brabantio in the first scene. In an effort to provoke Desdemona's father to a rage, he mixes ethnic slurs with erotic incitements: "An old black ram / Is tupping your white ewe"; "your daughter [is] covered with a Barbary horse"; she "and the Moor are now making the beast with two backs." To Roderigo he is "the thick-lips"; and in continuing the account of the marriage to Brabantio after Iago's departure, Roderigo enlarges on the image: even at that moment she is "in the gross clasps of a lascivious Moor," an "extravagant and wheeling stranger / Of here and everywhere."

This theme of alienation—Othello as a "wheeling stranger" in Venetian society—underlies his vulnerability to Iago's insinuations. While allusion to the racial difference between Othello and Desdemona is muted in later episodes, these earlier inciting remarks remain with the audience, reinforced throughout by the visual representation of the Moor as darker-skinned and, very often in contrast, Desdemona as a blond, blue-eyed northern Italian. Othello is often portrayed by a black actor (famously by Paul Robeson, and more recently by James Earl Jones) or by a Caucasian such as Laurence Olivier with heavy makeup. I am not convinced that Shakespeare was making a subtle racial statement here; he was simply adapting to the Elizabethan stage an old novella by an Italian writer, Giraldi Cinthio, in which Othello is a Moor and so remains one in the play. But the implications of a darker skin for modern and for Elizabethan audiences deserve comment.

Today we usually conceive, rightly or wrongly, of a person with a swarthy complexion as possessed of a passionate nature. Young men and women flock to sunbaked beaches to acquire a "savage tan," which in the mysterious chemistry of physical attraction is said to render them more appealing to the opposite sex. A dark skin implies vitality, sexual prowess, and emotional volatility, and however often the impression may disappoint, the appeal prevails. We entertain, further, the tradition of the "Latin Lover," a tawny Lothario, skilled in the art of seduction, barely concealing a steeped passion beneath a suave exterior and cool civility. Compared to the stereotypical image of the pale-skinned, tight-lipped, repressed, and proper Northerner, those whom harsh winters reduce to pragmatic, often puritanical, habits of survival, the Mediterranean races are seen as carefree and volatile, unrestrained by stiff custom and propriety. So, at any rate, goes the popular image of those who live in sunlit lands, in part accounting for the appeal of Caribbean islands to modern vacationers. Othello's dark complexion, then, suggests to modern audiences that beneath his austerely controlled exterior there smolders a deeply passionate nature that could flare up dangerously in moments of love or anger.

To an Elizabethan audience the Moors were all this and something more. They were a warrior race, one that conquered Spain in the eighth century and went on to occupy France as far north as the Loire River, until stopped there by Charles Martel at the battle of Tours. The patrons of Shakespeare's Globe Theater would have thought of the Moors as an alien presence in Christian Europe in their own time, a culture that had occupied portions of Spain until late in the fifteenth century.

To those patrons, then, the Moor was a respected warrior. But he was also an infidel who had been the scourge of Christianity, and Shakespeare worked artfully on the conflicting sentiments of an audience who perceived Othello as an alien presence but at the same time a man much like themselves, subject to the same dreams and passions. In the end Othello is defeated by those emotions in excess, inflamed by his sense of alienation from the society he sought vainly to embrace. Othello's weakness is his passion, attributed again rightly or wrongly to his color but implied strongly by his nature. It is kept strictly constrained in Venice, where he commands the combatants to "Keep up your bright swords"; but it emerges uncontrolled in Cyprus, where he plots the death of Cassio and Desdemona.

However composed Othello appears in the first act—properly deferential to Brabantio and dignified in the presence of the duke— the fact remains that his marriage to Desdemona is precipitous, an

act of thoughtless passion. He defies all the settled customs of an ordered society by wedding the daughter of a respected Venetian merchant and senator without the father's permission, knowing full well
that he would have forbidden it. Brabantio is surprised by it. Raging at Othello, he cannot understand how his daughter could have
"run from her guardage," a careful and caring home, and fled "to the
sooty bosom / Of such a thing as thou"; he finds it incomprehensible that she could "fall in love with what she feared to look on."

This rough soldier wins the heart of a young woman, properly
raised in the protective environment of a cultured society, and does
so with tales of his exotic adventures. "She loved me for the dangers
I had passed," he explains to the duke, "and I loved her that she did
pity them." And he marries her in impulsive disregard for the norms
of accepted behavior in the culture with which he aspires to identify.
Although at first glance this may seem a fragile basis for a marriage,
in truth it is no more or less substantial that the attraction between
any of Shakespeare's couples, who fall in love at first sight for no accountable reason.

Physical passion was difficult to portray on the Elizabethan
stage, where female roles were played by ornately costumed boys.
An athletic kiss or prolonged embrace was hazardous before an audience too well aware that beneath the powdered wig and generously padded brocade was the body of a prepubescent youth. It is in
the poetry of his lines that Shakespeare gives glimpses of Othello's
deep fire, prominently on the occasion of his reunion with Desdemona on his arrival in Cyprus. His mission to prevent a Turkish invasion of the island is aborted when a storm at sea scatters the enemy fleet, at the same time, of course, endangering his own. He
arrives safely, however, and greets his bride:

> O my soul's joy
> If ever after tempest come such calms,
> May the winds blow till they have wakened death.
> . . . . . . . . . . If it were now to die,
> 'Twere now to be most happy.

"I cannot speak enough of this content," he goes on, "it stops me
here." Othello loves Desdemona with his whole being. Later, after

she persuades him to hear the disgraced Cassio's account of the brawl with Montano, he gazes after her as she takes her leave and exclaims,

Excellent wretch! Perdition catch my soul
But I do love thee; and when I love thee not
Chaos is come again.

And by "chaos" he means not simply distress or disorder but the final dissolution of his world.

Iago detects a vulnerability in the Moor's soaring passion for his wife, and he exploits it. He preys upon the elements of Othello's character that mark him as different from Venetian society, hence from Desdemona. Dwelling on their incompatibility, he persuades Othello that he is unfamiliar with Venetian customs, especially the duplicity of their women, claiming that "In Venice they do let God see the pranks / They dare not show their husbands." Iago reminds him that "She did deceive her father, marrying you; / And when she seems to shake and fear your looks, / She loved them most." Othello is taken in completely by these insinuations, and in brief lines concludes that the gap between him and his wife in race, background, and age is so wide that it has led to her infidelity:

Haply, for I am black
And have not those soft parts of conversation
That chamberers have, or for I am declined
Into the vale of years.

This is the turning point in the scene: "She's gone," he concludes, "I am abused; and my relief / Must be to loathe her." "Chaos" has indeed "come again," a time when he "loves her not," when Othello comes to hate his wife with a passion as intense as that with which he loved her. In a mixture of pain and anger he rages that his life as a man and a husband is over: "O now for ever / Farewell the tranquil mind! Farewell content!" As is his life as a soldier:

Farewell the neighing steed, and the shrill trump,
The spirit-stirring drum, th'ear piercing fife,
The royal banner, and all quality,
Pride, pomp, and circumstance, of glorious war! . . .
Farewell! Othello's occupation's gone!

In the balance of the play, Othello is a tormented man, torn between twin passions—his love for Desdemona and his anguish at her supposed betrayal. And, true to his nature, he can countenance no way between the two—"To be once in doubt / Is once resolved." Still, it tears at his spirit—"But the pity of it, Iago! Iago, the pity of it, Iago!"—"yet she must die."

In the end, still unable to resolve these conflicting passions, Othello enters the bedchamber to perform an act that every fiber of his being, every particle of his spirit, resists, and he prepares himself by depersonalizing his role. He imagines himself a priest approaching a sacrificial altar, intoning a solemn chant—"It is the cause, it is the cause, my soul: / Let me not name it to you, you chaste stars, / It is the cause"—and then as an instrument of justice purging humanity of corruption—"Yet she must die, else she'll betray more men." He bends over to kiss her sleeping form, conflicted still: "O balmy breath, thou dost almost persuade / Justice to break her sword." As she awakens, his resolution returns, and he kills her in the bed where, he is persuaded, she has betrayed him.

To impart a tragic sense to the final scenes, Shakespeare restores the image of Othello we encountered at the outset, the noble Moor who commands "Keep up your bright swords" to prevent bloodshed and addresses the ducal court with restraint and dignity. In his final words, delivered with that same solemn dignity, he recalls that he has "done the state some service" and asks only that he be remembered as one who "loved not wisely but too well." And then, overcome by his folly and his loss, he takes his own life. Cassio's epitaph reminds us once again of his former stature: "He was great of heart."

Does that critical central scene of Act Three convince us, then, that a man so "great of heart" could be brought to such an end? Shakespeare has certainly done his part in portraying the depth of the Moor's passion and the differences between the lovers—Othello's racial background, the soldier's lack of sophistication, and his advanced years, the qualities that transform him in a single episode from ardent devotion to murderous jealousy. The ultimate test is in the performance, of course, in the actor's ability to convey the slow growth of doubt in Othello, culminating in that climactic "She's

gone" as he falls victim to Iago's unrelenting assault upon Desdemona's virtue.

How are we to think of Othello? As a noble mind, brought low
by his passions? As a rough barbarian who plucks a flower from the
cultivated garden of its protected life and then crushes it? As a simple soldier innocent of sophisticated culture who falls prey to the
subtle intrigues of a vindictive villain, one skilled in the deceptive
devices of an intricately mature society?

Yes, all of these. In the figure of Othello, Shakespeare unmasks
the tragic dual nature of mankind, portraying the human spirit as at
once noble and brutish. We, like the Moor, are gifted with the ca-
pacity to conceive a soaring vision of joy and fulfillment; but, again
like him, we can be reduced to primal rage when those riches are
snatched from us. Both a lesser angel and a greater ape, we swing
precariously between the two natures, unwilling to surrender the
one and unable to subdue the other.

# PETRUCHIO AND KATE

*"And where two raging fires meet together,*
*They do consume the thing that feeds their fury."*

IT SEEMS APPROPRIATE to consider Petruchio and Kate together, as we do Romeo and Juliet, since their fortunes are so intimately linked. Unlike the "star-crossed lovers," however, these two are locked in a battle of wills, a struggle between a man and a woman who in fact mirror one another in many respects. Both are headstrong, witty, high-spirited, and uncompromising individuals, who to all appearances find themselves in the end very much in love. In *The Taming of the Shrew*, however, the path to that realization does not begin with love at first sight. On Kate's part it seems rather to be hatred on first sight, though her initial reaction to Petruchio appears to be no different from her attitude toward the entire male population, a contempt that focuses on him as simply the most recent one to come to her attention.

Qualifying phrases such as "seems" and "appears to be" are most apt in this description because Shakespeare is typically ambiguous about what it is that brings about the final attraction between the two. The poet only hints at the reason in Petruchio's philosophical confidence that "where two raging fires meet together, / They do consume the thing that feeds their fury"; but Shakespeare goes no further to explain the outcome of their tumultuous affair. There are in effect three phases to their history: the courtship, the marriage, and the aftermath, though the period of marriage may well be seen as a continuation of the courtship. And in each phase Petruchio employs a different strategy to win the heart of "Katherine the curst," as she is widely known.

Katherina Minola, the "shrew" of the title, is the abusive, shrill-tongued, ungovernable daughter of Baptista, a wealthy merchant of

Padua. The source of her ill temper is left undefined—after all, each of us knows such people—but Shakespeare implies that it arises from envy of her sister Bianca, who aside from her beauty is a properly modest maiden, to all appearances obedient, temperate, and unassuming. And because of her outwardly pliant demeanor she has a host of suitors—four of them during the course of the play—while at the outset Kate has none. But though Kate appears to be jealous of Bianca's popularity, it is not clear whether this is the cause of her abrasive nature. It certainly provides an occasion for her to display her discontent, but she seems angry at life itself.

Kate, on first impression, is a rebellious young woman who defies her father's will and resents his apparent preference for Bianca. Baptista announces that Bianca cannot marry until Kate is claimed, and on leaving he orders her to stay while he confers with his favored daughter. Kate bristles at the slight—"Why, and I trust I may go too, may I not?"—and she stalks off in a huff. She has, then, a fiercely independent streak and rebels against parental or any other authority over her. Baptista exercises the father's traditional prerogative, here and in later episodes, to choose the men his daughters will marry, and they have little say in the matter, a custom that Kate clearly resents. There is certainly enough in Baptista's humiliating edict to inflame her, however, and for the moment all her anger is directed at Bianca. She seizes her sister, binds her hands, and abuses her verbally and physically until interrupted by their father. Kate then turns her wrath on him:

> Nay, now I see
> She is your treasure, she must have a husband;
> I must dance barefoot on her wedding-day
> And for your love to her lead apes to hell.*

She storms out to "sit and weep," she says, "till I can find occasion of revenge."

Petruchio, we find, is a handsome, robust, self-confident young man, though he seems at times somewhat brash and overly mercenary.

---

*A rather cruel saying of the time: Old maids lead apes to hell rather than children to heaven.

He has inherited his father's estate, he tells his friend Hortensio, one of Bianca's suitors, and has "come to wive it wealthily in Padua."* It doesn't matter to him if his wife is old, or ugly, or shrewish; it is not even important that he love her, so long as she is rich. Petruchio's unabashed pursuit of wealth may cast him in an unattractive light, but this is only one episode in Shakespeare's subtle ridicule of the practice of bartering for a bride. Later in the play Bianca's suitors confer with her father, each inquiring about the size of her dowry and boasting of his wealth in competition for her hand. Baptista bestows her on the richest one.

Hortensio persuades Petruchio to marry Kate so that he will be free to court Bianca, and his friend readily agrees, having been assured that she will come with a handsome dowry. Petruchio is not deterred by accounts of "Katherine the curst." He has every confidence that he can subdue her since, he claims, he can be "as peremptory as she is proud-minded," and besides, "I am rough and woo not like a babe."

In each of the aforementioned three phases of this courtship— Petruchio's rough wooing, the marriage, and the aftermath—he employs a different method. The character of these two, our subject here, reveals itself in their responses to each of these phases and will be most effectively observed by following the course of their encounter. Petruchio greets her quite amiably at first—"Good morrow, Kate"—and she replies curtly that she prefers to be called Katherine. In a design to establish his control from the outset, he responds by repeating "Kate" eleven times in six lines of verse, but then has to submit to a series of blistering insults, ending with a slap in the face. He seizes her to deter any further physical abuse, and as she struggles to free herself he insists perversely that she is not "rough, and coy, and sullen," as he has been led to believe, but rather "pleasant, gamesome, passing courteous, . . . soft, and affable." She is infuriated by her inability to escape his grasp as well as by his perversity, and he finds that he has to change his tone, announcing firmly that he will marry her despite her irascible disposi-

---

*A line that provides the title for one of the hit songs in Cole Porter's popular musical, *Kiss Me Kate*.

tion since her father has already agreed to the match. Moreover, he says, "I am he am born to tame you, Kate, / And bring you from a wild Kate" to one more submissive—lines that once again significantly repeat "Kate."

At the wedding, Petruchio's intent clearly is to humiliate her. First, he arrives late, reducing her to tears, and when he finally does appear he is outlandishly dressed and sits astride a decrepit horse. He behaves outrageously at the ceremony, striking the minister and throwing wine in the face of the sexton, and afterward he insists that they will not stay for the wedding feast but leave directly for his home in Verona. Kate reacts angrily to his presumption, declaring that she will not go with him: "I see a woman may be made a fool / If she had not a spirit to resist."

In response to her defiance, Petruchio insists that since they are now married she has no choice in the matter, and he replies with what must be the most outrageous description in all of literature of the relationship between husband and wife. The custom of the time certainly dictated that the father ruled over his family, even as the king ruled his country, and that when a woman married, all that she possessed passed into the hands of her husband. But Petruchio's portrayal of the tradition proves especially provocative:

> I will be master of what is mine own.
> She is my goods, my chattels, she is my house,
> My household stuff, my field, my barn,
> My horse, my ox, my ass, my any thing,
> And here she stands.

He seizes Kate and, brandishing his sword, carries her off, to the amazement of some—"Of all mad matches never was the like"—but to the satisfaction of Bianca: "Being mad herself, she's madly mated."

Once the couple arrive in Verona, after a long, tiring ride, Petruchio adopts a new strategy. He appears to be a harsh, abusive master in his own household, railing at his servants for their apparent neglect: "You logger-headed and unpolished grooms!" "You peasant swain, you whoreson malt-horse drudge!" He beats one for supposed clumsiness in removing his boots and strikes another, "a whoreson beetle-headed, flap-eared knave!" for dropping a bowl of water. Kate looks on helplessly at his display of rancor. She is tired, wet, cold, and hungry, and Petruchio is deceptively courteous and sympathetic toward her, insisting that his anger is directed at his servants, who, he fumes, are not properly prepared to receive her. When food is finally brought, he claims the meat is burned and throws the dishes at the servers. When the couple retires for the night, having eaten nothing, he tears the bed apart, raging that it was carelessly made, and continues his tirade into the morning hours, depriving Kate of sleep.

Kate is given to acts of physical violence. She has already abused Bianca, broken a lute over Hortensio's head, and slapped Petruchio; and his rough usage of his servants may well be a not so subtle message that she would do well not to repeat that behavior. He discloses his intent in a soliloquy, comparing his strategy to the taming of a hunting falcon. Kate is by now hungry and exhausted, a condition, he says with satisfaction, that he has brought about on the pretext "that all is done in reverend care of her." "This a way to kill a wife with kindness," he goes on, "and thus I'll curb her mad and headstrong humour."

He continues his campaign the following day. Hortensio has joined him, having abandoned his pursuit of Bianca, and at breakfast Petruchio urges him to consume the food before Kate can do so. Then comes the episode of the tailor. Kate, we must assume, having been carried off so abruptly, is still in her wedding gown, now somewhat the worse for wear, and Petruchio has generously ordered a new outfit for her in preparation for their return to Padua. But he finds fault with the tailor's efforts, beginning with the cap. And we find that he has embarked on a new strategy. He dismisses the cap as "lewd and filthy," but Kate insists that it is perfectly proper, that "gentlewomen wear such caps as these." He responds now with an openly stern reproof, playing on the word: "When you are gentle, you shall have one too, / And not till then."

This blatant admission of his intent incites a spirited response from Kate, who despite her fatigue shows sparks of her earlier defiance:

> Why, sir, I trust I may have leave to speak,
> And speak I will. I am no child, no babe.

> Your betters have endured me say my mind,
> And if you cannot, best to stop your ears.

Petruchio has no answer to her sudden display of resolve and deflects it by turning promptly to the question of the gown, which he also rejects, abusing the tailor with insults appropriate to his trade— "thou thread, thou thimble." So Kate must return to her father's house in the same dress, now spattered and torn, that she wore on leaving it.

Having humiliated, starved, and exhausted Kate, Petruchio now sets out on the last stage of his campaign to reduce her to obedience. He begins to accuse her openly of continued resistance to his will and holds over her a threat to cancel the return trip to Padua unless she subsides. He does so cleverly by making statements that are obviously contrary to reality and insisting that she agree with him. As they are preparing to leave, he notes that it is seven o'clock, and when she draws his attention to the fact that it is actually "almost two," he flies into a mock rage: "Look what I speak, or do, or think to do, / You are still crossing me." And he insists that if they are to leave, "It shall be what o'clock I say it is."

Kate begins to get the message and plays along. When on the trip Petruchio remarks on "how bright and goodly shines the moon," she indiscreetly observes that it is actually the sun he is looking at, causing him to repeat his complaint, "Evermore crossed and crossed, nothing but crossed" and order that they turn back. She quickly agrees that it is indeed the moon, and when he insists that it is after all the sun, she replies in exasperation, "What you will have it named, even that it is, / And so it shall be so for Katherine." The charade is repeated when they meet an aged man on the road, whom Petruchio insists is a "fair lovely maid." Well into the game now, she agrees, only to be reprimanded for mistaking "a man, old, wrinkled, faded, withered" for a young woman. So she apologizes to the bewildered man for her error: "Pardon, I pray thee, for my mad mistaking." Anything to get back to Padua!

What is going on here? Is Kate truly being "tamed"? At this stage her shrewish behavior is certainly subdued, though not her independent spirit. Her responses to Petruchio's absurdities are prompted more by sufferance than submission. If he says the sun is the moon, so be it; if he says the old man is a blushing maiden, let him have his way. If this is some game, she can play it as well as the next person.

And what of Petruchio? Is he really the abusive master of his household, beating his servants for every slight slip and demanding his wife's obedience to his every whim, however ridiculous? A brief exchange between two of those servants offers some insight:

> *Nath.* Peter, didst ever see the like?
> *Peter.* He kills her in her own humour.

They apparently find his behavior entirely out of character and are aware of the purpose behind it. Petruchio is surely brash, self-assured, and clever, but there is no reason to think him cruel. He carries Kate off against her will and subjects her to privation—always, he insists, in the interest of her well-being—and then he tests her subservience with a series of absurd issues. And it would appear that he is entirely successful in his design.

And what is the evidence of his success? In the streets of Padua he asks her for a kiss, and she replies that it is not proper for them to do so in such public place. He responds with another threat to return to Verona; but he does so here only playfully, and she takes it as an amorous gesture, coyly agreeing to his desire, not in submission but in obviously willing acceptance of it. What has happened since these two "raging fires" first met? Have they in fact consumed "the thing that feeds their fury"? Some interpreters suggest that they fell in love at the moment of their first encounter, attracted to one another by kindred high spirits, and that all the ensuing events are like the courtship of eagles that couple violently in midair. Perhaps. What seems more evident is that Petruchio comes upon a woman who can match his restless energy and independent spirit, and that in time he recognizes the priceless value in her. On Kate's part, she clashes with a man who is willing to take extraordinary pains to capture her affection, a suitor who is equal to her fiery temperament. The two eventually fall in love, seeing in each other the qualities that they value most in themselves; and though their future may not prove tranquil, it will never be dull.

Any doubt of the loving amity between Petruchio and Kate is dispelled by her final speech, in which she scolds the other wives, Hortensio's widow and Bianca, for their sullen disregard of their husband's wishes. How dare they, she asks, disobey "thy lord, thy king, thy governor." "Thy husband is thy lord, thy life, thy keeper," she continues, "thy head, thy sovereign [who] craves no other tribute at thy hands / But love, fair looks, and true obedience." It is unthinkable that they should "seek for rule, supremacy, and sway, / When they are bound to serve, love, and obey." Petruchio is delighted with her declaration: "Why, there's a wench! Come on, and kiss me, Kate."

But can she possibly mean what she says? Generations of directors have struggled with Kate's troublesome speech, wrestling with the contention that earlier developments in the play fail to justify such a dramatic transformation. The best that can be said of it in this regard is that by demeaning Bianca she finally enjoys the "revenge" she had promised earlier. Some directors, perhaps more ideologically inclined, are appalled by her words, shocked that a woman so independent minded could utter such heresy. They solve the dilemma by disassembling the speech, distributing parts of it to other, more chauvinistic members of the cast.

Others contend that she delivers the lines ironically, that is, undercutting her own words with a contemptuous tone of voice. The speech itself gives some substance to this approach, since if one says the same thing over and over it eventually takes on its opposite meaning, as in Mark Antony's repeated characterization of Caesar's assassins as "honorable men." After all, how many times and in how many ways does one have to repeat the claim that the husband is lord and master. Say it often enough and it soon becomes clear that he is anything but. Then too, Kate's assertion of her husband's exalted status is so outlandish that it may be said to discredit itself.

Still other productions stage the scene persuasively as a private joke devised by Petruchio and Kate, now very much in tune with each other, to ridicule the other women's new husbands who are faced with an unanticipated reality of marriage, a wife who is not as compliant as she seemed during courtship. The two principals, it may be said, have already worked their way through the contest of wills that eventually follows the fading of "that first fine careless rapture," and so can anticipate a union untroubled by such marital push and pull. Perhaps. It is a resolution that at least justifies Petruchio's delight in her speech. He is certainly not deaf to irony.

How Shakespeare intended his audience to respond, we'll never know. However we may interpret its controversial outcome, *The Taming of the Shrew* is an engaging comedy. The poet pursues one of his most pervasive themes, the perennially entertaining contention of men and women in their pursuit of love. The quest is never easy, he reminds us, but it is rich in its rewards. Kate is a high-spirited, defiant young woman eventually tamed, but not subdued, by love; and Petruchio is a clever, uninhibited, devil-may-care rascal whose affections are finally captured by a woman who is every bit his equal in fire, wit, and ardor.

# PORTIA

*". . . an unlessoned girl, unschooled, unpractised,*
*Happy in this, she is not yet so old*
*But she may learn."*

WHEN YOUNG BASSANIO wins the hand of Portia in *The Merchant of Venice*, she is overjoyed and addresses him in a speech that has some puzzling lines. It may be troubling to twentieth-century ears to hear her say that she commits herself to him,

> to be directed,
> As from her lord, her governor, her king.
> Myself, and what is mine, to you and yours
> Is now converted.

But such was the custom in Shakespeare's time, when legally the bride's wealth and property came into the possession of the groom.

Especially puzzling, however, is Portia's characterization of herself as "an unlessoned girl, unschooled, unpractised, / Happy in this, she is not yet so old / But she may learn." Of course her declaration can be attributed to maidenly modesty as she faces her future husband with obvious delight, but it appears to contradict everything we have come to know of her thus far in the play or will learn from this point forward. Our first impression of Portia is that she is a confidently poised young woman who greets her many suitors with grace, dignity, and composure. And we are to discover that she is adventurous, resourceful, clever, and commanding; and far from "unlessoned" and "unschooled," she is impressively learned.

Portia is a dutiful daughter. Fathers in those times reserved to themselves the prerogative to choose their daughters' husbands, though the recently deceased father in this case seems to have taken his responsibility in the matter very seriously indeed, by exercising his prerogative from beyond the grave. He has bequeathed all his wealth to his daughter but required that she marry the man who chooses the casket from among three—of gold, silver, and lead— that contains her portrait. It is an old, familiar tale that Shakespeare adopts for his purpose, providing him with an opportunity to depict comic caricatures of pompous princes who scorn the common lead casket. When Bassanio arrives, an obviously more attractive alternative to her former suitors, she releases him to the task with a song in two verses. The first suggestively ends in words all of which rhyme with "lead." The second urges him to disregard "Fancy," that is, the glitter of silver and gold. Bassanio takes the hint, whether consciously or subconsciously, and selects the correct lead casket, the occasion for Portia's curiously self-effacing speech, which though obviously heartfelt in its sentiment, can only be described as disingenuous.

How disingenuous soon becomes apparent. Bassanio receives news that his great friend Antonio has had to default on a loan that the young man received from Shylock on the merchant's credit, and that the Jew now demands the penalty agreed upon if the money is not returned on time, a "pound of [his] fair flesh." Portia, impressed by the close bond between Bassanio and Antonio, generously supplies funds sufficient to repay the loan and releases her betrothed to defend the merchant, though not before the marriage ceremony.

Determined to have a hand in the trial, she adopts the disguise of a learned doctor of laws, Balthazar, and at the duke's invitation assumes control of the court. Portia dominates the scene, first, in famous lines, urging Shylock to be merciful:

> The quality of mercy is not strained,
> It droppeth as the gentle rain from heaven
> Upon the place beneath: it is twice blest,
> It blesseth him that gives, and him that takes.

When the Jew adamantly refuses repayment and demands his "bond," she passes judgment: the law must be observed, and Shylock is awarded his "pound of flesh." Apparently incredulous that he should actually attempt to collect the penalty, she watches quietly as

Antonio takes his leave of Bassanio and Shylock prepares his knife. Not until it is unmistakably obvious that Shylock fully intends to carve on the merchant does she intervene to stop him. She cites other, more obscure Venetian laws that condemn the Jew to death for threatening the life of a citizen.

Having saved Antonio from certain death, Portia now presides over the sentencing of Shylock. The duke remits the death penalty, reducing it to a fine, but insists that half the Jew's wealth be surrendered to Antonio. Turning to the merchant, Portia asks, "What mercy can you render him, Antonio?" In response, he asks that the fine be remitted as well, and that he will keep his half in trust for Shylock's daughter, Jessica, and her Christian husband, Lorenzo, on condition that Shylock bequeath all his wealth to them upon his death. And, further, he requires that the Jew agree to "become a Christian." Portia turns to Shylock now: "Art thou contented Jew? what dost thou say?" He consents, and she orders that the deed be drawn.

Bassanio and Antonio urge Portia/Balthazar to accept payment for her services, but she refuses all monetary reward, asking only for a ring Bassanio wears as a token of their gratitude. The ring is actually one she had given him on their betrothal with the caution that if he should ever "part from, lose, or give [it] away, / Let it presage the ruin of his love." Bassanio is reluctant at first, but at Antonio's urging he finally agrees.

Portia's deception culminates in the comic fifth act of the play, in which she proves to be as impressive in her own right as she was in the guise of a doctor of laws. Once more she dominates the act, as she had the trial scene. First she reveals that she has the ring, then that she received it from Balthazar, and finally that the learned doctor gave it to her as a gift when she shared his bed. Bassanio is struck speechless, but she quickly relieves her husband's bewilderment by revealing that she had indeed masqueraded as Balthazar and it was she who secured the verdict against Shylock. The play ends on a note of reconciliation and the promise of future happiness, as is appropriate for a comedy.

But what does this deception about the ring accomplish, except to supply Shakespeare with a situation rich in comic possibilities?

Portia's actions suggest that she has a purpose somewhat more serious than simply playing a harmless trick on her husband. To return briefly to the trial scene: When it appears that Antonio will indeed be forced to surrender his pound of flesh and inevitably his life, Bassanio embraces his friend, exclaiming passionately:

> Antonio, I am married to a wife
> Which is as dear to me as life itself,
> But life itself, my wife, and all the world
> Are not esteemed with me above thy life.

Portia responds to her husband's declaration in a sardonic aside: "Your wife would give you little thanks for that / If she were here to hear you make the offer." Bassanio's emotional outburst, along with some of his earlier remarks about his friendship with Antonio, alerts her to the close bond between the two men—a bond, she wisely suspects, that could rival her husband's commitment to their marriage. The trickery with the ring is a strongly implied reminder to him that, whatever his past attachments, he owes his affection and his duty in the future to his wife. It is, in brief, a lesson in marital fidelity. Portia never explicitly says as much—she is far too subtle for that—but her intent is unmistakable.

Portia is not, then, an "unschooled" and "unlessoned girl," as she modestly describes herself to Bassanio. She is rather a highly able and sophisticated young woman, who in a display of ingenuity and intelligence saves the life of an innocent man, orchestrates the indictment and merciful sentencing of his vengeful assailant, and "lessons" her husband on his marital obligations. She is probably best described by Shylock's daughter, Jessica:

> It is very meet
> The Lord Bassanio live an upright life
> For having such a blessing in his lady,
> He finds joy of heaven here on earth,
> . . . . . . . . . . for the poor rude world
> Hath not her fellow.

# PROSPERO

*"By my so potent art."*

PROSPERO is many men in one. Those he encounters see him as a
wizard, a harsh master, a father, a god, and finally a human being
like themselves. And some would have it that he is Shakespeare himself. However we may view the figure, *The Tempest* is a magical play,
in both its appeal to audiences and the "so potent art" of Prospero.
Unearthly spirits haunt its air and they appear in many guises, at
times entertaining, at others enticing, and to the wicked menacing.

Prospero's magic powers emanate from books the kindly Gonzalo secured for him when he and his daughter Miranda were exiled
from Milan, cast adrift on "a rotten carcass of a butt [boat]" by his
devious brother Antonio, who deposed him as Duke of Milan. The
knowledge gained from these books is the source of his hold over the
spirits—chief among them Ariel—that inhabit the isolated island
on which he and his daughter are marooned. At times the wizard exercises his powers directly, as when he renders Ferdinand powerless,
summons spirits to perform a masque and calls for "some heavenly
music," and reduces his enemies to a painful paralytic state. More
frequently, however, it is Ariel who does his bidding to perform
marvelous deeds, raising the tempest, rescuing the shipwreck victims, luring them to Prospero's cave with a "sweet air," or terroriz-
ing the Italian lords in the form of a harpy.

This wizard's rule of his small realm is absolute, and he can prove
a harsh master. Ariel fears him. Years before, Prospero had released
him from a tree where he had been imprisoned by "the foul witch
Sycorax" who then died, leaving him there, and ever since the spirit
has served his rescuer, though longing to be free of his servitude.
When Ariel reminds Prospero that he had promised him freedom,

he turns on the spirit savagely, threatening to return him to his forest prison if he doesn't behave. Ariel subsides and remains respectfully obedient.

The master is most fearsome to the subhuman Caliban, the son of Sycorax and the only inhabitant of the island when the two exiles arrived. At first Prospero took pity on the creature, treating him kindly and teaching him language, but when he discovered Caliban threatening to molest Miranda, he reduced the brute to the level of a slave, hauling water and firewood, washing dishes, and cleaning their cave. If Caliban becomes rebellious, Prospero asserts control by inflicting him with "cramps, / Side-stitches that shall pen thy breath up," and pinches "as thick as honeycombs, each pinch more stinging / Than bees had made them." The slave remains defiant, claiming that "this island's mine" and complaining of his servitude, but he is forced to obey since, as he admits, Prospero is more powerful than his "dam's god Setebos."

At the same time this harsh master can be merciful and forgiving. He had been overthrown as Duke of Milan in a conspiracy by the ravenous lords of Italy, his brother Antonio, Alonso, the King of Naples, and his brother Sebastian. Now, with Ariel's aid, he casts a spell that subdues them to paralytic immobility, and he rejoices in his victory: "At this hour / Lies at my mercy all mine enemies." Struck, however, by Ariel's remark that "were I human," he would have pitied them, he relents, reasoning that

> The rarer action is
> In virtue than in vengeance: they being penitent,
> The sole drift of my purpose doth extend
> Not a frown further.

Later, having thwarted a conspiracy to take his life—one concocted by Caliban, the king's drunken butler Stephano, and his jester Trinculo—Prospero pardons them all, demanding only that they "trim" his cave. And in the end he gives Ariel his freedom.

This image of Prospero as a harsh master has been the subject of critical commentary in recent years. Some scholars see him as Shakespeare's condemnation of the slave trade, a growing industry at the time with the opening up of the Americas and Africa to European exploration. Caliban in their view is representative of oppressed races whose labors were being exploited to amass riches for their masters, who are mindless of the suffering they impose, and Prospero to this way of thinking is an example of the oppressors. Shakespeare, in brief, is making a statement about human rights. Well, perhaps.

Such judgments tend to reduce Prospero to a one-dimensional figure when there are in fact many sides to him. He is also, for example, a doting father, anxiously concerned about the welfare of his daughter. When we first see them, he puts his wizard robes aside and attempts to relate to Miranda the story of their lives. Like any parent, he takes pains to inform her of her heritage, and like any child she is less than attentive. Their dialogue takes place within sight of the ship foundering in the tempest Ariel has raised, and her eyes turn to it sympathetically as her father tells his tale. He finds it necessary to recall her notice repeatedly to his account: "Dost thou attend me?" "Thou attend'st not!" "Dost thou hear?" She is drawn to the spectacle of the distressed vessel, which in her innocence she is convinced contains "some noble creature in her," a sentiment that contrasts ironically with her father's description of those "noble creatures" as in reality the villainous lords of Italy who are responsible for their exile.

The father, again, stands careful guard over his child's innocence. When he observes Caliban's prurient interest in her, he restrains the creature with cramps and pinches. Prospero, like any father of Shakespeare's time or our own, is concerned that his daughter engage in a favorable marriage. Ferdinand, the son of King Alonso, survives the tempest, as does the ship in fact, and all aboard her. Prospero brings the two together, and they are immediately smitten with one another, much to the father's delight: "It goes on I see, / As my soul prompts it." "At the first sight / They have changed eyes. Delicate Ariel, / I'll set thee free for this."

He is apprehensive, however, that their sudden attraction may have proven too easy, that in a sense they will not value their love if it comes without trial. He feels that he must provide obstacles to their union, "lest too light winning / Make the prize light." To that end he condemns Ferdinand harshly as a spy and a traitor, to be held captive and punished by assuming Caliban's task, fetching in fire-wood. Miranda is distraught, pleading with her father, "this / Is the third man that e're I saw; the first / That e're I sighed for"; but he is adamant, reproaching her as "an advocate for an imposter." This test of the young man's worthiness in time proves him constant, and Prospero eventually relents, bestowing his blessing on their be-trothal. He displays an almost comic anxiety, however, that their youthful passion might betray them, and he warns Ferdinand sternly that to "break her virgin-knot" before marriage would condemn their union to "barren hate, / Sour-eyed disdain, and discord." Shortly thereafter, observing them perhaps sitting too closely to-gether, he warns him again: "Look thou be true: do not give dal-liance / Too much the rein." To celebrate the occasion, demonstrate his pleasure at their betrothal, and entertain them he has his atten-dant spirits put on a performance of poetry, dance, and song, all in ceremonial praise of marriage.

Shakespeare's Prospero is also in many ways a godlike figure, a deity presiding over all creation, over every level of existence. Ferdi-nand, hearing unearthly music, assumes that it emanates from "some god o'th'island," and so it seems with Prospero. He reigns over creatures of the supernatural world, Ariel and his attendant spirits, and at the next level below over the realm of humankind. Further down the chain stands Caliban, the "monster," as Stephano calls him, a link between mankind and the animal kingdom. And below him lies the natural world, the island itself which, as Gonzalo observes, contains "every thing advantageous to life." Finally comes the inanimate stone, the stuff of Prospero's cave. Every step in the hierarchy of the visible and invisible universe comes under the sway of this powerful deity.

Caliban sees Prospero as a god more potent than his Setebos, one that we find often resembles the Old Testament Yahweh, raging with wrath and vengeance. And like the ancient Israelites, Caliban chaffs under the Almighty's dominion, in his pathetic simplicity turning to false deities, pleading with the drunken butler Stephano to "be my god." If Prospero is a god of justice, however, he is also a god of mercy, forgiving those who conspired against him, as we have seen, and pardoning Caliban for his murderous intent.

This "god o'th'island," then, is omnipotent and merciful. He is also omniscient, possessing knowledge of the past and future. During the masque he stages to celebrate the betrothal of Ferdinand and Miranda, he is suddenly struck with the thought of Caliban's plot on his life, and he abruptly sweeps his spirits away. Noting that Ferdinand is distraught at the precipitant dissolution of the masque, he attempts to calm the young man, and in one of Shakespeare's most memorable poetic passages he prophesies the end of the world:

> Be cheerful, sir.
> Our revels now are ended. These our actors,
> As I foretold you, were all spirits, and
> Are melted into air, into thin air,
> And, like the baseless fabric of this vision,
> The cloud-capped towers, the gorgeous palaces,
> The solemn temples, the great globe itself,
> Yea, all which it inherit, shall dissolve,
> And, like this insubstantial pageant faded,
> Leave not a rack behind: we are such stuff
> As dreams are made on; and our little life
> Is rounded with a sleep.

For all his powers, however, Prospero is but a man, one whose only desire is to return to the familiar world of men. Once the wrongs done him have been justly dealt with and he is restored to his rightful role as Duke of Milan, he wants no more of magical powers, realizing perhaps that they have no place in that world, where they might become an instrument of evil rather than good. He is resolved, therefore, to discard them:

> I'll break my staff,
> Bury it certain fathoms in the earth,
> And deeper than did ever plummet sound,
> I'll drown my book.

And in the end he frees Ariel, with some sadness we may assume, as one who must bid "fare thou well" to a cherished friend.

It is tempting to imagine, as have many, that Prospero's decision to drown his book "deeper than did ever plummet sound" is a reflection of Shakespeare's desire to put aside his pen. *The Tempest* is said to be his last complete play,* and the image of the ancient wizard surrendering his powers and returning to Milan, where "every third thought shall be of the grave," calls to mind the poet leaving the London stage, where he had reigned for twenty years, to seek the comfort of retirement in his native Stratford. The parallels are intriguing. Prospero reviews the many wonders his magic has summoned:

> I have bedimmed
> The noontide sun; called forth the mutinous winds,
> And 'twixt the green sea and the azured vault
> Set roaring war. . . . graves at my command
> Have waked their sleepers, op'd, and let 'em forth
> By my so potent art.

These are, of course, some of the same wonders that Shakespeare has evoked in his plays—Lear beset by the storming elements, for example, and ghostly apparitions in the streets of Rome on the night before the assassination of Caesar. Perhaps, some think, Shakespeare is here looking back on his own "so potent art" once he has chosen to abandon it.

Who is this Prospero, then? Is he the powerful wizard, the harsh master, the omnipotent, omniscient god of wrath and mercy, the anxious father concerned for the welfare of his child, an old man longing for the comfort of his homeland? Or is he Shakespeare himself? He is, of course, no one of these alone, rather all of them in one. In his many guises Prospero plays a variety of roles that evoke the image of a just figure of authority. He protects the innocent, holds evil in check, counsels the young, dispenses even justice, shows mercy to his enemies, pardons those who err out of ignorance, and in the end surrenders his high powers with grace and wisdom.

---

*\*Henry VIII* appears to have come later, but it is generally agreed that some of its scenes are by another hand, possibly John Fletcher.

# RICHARD II

*"Tell thou the lamentable tale of me."*

OUR SENTIMENTS toward Richard II range widely during the course of the play. We respond at one time or another with disgust at his heartless arrogance, dismay at his disabling self-pity, admiration for his eloquence, and finally deep sympathy as he confronts his fate.

Richard is a weak king who rules in the shadow of towering ancestors. A glance at his history will offer insight into his character, for though Shakespeare makes only passing reference to earlier events in the play, they were surely on his mind as he shaped this tragic figure. Richard was the grandson of Edward III, the warrior-king who humiliated the French at Crécy (1346) and Poitiers (1356), and the son of Edward the Black Prince, the king's eldest son, equally famous for his martial prowess. Edward III had seven sons, two of whom have prominent roles in the play—the Dukes of Lancaster and York—and a third who was murdered before the initial scenes—the Duke of Gloucester, or "Woodstock," as he was known.

The Black Prince died a year before his long-lived father, and Richard, as the son of the eldest son, inherited the throne at the age of eleven. During the first years of his reign he ruled under the careful supervision of his powerful uncles, and on coming of age he found that he had to struggle against their influence to establish himself on the throne. To do so, apparently, he was not above treachery. The early scenes of the play include accusations that he was responsible for the death of Woodstock through the agency of his loyal accomplice, Thomas Mowbray, Duke of Norfolk.

We first see Richard in a highly ceremonial role, presiding over the controversy between Mowbray and Henry Bolingbroke, son of the Duke of Lancaster, and it is apparent that he is enjoying his royal eminence. The scenes are filled with medieval pageantry and long speeches by the disputants proclaiming their fervent devotion to their king, which he receives as his just due. Shortly thereafter we see him in private conference with a group of his close supporters— Bushy, Greene, Bagot, and York's son, the Duke of Aumerle—and some of his more unpleasant character traits come to light.

Richard is apparently enjoying his role entirely too well, in the process exhausting the royal treasury in extravagant expenditures on, as he admits, "too great a court / And liberal largess." Confronted with the need to finance an expedition against the Irish, he rents out royal lands and, should revenues by that means prove insufficient, supplies his courtiers with blank charters empowering them to impose taxes at will. Further, he adopts the practice of confiscating the estates of his deceased uncles. Woodstock's widow, the Duchess of Gloucester, laments her return to a castle of "empty lodgings and unfurnished walls, / Unpeopled offices, untrodden stones," and on the death of John of Gaunt, Duke of Lancaster, the king takes possession of all his "plate, coin, revenues, and moveables."

Two other impressions arise from this glimpse of the private Richard. He is callously indifferent to the passing of his uncles. When informed that Gaunt, who is close to death, requests a meeting, he goes with a tasteless jest: "Pray God we may make haste and come too late!" Further, there is an air of decadent eroticism within his close circle of friends at court, an impression heightened by Bolingbroke's later condemnation of Bushy and Greene, whom he accuses of having "made a divorce betwixt his queen and him, / Broke the possession of a royal bed."

Richard at this stage, then, we find to be a profligate king, laying waste the wealth of England in frivolous expenses to adorn his court; he has no reservation about taxing his subjects to support his irresponsible extravagance; and there are implications of erotic involvement with members of his inner circle. Shakespeare leaves us with the unmistakable conviction that such a man is unfit to wear a crown.

This impression is reinforced by how readily he surrenders it, and we may find ourselves dismayed by how docilely he does so. On

the death of Gaunt, Bolingbroke defies the king's decree and returns
from exile, claiming that he comes only to assert his right to the title of Duke of Lancaster. Disgruntled lords join his cause, and soon
he confronts Richard at the head of a substantial army. The king responds to the threat in wide emotional swings, ranging from defiance to despair.

Richard, returning from Ireland, is supported by the loyal
Bishop of Carlisle and York's son, the Duke of Aumerle, and he is
initially confident that he can face down any rebellion simply because he wears the crown:

> Not all the water in the rough rude sea
> Can wash the balm off from an anointed king;
> The breath of worldly men cannot depose
> The deputy elected by the Lord.

But his resolve crumbles as he receives a series of disheartening reports. First he learns that the Welsh army, which he anticipated
would join him upon his arrival, has grown impatient of his tardy
return and disbanded, leaving him with no soldiers at his command. He despairs at the news, advising his few retainers, "All
souls that will be safe, fly from my side, / For time hath set a blot
upon my pride"; but he quickly recovers, "I had forgot myself, am
I not king? / Awake, thou coward Majesty!" His resolve is shallow,
however, for he greets a messenger even before he delivers his report: "Say, is my kingdom lost? Why, 'twas my care, / And what
loss is it to be rid of care?"

The report is discouraging: Bolingbroke has been received joyously throughout the kingdom and has executed Richard's cherished
courtiers, Bushy and Greene. The king is crushed, "of comfort no
man speak. / Let's talk of graves, of worms, and epitaphs," and he
succumbs to despair: "For God's sake let us sit upon the ground /
And tell sad stories of the death of kings." He ends with a plaintive
appeal to his remaining supporters, pleading a common humanity
with them: "I live with bread like you, feel want, / Taste grief, need
friends—subjected thus, / How can you say to me, I am a king?" His
spirits revived by encouragement from Carlisle and Aumerle, he is
once more defiant: "Proud Bolingbroke, I come / To change blows

with thee for our day of doom." But the mood quickly passes when he learns that York is in the company of the enemy: "Discharge my followers; let them hence away, / From Richard's night, to Boling-broke's fair day."

Richard's confrontation with Bolingbroke is marked by these same wide swings between defiance and despair. Bolingbroke sends the sturdy Earl of Northumberland to speak for him—a presump-tuous act in itself, a duke appointing an earl as emissary to a king. Richard is outwardly defiant at first, claiming divine sanction for his royal office:

> Yet know, my master, God omnipotent,
> Is mustering in his clouds on our behalf,
> Armies of pestilence, and they shall strike
> Your children yet unborn, and unbegot,
> That lift your vassal hands against my head,
> And threat the glory of my precious crown.

But to his friends he is despondent: "What must the King do now? Must he submit? / The King shall do it. Must he be deposed? / The King shall be contented." He will exchange all the splendors of the royal court, he says, and his "large kingdom for a little grave, / A lit-tle little grave, an obscure grave." "What says King Bolingbroke," he asks Northumberland, "will his Majesty / Give Richard leave to live till Richard die?" And in the end he surrenders meekly: "What you will have, I'll give, and willing too," since as he says, "do we must what force will have us do."

Shakespeare at times offers cogent commentary on his charac-ters, often in the speeches of ordinary citizens who voice their judg-ment of the great and mighty. Here the most acute evaluation of Richard's downfall is that of a minor figure, the Duke of York's gar-dener. The image of the garden as a microcosm of the world is a commonplace in literature, and Shakespeare employs the convention to characterize the failings of the fallen king. The gardener looks upon his domain as a kingdom and regularly uses the language of politics to define his role in its upkeep. He speaks of relieving "op-pression," serving as an "executioner" in "our commonwealth," and preserving good "government."

Speaking of Richard, he calls it a pity that the king "had not so trimmed and dressed his land / As we this garden." It is good husbandry, he says, to "wound the bark" of trees, lest they become "over-proud in sap and blood"; and had Richard done the same to "great and growing men, / They might have lived to bear, and he to taste / Their fruits of duty." Further, "superfluous branches / We lop away, that bearing boughs may live." It is because of the king's neglect, he concludes, his "waste of idle hours," that he has been "quite thrown down." And so it seems. Richard's preoccupation with the splendors of his court, the outward trappings of the monarchy, and the pleasures of the crown have left him unconcerned with the threat of "great and growing men" until it is too late to "wound" them or "lop away" their power.

But Shakespeare will not allow us an unmixed satisfaction at Richard's downfall, no matter how much we may feel that he richly deserves it. Yes, he has been a profligate monarch who has leeched the wealth of his kingdom for his own gratification, imposed arbitrary taxes on and confiscated the property of his subjects to defray the cost of his lavish court. He has such an exalted vision of his role as a "deputy elected by the Lord" that he feels no concern for the mundane lives of his subjects or the loyalty of his powerful nobles. Subject daily to the flattery of sycophant courtiers, he is so caught up in the ceremonial trappings of the monarchy that he gives little thought to the obligations of the crown.

And yet, despite his arrogance, his decadence, and his haughty self-regard, our response to the figure is a contradictory mixture of frustration and sympathy. We watch in dismay his regression into paralyzing self-pity and his servile submission to Bolingbroke's demands. Is he so weak-willed that he could not do so with more dignity, resisting the "bully Bolingbroke" with more resolve? Has despair drained him of all defiance? But it is precisely his poignant expression of that despair that elicits our pity. We have all known such a time, and here before us is yet another soul who laments a devastating loss in stirring poetry that evokes the memory of all the darker passages of our lives.

Our sentiments at this point in the play are voiced later by the queen when she meets her husband under guard on his way to the

Tower. She asks why he is so passive, why he is not incensed at Bolingbroke's presumption. "The lion dying thrusteth forth his paw," she says, "and wounds the earth, if nothing else, with rage / To be o'erpowered." Why, she asks, does he, "pupil-like, / Take the correction mildly, kiss the rod," and accept his fate with such "base humility"? And we must wonder as well.

Thus we witness Richard's downfall with a mixture of satisfaction at his overthrow, frustration at his servile weakness, and pity for his anguish. And there is more to come. In the scene where Richard finally relinquishes the crown, he shows a flair for the dramatic, and we sit in admiration at his eloquence.* Despair is still the theme of his expression, but it has a defiant edge to it. His enemies expect him to play a docile role in the ceremonial passing of the crown, but Richard takes control of the occasion. He upstages the stoic Bolingbroke and impassive Northumberland, who are reduced to mere props in his performance. Seizing the crown, he thrusts it at Bolingbroke, who, nonplussed at the gesture, grabs hold of it in surprise. The result is a dramatic visual effect: the two kings stand side by side holding the golden prize between them at this climactic moment in the play. Before releasing it, however, Richard declaims on the occasion: The crown is a well and they are two buckets in it, Bolingbroke the one above, "dancing in the air," and he the one below, "unseen, and full of" the water of his tears. Bolingbroke, taken aback by this sudden eloquence, is reduced to one-line rejoiners: "I thought you had been willing to resign." "Are you contented to resign?"

Northumberland then presents Richard with a list of the crimes he is accused of and bids him read it, but he dismisses the document, proclaiming that his only crime has been to assist in "the deposing of a king." He calls for a mirror, and after glancing at his reflected image he dashes it to to the ground, declaring that "A brittle glory shineth in this face; / As brittle as the glory is the face." It is another dramatic display of mixed anguish and obstinance, which he concludes with a scornful request that he have "leave to go" anywhere

---

*This episode, known as the "deposition scene," was omitted from printed editions during the reign of Queen Elizabeth as perhaps too provocative for the aging monarch. Shortly after the ill-starred rebellion of the Earl of Essex, she is said to have remarked, "I am Richard II, know thee not that?"

"so I were from your sights." Bolingbroke directs that he be conveyed to the Tower.

It is while en route to that prison, fatal to more than one English king, that Richard encounters his queen, who asks why, like "the lion dying [who] thrusteth forth his paw," he has not opposed his deposition. But all defiance has drained from him now, leaving only abject resignation: "Think I am dead," he replies, and asks her in future times to "tell the lamentable tale of me," one that he predicts will "send the hearers weeping to their beds."

Shakespeare artfully arouses our sympathy for Richard, in anticipation of his death. When last we see him, he broods over the comparison between his prison cell and the world in a long, moving soliloquy. Hearing music, his thoughts turn to its rhythm, or "time," leading to his melancholy admission that "I wasted time, and now doth time waste me." A loyal groom visits him, expressing regret at his misfortune; and then a keeper enters, dismissing the groom and offering Richard food. He insists that the keeper taste it first, as was customary among monarchs to prevent poisoning, but the man refuses, he says, on orders from the king. At that—finally!—Richard flies into a rage and attacks the keeper, swearing, "The devil take Henry of Lancaster, and thee! / Patience is stale, and I am weary of it!" His outburst is a signal for the entrance of his assassins, who after a brief struggle murder him.

Richard II is a difficult man to like. His arrogant pride, his extravagance, and his callous indifference to his subjects are repelling at first. He is not, to all appearances, tyrannical or cruel; but he has an exaggerated notion of his privilege and importance as "the figure of God's majesty, / His captain, steward, [and] deputy elect," in the words of Carlisle. It is remarkable that Shakespeare is able to arouse our sympathy for such a figure, for while we acknowledge that he is unfit to rule and may well deserve his deposition, at the same time we deplore the self-pity that drains his resolve to resist it. And his death in the end strikes us as a tragic loss.

# RICHARD III

*"I am determined to prove a villain."*

RICHARD, Duke of Gloucester, is not a complex figure. He has a single goal in life, to rule England as Richard the Third, and he sets out to achieve it with unwavering resolve, untroubled by doubts or the pull of conscience. Not for him is the inner turmoil that furrows the brows of Shakespeare's more sympathetic figures, those who ponder the balance of their allegiance to conflicting values—justice and mercy, love and duty, devotion to family welfare and the obligations of public office. He is not moved by vengeance, or jealousy, or love, or honor, or family ties, but by pure, unalloyed ambition, nothing more and nothing less. And as he schemes his way to the crown, dexterously disposing of those who stand in his way, he is vastly entertaining, the villain we love to hate.

We encounter Richard in three of Shakespeare's history plays, *Henry VI, Parts 2* and *3*, and *Richard III*. He is the third son of another Richard, the Duke of York, who raises a rebellion to depose King Henry and mount the throne of England himself. In this so-called War of the Roses, the fifteenth-century civil conflict between the houses of York and Lancaster, the duke is ably supported by his eldest son, Edward, by the next in line, George, and by Richard. York is taken prisoner in battle, however, and is murdered by his Lancaster foes, leaving Edward to inherit his title and his claim to the throne.

Richard is unconditionally committed to his brother's cause and proves to be a formidable and resourceful warrior. Despite the physical deformity that tradition has attributed to him—a hunched back, a stunted leg, and a withered arm—he is fierce in battle and a highly effective leader of men. At one point, when the York forces

suffer a defeat, he rescues Edward from his enemies, and later he returns with his brother to overcome them and secure the crown for
good. Richard, further, is utterly ruthless in pursuit of the York ambitions. He joins others in the slaughter of Henry VI's son, the
Prince of Wales, and later murders the king himself, at the time a
prisoner in the Tower of London.

In a lengthy soliloquy midway through *Henry VI, Part 3*, Richard
reveals his ambition: "I do wish the crown," he reflects, and he will
take any measure to achieve it, performing deeds so dark and devious
that they will "set the murtherous Machiavel to school." In the closing scenes of the play, after killing King Henry, he sets his sights on
the next obstacles in his path to the throne, his elder brother George,
Duke of Clarence—"I'll be thy death"—and Edward's young son and
heir—"I'll blast his harvest." Richard is well aware of the depth of
his iniquity and he makes no apologies for it. He is refreshingly clear-
eyed about his own character: "I that hath neither pity, love, nor fear
. . . am myself alone." He expects no sympathy, and we may be assured that any such sentiment would be wasted on him.

*Richard III* opens with the famous soliloquy beginning "Now is
the winter of our discontent," in which Richard, at the time Duke
of Gloucester, laments that he, who had made his name on the battlefield, must now endure "this weak piping time of peace." "I hate
the idle pleasures of these days," he complains, since he cuts an awk-
ward figure in court, being "deformed, unfinished, sent before my
time / Into this breathing world, scarce half made up." It has been
suggested that Richard's wickedness can be traced to his deformity,
that his mind is as twisted as his body; and it can be argued quite
plausibly that he senses himself an object of ridicule in a court of
handsome lords and ladies and seethes with anger at their scorn,
seeking vengeance for the indignity. Shakespeare, however, is not
concerned with exploring the psychological or social origins of evil.
In a play, a "two hours' traffic of our stage," he is more interested in
dramatizing the consequences of evil, hence for his purposes it simply exists, as it does in figures like *Othello's* Iago, *Cymbeline's* Cloten,
and the malignant Aaron of *Titus Andronicus*. Such characters—and
more could be named—illustrate that evil is abundantly evident in
human action, whether the human be deformed or not.

Indeed, it must be acknowledged that evil is both interesting and entertaining, far more so certainly than good; and it provides a wider scope of effects for the pen of a playwright or novelist. So, says the Bard, let me show you how it works in the case of a wicked man in a wicked world. We may imagine him advising us: "Don't fret, leave your moral indignation in the cloakroom. Just sit back and enjoy this fascinating figure whom I shall fashion for you to watch as he carves his way to the crown."

It is not contradictory, then, or perverse to suggest that Richard is both wicked and entertaining. We do not find that his allusions to his twisted body, in his opening soliloquy or elsewhere, carry a note of bitterness or self-pity. Rather, he speaks of his deformity in an almost lighthearted vein, citing it first in half jest as a justification for his ambition: "Since I cannot prove a lover . . . I am determined to prove a villain." In a later scene he makes use of his withered arm as a pretense for condemning to death a courtier who opposes his intention to assume the throne. His misshapen body is but one weapon in the armory of devices he employs to gain his ends.

A glance at several episodes in the play will illustrate how Richard can be at once malicious and amusing, evil and engaging. His first target, as he tells us, is his brother, George, Duke of Clarence. King Edward is ill, and should he die, George will become the lord protector, exercising the power of the throne during the minority of the eleven-year-old Edward V. So George will have to go. Richard circulates the report of a prophecy that someone whose name begins with "G" will murder the king's heirs (a delightfully ironic calumny, since after all he is the Duke of *G*loucester). Alarmed, Edward orders George imprisoned and put to death, but he later rescinds the sentence. Richard commiserates with his brother, promising sympathetically to plead his case with the king, but he quickly ensures that George is executed before the king's pardon can arrive. His hired assassins perform the deed and, just to be sure, dump his body into a barrel of wine. On Edward's death, then, Richard will become lord protector. So far, so good.

There is then the need to enhance his position by way of an auspicious alliance. In what is perhaps the most outlandish wooing scene in stage history, he persuades young Anne, of the powerful

Warwick family, to marry him, despite the fact that he has murdered her husband, the Lancaster Prince of Wales, and her father-in-law, Henry VI. He encounters her as she accompanies the king's body to burial and is immediately showered with her curses for his role in their deaths. He attempts to turn her anger aside by protesting that he did it all for her:

> Your beauty was the cause of that effect—
> Your beauty that did haunt me in my sleep
> To undertake the death of all the world,
> So I might live one hour in your sweet bosom.

This approach fails to have the desired effect, however, so he resorts to a dramatic gesture. He offers her his sword and bares his breast, bidding her to kill him, insisting again that "'twas thy beauty that provoked me" and "thy heavenly face that set me on." This seems to work; she accepts his ring and agrees to meet him later.

Richard is elated by his success and cruelly scornful of Anne— "Was ever woman in this humour wooed? / Was ever woman in this humour won?"—and he concludes with grim satisfaction, "I'll have her, but I will not keep her long." Here again he makes light of his deformity in expressing his disdain:

> I do mistake my person all this while!
> Upon my life, she finds—although I cannot—
> Myself to be a marv'lous proper man.

I'll have to get a mirror and have another look, he goes on ironically, and employ tailors so as to "study fashions to adorn my body." Indeed they do marry, and in time Anne becomes Queen of England, but Richard quietly disposes of her when she no longer serves his purpose.

In another scene he adopts a pose of amity to all the contentious nobles of the court, and though some of them know him well enough to scorn his performance, he is a pleasure to watch. The court of Edward IV is split into wrangling factions, groups of rather colorless characters who spit hatred at one another—fertile ground, as Richard observes sardonically, for him "to bustle in." The queen's family contends with the royal council for power, and the dying king requires them to enact a ceremony of reconciliation in the hope that he can leave the kingdom at peace. At the king's insistence, these deadly enemies vow eternal love for one another and embrace with stiff reluctance. It's all hypocrisy, of course, a charade of accord that will promptly dissolve on Edward's death, on the whole a distasteful and rather dull scene. We await Richard's entrance impatiently to see how he will enliven this stilted ceremony, how he will outdo them—and he doesn't disappoint. Coming upon them, he protests that "'Tis death to me to be at enmity, / I hate it, and desire all good men's love." And then, with an extravagant flourish:

> I do not know that Englishman alive
> With whom my soul is any jot at odds,
> More than the infant that is born to-night.
> I thank my God for my humility.

We delight in his show, for after all he is simply echoing their false display of amity, and indeed outdoing them at it. Since he is well aware that they consider his pose no more sincere than their own, his extravagant claims are, as much as anything else, a blatant mock of their hypocrisy.

Richard is endlessly inventive. He ruthlessly disposes of those in the court who oppose his coronation, and in another episode spreads rumors that Edward's heirs, and Edward himself, were born illegitimately, hence that none of his line have a just claim to the throne. (Richard here accuses his own mother of adultery. Nothing is sacred!) The charge has the desired effect. Richard and his close ally, the Duke of Buckingham, orchestrate a ludicrous charade in the presence of the mayor and citizens of London. He appears on a balcony above, prayer book in hand and flanked by two bishops, "props of virtue for a Christian prince," as Buckingham calls them. The duke urges him to mount the throne "by right of birth," and he at first refuses, pleading that he prefers a life of prayer and meditation. Pressed to accept, he finally agrees but with a pose of painful reluctance: "Will you enforce me to a world of cares?" "God doth know," he insists, "and you may partly see, / How far I am from the desire of this." His brazen effrontery is a joy to watch.

As much as we enjoy Richard's iniquity, however, we are constantly reminded that we are in the presence of naked evil. The torrent of abuses hurled at him, chiefly by women, will not let us forget just who and what he is. When Anne first encounters him, for example, she exclaims, "Avaunt, thou dreadful minister of hell" and accuses him of respecting "no law of God nor man." Queen Margaret, the widow of Henry VI, whom Richard murdered, is the most virulent, calling him among other things an "elvish-marked, abortive, rooting hog," "a bottled spider," and a "poisonous bunch-backed toad." His own mother, the Duchess of York, regrets that she had not strangled him "in her accursed womb" and predicts, "bloody thou art; bloody will be thy end." Richard deflects these oaths, some with witty retorts, others with easy indifference. They seem never to anger him, even those from his mother, nor do they deter him from his determined intent. They are to him petty annoyances; but they color our response to the figure, suggesting that perhaps we are enjoying him too much.

Once on the throne, his life's goal achieved, Richard's character changes noticeably. Less now the carefree schemer, delighting in his own deviousness, he begins to display a strain of petulance, a tendency to bristle at the slightest sign of disagreement. He mistrusts everyone about him, even his closest allies, notably the Duke of Buckingham, who has been complicit in all his schemes to gain the crown. When Richard proposes that the young princes, Edward V and his brother, be disposed of, the duke does not promptly concur and in the end pays for his hesitation with his head. Meanwhile forces gather to oppose Richard's rule, rallying around the Earl of Richmond, who is a descendant by a circuitous route from the house of Lancaster.

The armies confront one another at Bosworth Field, and on the night before battle we are witness to a scene that shows Richard in a somewhat different light. We have delighted in his jaunty villainy, have watched him cut his way to the throne free of any qualms of conscience as he devises ingenious schemes to eliminate those standing in his way. He has arranged for the death of the princes, an unforgivable act to be sure; but he did so, it seems, without malice toward them.* He thought the deed a practical, necessary measure to

---

*Except perhaps in his encounter with the precocious young Duke of York, who draws attention to his deformity by asking for a ride on his humped back.

remove any rivals to his crown. But our delight in Richard is rapidly draining away—he is considerably less amusing in the closing scenes. The heartless murder of two innocent boys brings stage center a question that has been hovering in the wings for the entire play: Is there no glimmer of conscience in this man, no hint of guilt about the trail of blood he has left behind him on the way to the throne?

On that night before the battle, Richard has a dream in which a procession of his victims' ghosts, all eleven of them, parade before him, each condemning him to "despair and die." Starting awake, he is beset by doubts: "Is there a murderer here? No. Yes, I am!" "I am a villain—yet I lie, I am not!" He sinks for a moment into a swamp of self-pity—"There is no creature loves me, / And if I die, no soul will pity me"—but then quickly recovers—"And wherefore should they, since that I myself / Find in myself no pity to myself?" The fit passes and he is once more all energy and purpose, stalking out into the night to check on the loyalty of his followers, crisply setting his army in battle order as the enemy approaches, and calling for his armor and horse. This has not been an attack of conscience, only a momentary distress at a ghostly visitation, which could unnerve any man. "Conscience," he protests shortly thereafter, "is but a word that cowards use, / Devised at first to keep the strong in awe." Shakespeare wisely does not allow him to wallow in a sty of guilt here at the end. He is as resolute as ever, and anything less would be an offense to our perception of Richard as an essentially evil man, unmoved by any touch of remorse.

Shakespeare takes nothing away from Richard as a warrior in the final scenes. He suffers defeat at Bosworth Field and pays for his crimes with his life, as seems only right, but only because his followers desert him and by chance he loses his horse. His end may be morally satisfying, but we're sorry to see him go. Shakespeare's Richard III, we have found, is bold, witty, resolute, and resourceful. But he is also cruel, treacherous, utterly ruthless, and completely without conscience. We have both deplored and delighted in his iniquity, a measure of Shakespeare's skill in placing before us an irredeemably wicked and endlessly entertaining villain.

# ROMEO AND JULIET

*"O, I am fortune's fool!"*

*"My only love sprung from my only hate."*

IT WOULD BE FRUITLESS, and redundant, to consider these "star-crossed lovers" separately. The chief "character" of the play is the love between them, and they are so alike that theatergoers worldwide imagine them as one and speak of them in a single phrase. They are both young, innocent, impetuous, ardent, consumed by a love mutual in its passion, and subject tragically to the same fate as a result of it. Their youth distinguishes them from other famous couples in Shakespeare's tragedies, those such as Antony and Cleopatra, who are seasoned adults when they meet, both by that time highly experienced in amorous adventures, or Othello and Desdemona, he already "declined / Into the vale of years" and she to all appearances a mature woman. Such figures, further, are significantly dissimilar in background and character, calling for analysis as individuals, while Romeo and Juliet are so alike that they are better considered together.

Romeo's age is unspecified, but when we first meet him he leaves an impression of unripe youth. He is in love; indeed Romeo is in love for the entire play, but in the early scenes not with Juliet. He is in a pitiable state of melancholy, pining away for a young woman, Rosaline, who wants nothing to do with him. Shakespeare depicts him as the traditional chivalric lover, who is rejected by the unattainable object of his desire and suffers from symptoms of the "love-sickness."* The figure is the object of gentle satire in Shakespeare,

*See "Silvius," pp. 278–281.

and we watch with amused compassion as Romeo seeks solitude and wanders inconsolably in the night, afflicted with sighs and groans.

Juliet's age is clearly stated, indeed is the subject of some discussion. When Paris, a thoroughly respectable young man, a "kinsman of the prince," asks permission of her father to seek her hand in marriage, Capulet replies that she is not yet fourteen. Paris reminds him that "Younger than she are happy mothers made," and Capulet reluctantly agrees, stipulating, however, that the decision is entirely up to her. Juliet is a properly respectful and obedient daughter, well aware that, as was the custom of the time, her father has the final word on the choice of her husband. She has been raised in a well-to-do protective household, one in which her "honor," or chastity, has been carefully guarded as an essential prerequisite for an advantageous marriage. We can expect that as a child nurtured by the earthy Nurse, however, she is not unaware of the facts of life, though she has yet to experience the full emotive force of love.

Shakespeare's challenge is to dispel the impression that we are witness to the excesses of a lovesick young man on the rebound and an immature teenager caught up in a romantic fantasy. Their initial attraction may seem to some a flaw in character, a precipitate infatuation of the kind that occasionally inflicts itself on the injudicious young—an impression, fortunately, that is in all likelihood limited only to those in the audience who look upon youth itself as a flaw.

Shakespeare achieves the effect of mature love in two ways. First, he places the encounter in the context of an implacable feud between two families. Romeo and Juliet live not far from one another in the provincial town of Verona. In time and in the normal course of events they may well have met, fallen in love, married, and thereafter experienced the joys and trials of any couple. Indeed, they do meet, fall in love, and marry, but they are denied those normal joys and trials because he is a Montague and she a Capulet, two clans that hate each other. Shakespeare does not explore the origins of their animosity, and we do not ask, aware as we are that such things can happen to one degree or another in any community. He implies only that it has arisen from ancient grievances, long forgotten by both sides, only to be renewed by succeeding generations, fueled by repeated insults, beatings, and murders that call for yet more acts of vengeance. The play opens on a violent confrontation between servants of the two houses, one that spreads quickly to include the principals, until the Prince of Verona steps in to demand an end to these "civil brawls." Any further such incidents, he warns angrily, will be punished by death.

Romeo and Juliet become, then, not two overwrought adolescents but tragic victims of a mindless enmity, and they are raised to the stature of martyrs on the altar of their elders' ancient grudges, an antagonism that stretches back beyond the memory of those who harbor it. As these families hate simply because they hate, these two love simply because they love.

Shakespeare enhances the impression of mature love further by endowing Romeo and Juliet with matchless poetry, conveying a passion and understanding that seem beyond their years. Their lines are familiar to the ears of those who may not otherwise know the play:

> *Rom.* But soft, what light through yonder window breaks?
> It is the east and Juliet is the sun.

> *Jul.*                                 That which we call a rose
> By any other word would smell as sweet.

> *Rom.* He jests at scars that never felt a wound.

> *Jul.* Good night! Good night! Parting is such sweet sorrow,
> That I shall say good night till it be morrow.*

*Romeo and Juliet* is above all else a love story. The youth, joy, and innocence of these two is infectious, engaging our complete sympathy. We witness the evolution of their love from its inception to its consummation to its crisis and finally to its tragic end, and we watch them grow as they meet its challenges.

The two meet when the adventuresome Montague youths, accompanied by their irrepressible friend, Mercutio, dare to crash a masked ball to be held by the Capulets. Romeo is recognized by Juliet's hotheaded cousin Tybalt, who calls for his rapier and has to be restrained from attacking him by the elder Capulet, insisting that violence not mar the occasion. Tybalt is incensed by Romeo's insolent intrusion, however, and vows revenge.

---

*Equally familiar is Mercutio's "A plague o'both your houses!"

The lovers spy one another and are instantly smitten, as are many such couples in Shakespeare, who is not inclined to dwell on the phenomenon, implying simply that such things happen, so let's get on with the play. Under the protective anonymity of their masks, he impulsively asks her for a kiss; she coyly agrees to one, and then to another—and the bond is sealed.* Neither is as yet aware of the other's sudden infatuation, nor for that matter of the other's identity. When Juliet learns that he is a Montague, she is inconsolable, "My only love sprung from my only hate!" and he, on hearing that she is a Capulet, laments that he is now under the sway of an enemy.

With the impetuosity of youth, however, Romeo is determined to have another sight of her, and, mindless of the danger, he climbs the Capulet garden wall and secrets himself in the dark beneath her balcony. Romeo loses himself in thoughts of his devotion, wishing wistfully that she knew of it. This a magic moment in any love's history, when each discovers miraculously that they share the same passion. When she speaks and he hears that she returns his affection, he reveals himself and pours out his ardor:

> With love's light wings did I o'erperch these walls.
> For stony limits cannot hold love out,
> And what love can do, that dares love attempt.

When Juliet first encounters Romeo at the Capulet ball, she is completely unprepared for the flood of emotion he arouses in her. Hers is first love, an exciting and unsettling experience for any young woman, and when she discovers that he is enamored of her as well, the unfamiliar and unexpected sensation overwhelms her. She is not so overcome, however, as to be unaware of her vulnerability:

> O gentle Romeo,
> If thou dost love, pronounce it faithfully.
> If thou thinkst I am too quickly won,

---

*Staging is a challenge here since they fall in love while masked. The problem is variously resolved by inventive directors, who either dispense with the masks altogether or have Romeo raise his at the sight of her. Tybalt recognizes him by his voice.

I'll frown, and be perverse, and say thee nay,
So thou wilt woo; but else, not for the world.

She seems more sensible than he to the abruptness of their mutual attraction—"It is too rash, too unadvised, too sudden"—but she embraces its promise—"This bud of love, by summer's ripening breath, / May prove a beauteous flow'r when next we meet."

Juliet remains sufficiently levelheaded to respond to Romeo's high words and fervent vows by asking when he means to fulfill them, that is, "Where and what time thou wilt perform the rite." He is ecstatic and eagerly prepares to rush off and make arrangements, only to be held back momentarily by her desire to prolong the encounter; and it is only repeated calls from the Nurse that force her to end it.

Romeo engages the aid of a sympathetic priest, Friar Laurence, and they are married, only to be painfully separated after the rites. In an effort to stop a duel between Juliet's quarrelsome cousin Tybalt and his good friend Mercutio, Romeo is inadvertently responsible for the latter's death. Wracked with guilt and anger, and again unmindful of the consequences, he avenges Mercutio's death by killing Tybalt. In this encounter Romeo reveals himself as hotblooded as any of his volatile kin, a youth who has inherited the mandate of his clan that blood must be avenged with blood. As he stands over the body of the dead Capulet, he is suddenly aware of the folly of that tradition and of its consequence for him: "O, I am fortune's fool!" Word of Tybalt's death leaves Juliet equally distraught. Bewildered by the conflicting emotions aroused by the murder of a much-cherished cousin by her beloved, she cries out at the frightening irony of the event, calling Romeo a "beautiful tyrant! fiend angelical!" a "damned saint," and "an honorable villain!"

A compassionate Prince of Verona banishes Romeo for his rash act rather than condemn him to death as he had first threatened, and the lovers respond to the sentence with equal anguish. For those newly in love, any time apart, be it for an hour or a day, is but an empty interval until they can once more join hands and hearts; they simply want to *be* with one another. To Romeo and Juliet, then, his exile seems a kind of dying, and each echoes the other's dismay at the prospect of separation. To Juliet, "'banished' / Is death, mistermed"; and for Romeo, "There is no end, no limit, measure, bound, / In that word's death."

They undergo a change with this turn of events, each displaying new depths of character. Juliet seems at first too young to meet the trials she faces, and they mount. Her father, impatient now, insists that she wed Paris and is enraged at her refusal, and she is confronted with the desperate need to conceal her marriage with a Montague—a Montague moreover who has just slain a Capulet. Shakespeare transforms her earlier spontaneous desire to prolong their first meeting into a strain of steel resolve never to be apart from him. She embraces a scheme proposed by the well-meaning Friar Laurence, who gives her a potion that will reduce her to a deathlike trance for forty-two hours. The Friar predicts that her parents, thinking her dead, will lay her out in the Capulet crypt, from which Romeo can rescue her once she wakens.

She drinks the potion despite her doubts and fears about its effects, but the plan goes array, as Romeo hears only of her death. On receipt of the word, he has no second thoughts, no time of mourning, no regrets—he is beyond sorrow. No longer the melancholy youth we first met mooning over the unresponsive Rosaline, he decides that life is unendurable without his Juliet. He greets the news with profound, unspeakable despair, an almost stoic acceptance that his fate must be sealed with hers, and he returns to Verona determining to live one more moment with her and then take his own life. Romeo arrives at the crypt, kisses the apparently lifeless Juliet, and then kills himself. When she awakens to find his body by her side, she is overcome by a devastating sense of loss and without further thought joins him in death.

Romeo is Shakespeare's consummate portrait of a young man in love. He is a thoroughly appealing youth, engagingly pathetic in the early scenes for his unrequited passion, and good-natured when subjected to the playful derision of his friends, who taunt him about his obsession for Rosaline (they are unaware until the end that he has shifted his affections). He is impulsive, audacious, and resolute in his pursuit of a match with Juliet, one which he dooms because of intemperate anger and grief over Mercutio's death. In a word, he is young, but rather than fault him for his youthful indiscretion, we fondly indulge his excesses as we would anyone of his years who is moved by such a familiar passion, a man exalted by love and then shattered to have it snatched from him as a result of his own rashness. His decision to seek a common grave with Juliet, once he has learned of her supposed death, elevates him to a new level in our sympathies; he is determined to die rather than live without her.

Juliet is young as well, and equally appealing in her innocence and her ardor, and she matures rapidly in the face of adversity. Her death is not the consequence of an adolescent infatuation but the tragic end of a young woman who, once deprived of her love, is resolved that life is not to be endured without him. And the couple die not because of romantic impetuosity or immaturity but because two families are locked in a feud over ancient grudges in a society, as the Chorus tells us at the outset, "where civil blood makes civil hands unclean." It is this senseless hatred that is responsible in the end for the deaths of "Juliet and her Romeo."

# ROSALIND

*"Love is merely a madness."*

*As You Like It*, like so many of Shakespeare's comedies, is a play about love, but it explores the subject with a wit and scope unequaled in his other works. The four couples that populate the play—Orlando-Rosalind, Touchstone-Audrey, Silvius-Phebe, and Oliver-Celia—offer a dizzying array of love's dimensions—its joy, its despair, its disillusion, its aftermath, and its underside.

But our subject here is Rosalind, and she presents complexities enough to dazzle an audience with the various roles she plays. First, she is a young woman in love. Next, she appears in disguise as Ganymede, a worldly-wise young man who ridicules romantic notions. And finally, she takes on the role of a capricious woman who scolds her lover sharply and shows every indication of becoming an inconstant, perverse, and quarrelsome wife. The fact that in Shakespeare's time female roles were played by prepubescent boys makes these multiple impersonations even more complicated—a male plays a female who disguises herself as a male who in turn adopts the role of a female.

When we first see Rosalind, she is a young woman in trying circumstances. Her father, Duke Senior, has been deposed by his brother, Duke Frederick, and has taken refuge in the nearby Forest of Arden.* Rosalind is allowed to remain in court only because of her close friendship with the duke's daughter, Celia. But Frederick decides to banish her as well, despite her spirited defense and Celia's

---

*Shakespeare leaves the location of the court undefined. The Forest of Arden is in England, of course, close to Stratford, but the names of some of the minor characters—Le Beau, Amiens, Jaques—suggest France.

appeal, because, as he says curtly, "I trust thee not." Rosalind assumes the disguise of a young man Ganymede, and joined by Celia as the maiden Aliena, leaves to join her father in the forest.

Our first impression of Rosalind, then, is that she is a proper young woman of her time, respectful and obedient, but able to hold her own in the face of the duke's displeasure and undaunted by his edict. She is typical of Shakespeare's comic heroines in that she has fallen in love, in this instance with Orlando, as he has with her. But Orlando has troubles of his own. His elder brother Oliver hates him and plots against his life, so he is forced to flee, as it happens, to the Forest of Arden. As a consequence of the various animosities at court, therefore, by the middle of the second act all the principal characters of the play have been transported to the forest, where as so often proves the case in Shakespeare, good things happen.

Rosalind's disguise as Ganymede calls for her to adopt more intricate degrees of deception once she discovers that Orlando is in the forest and is inanely tacking amorous poems to her on the trees. She decides to approach him, not as herself, but as Ganymede, posing as a worldly young man experienced in the ways of lovers and cynical of all those so afflicted. She attracts his attention with a witty discourse on time and then indirectly brings up the subject of love.

At this point in the play a theatergoer may reasonably wonder why she doesn't just reveal herself to him. Aside from the practical matter that if she did there would be no play, her continued impersonation of Ganymede has precedent in other works of Shakespeare, though his heroines elsewhere seem to have better reason for concealing their identity. In *Twelfth Night*, for example, were Viola to abandon her disguise as Cesario she would be dismissed from the court of Duke Orsino, with whom she has fallen in love. Again, in *Cymbeline*, Imogene persists in her identity as Fidele because her jealous husband Posthumus seeks her death, and she is determined to prove her fidelity to him, as her adopted name implies.

Rosalind's retention of her disguise is of a different order, however. She uses it, as do still other heroines in Shakespeare, to test Orlando's devotion. It is device akin to Portia's impersonation of the doctor of laws, Balthazar, in *The Merchant of Venice*, which she retains after Shylock's trial so to impress her husband Bassanio with his marital obligations. Shakespeare's heroes are frequently put to one test or another to confirm their constancy. In a more broadly comic vein, the ladies in *Love's Labour's Lost* propose onerous tasks for their suitors to prove themselves worthy.

Orlando confesses that he is indeed hopelessly in love, and Rosalind, as Ganymede posing as an expert in such matters, scoffs at the notion, declaring that he has none of the customary marks of a lover:

> A lean cheek, which you have not; a blue eye and sunken, which you have not; an unquestionable [irritable] spirit, which you have not; a beard neglected, which you have not. . . . Then your hose should be ungartered, your bonnet unbanded, your sleeve unbuttoned, your shoe untied, and everything about you demonstrating a careless desolation. But you are no such man.

Rosalind alludes to the tradition of the courtly or chivalric lover, a figure that Shakespeare gently satirizes here and with such frequency elsewhere in his plays.* The courtly lover in some instances was said to worship his lady from afar, content simply to serve her, at times in menial tasks, at others as a valiant knight who to prove his devotion ventures forth to slay dragons and subdue Turks. In other accounts he is despondent that she rejects or takes no notice of him despite his exploits. He is reduced to a state of abject melancholy at her indifference and neglects himself, exhibiting symptoms of the "love sickness" that Rosalind finds lacking in Orlando. This condition, if left unrelieved, it was said, could result in dementia or death.

Rosalind, still as Ganymede, is finally convinced of Orlando's love, and she proposes to cure him of it! She has some experience in the remedy, she says, having once treated a man by posing as his beloved and setting him the task of wooing her:

> At which time would I, being but a moonish youth, grieve, be effeminate, changeable, longing and liking, proud, fantastical, apish,

---

*As in *The Two Noble Kinsmen*, Romeo's laments in Act One of the play, and Hamlet's distress as interpreted by Polonius: "This is the very ecstasy of love." See "Silvius," pp. 278–281.

shallow, inconstant, full of tears, full of smiles; . . . would now like him, now loathe him; then entertain him, then forswear him; now weep for him, then spit at him.

In this way, she claims, she was able to persuade him "to forswear the full stream of the world and live in a nook merely monastic." Ganymede proposes to "cure" Orlando of his affliction if he will woo him as if he were his Rosalind; and, intrigued by the "pretty youth," he agrees. With this device Shakespeare creates a situation packed with comic possibilities. Rosalind is at times herself, at others the skeptical Ganymede, and at still others the peevish, sharp-tongued woman whom, to avoid confusion, we shall call "Ganymede's Rosalind."

At times, however, it is uncertain which Rosalind is speaking. There is no ambiguity when she unburdens herself to Celia as the appealingly vulnerable young woman who is very much in love with Orlando. When he is late for his appointment to be "cured," she is anxiously impatient, questioning, "why did he swear he would come this morning and comes not?" And when he leaves, she is desolate: "I tell thee Aliena, I cannot be out of the sight of Orlando. I'll go find a shadow and sigh till he come." And there is no question that it is the cynical, worldly Ganymede who scoffs at the notion: "Love is merely a madness, and I tell you, deserves as well a dark house and a whip as madmen do."

But she seems to slip in and out of her several roles, particularly that of the waspish Ganymede's Rosalind. She greets Orlando, who as mentioned is late for his appointment, with a curt dismissal: "Why how now Orlando, where have you been all this while? You a lover! And you serve me such another trick, never come in my sight more." But shortly thereafter she exclaims, "Come, woo me, woo me; for now I am in a holiday humour and like enough to consent." Ganymede's Rosalind is playing the part, but Rosalind means it! She asks him what he would do if she should reject him, and, accepting his role in the charade, he answers with the traditional, "Then in mine own person, I die." She responds by citing well-known figures from classic literature, Troilus and Leander, who are said to have died for love, and, sounding more like Ganymede, she scoffs at the whole idea: "But these are all lies: men have died from time to time and worms have eaten them, but not for love."

It is clearly Ganymede's Rosalind who arranges for a mock wedding with Celia acting as the priest. The ceremony over, she predicts what Orlando will have to contend with in the marriage:

> I will be more jealous of thee than a Barbary cock-pigeon over his hen, more clamorous than a parrot against rain, more new-fangled than an ape, more giddy in my desires than a monkey. I will weep for nothing, like Diana in the fountain, and I will do that when you are disposed to be merry. I will laugh like a hyena, and that when thou art inclined to sleep.

This last calls to mind Cleopatra's strategy to retain her hold over Antony: "If you find him sad, / Say I am dancing; if in mirth, report / That I am sudden sick."

On several occasions the mask seems to slip, and the real Rosalind reveals herself. One is the aforementioned time when Orlando is late and she is genuinely upset. Another occurs when he announces that he must leave for two hours to "attend the Duke at dinner." Her immediate response seems to be sincere distress: "Alas, dear love, I cannot lack thee two hours." But she quickly recovers and reassumes her role as Ganymede's Rosalind: "Ay, go your ways, go your ways. I knew what you would prove. My friends told me as much, and I thought no less. That flattering tongue of yours won me."

Occasions are bound to arise during courtship when the man seems to show evidence of inconstancy or a lack of consideration. At such times the woman may have to wait with growing impatience for her tardy lover, or she finds that he cuts a meeting short because of another appointment, answering the call of concerns outside their loving relationship to engage in business, family affairs, "a night with the boys," or dinner with the duke. What young woman would not entertain doubts about her lover on such occasions? Whatever she may think, however, prudence resigns her to holding her tongue, at least in the early stages of their courtship. But Ganymede's Rosalind need have no such inhibitions; she is free to speak her mind and does so with stinging sarcasm, questioning Orlando's devotion. In how much of what she says, we may ask, is she playing the part

of Ganymede's Rosalind, and how much of it reflects Rosalind's true
sentiments toward him?

The two Rosalinds seem to share a common concern on another
occasion when she receives the news that Orlando has saved the life
of his brother Oliver by protecting him from the attack of a lion—
the Forest of Arden is not entirely benign. Orlando is slightly
wounded in the encounter and sends Oliver to make amends for
what promises to be yet another tardy arrival. Oliver bears a bloody
"napkin" that bound his brother's wound as evidence of his unanticipated delay—and Rosalind faints at the sight of it! Recovering
quickly, however, she attempts to pass off the lapse as part of her act:
"Ah, sirrah, a body would think this was well counterfeited. I pray
you tell your brother how well I counterfeited. Heigh-ho!" Oliver is
not so sure, however; indeed he addresses Ganymede ambiguously
as "Rosalind."

Thus in *As You Like It* we have three Rosalinds. Which is the
real one—the properly modest young woman, the clever, cynical
Ganymede, or the peevish lover who utters disturbing truths without restraint and predicts an uneasy future for her husband? This fascinating figure, of course, is something of each, a composite, one
might say, of them all. She is a warm, engaging young woman who
readily attracts friends and admirers; she is witty, imaginative, and
incisively aware of human nature; and she is high-spirited, able to
stand on her own and speak her mind.

The chief concern of these pages is the character of Rosalind, a
focus that does not allow for a full appreciation of Shakespeare's
richly varied exploration of love in *As You Like It*. The cast includes
three other couples who, with Orlando and Rosalind, define different dimensions of the subject. The pitiable shepherd Silvius is enamored of the shepherdess Phebe, who wants nothing to do with
him. In his pathetic pleading he mimics the symptoms of the love
sickness, imploring her to "pity" him and begging for a "scattered
smile" from her every now and then. The relationship becomes even
more strained when Phebe falls in love with Ganymede, providing
occasion for more of Rosalind's straight talk on the subject. The redemptive power of love is portrayed in the conversion of Orlando's
brother Oliver, who sees the error of his ways when he falls in love

with Celia. And the court jester Touchstone is an example of the underside of these romances. In his attempt to seduce the simple but virtuous goatherd Audrey, he reminds us that beneath all the elaborate protocol of courtship and fervent vows of constancy and devotion lies the stark reality of the matter, the primal prurient urge— in a word, lust.

The figure of Rosalind dominates the play, however, and in her various roles she gives voice to the joys, the anxieties, and the trials of those in love. In the end she orchestrates the revelation of her identity so that the play concludes with a stately wedding ceremony in which all four couples are happily joined. One may wonder, as does the melancholy Jaques, just how lasting and happy one or two of these marriages will prove, but such thoughts are not allowed to cast a shadow over the bright promise of the closing festive scene— not in a comedy, at any rate. In Duke Senior's final words, the unions will all end "in true delights."

# SHYLOCK

*"Hath not a Jew eyes?"*

SHAKESPEARE never leaves us entirely comfortable with a character, never able unconditionally to reject his villains or embrace his heroes. His figures have familiar human flaws that often impel them to tragically destructive acts, but at the same time they appeal to our sympathy precisely because those flaws are so very human and familiar. Coriolanus is insufferably arrogant, but he is a valiant warrior devoted to his country. Othello is a vengeful murderer eaten with jealously, but he never entirely loses the aura of "the noble Moor." Hamlet is distressingly indecisive, but he is reasonable and thoughtful when confronted with the task of killing his stepfather. Romeo is impulsive and hotheaded, but he is young and we forgive him his youthful excesses.

In this regard Shylock presented the ultimate challenge to Shakespeare. Can he arouse sympathy for a man who is determined to carve the flesh of another? Almost universally reviled in the poet's time, the Jews were either isolated in guarded quarters of a city or banished entirely from a kingdom, as they were from England in the thirteenth century by Edward I. Cosmopolitan Venice was more tolerant than most, but Jews were still confined to the "ghetto" district of the city and subjected to such indignities as the requirement to wear distinctly colored hats when they ventured into the streets. They were traditionally banned from ownership of property and in consequence gravitated toward professions such as banking, the jewelry trade, and medicine. An industrious and resilient people, many acquired great wealth, often lending large sums to kings, who when their debts mounted found it convenient from time to time to balance their books by banishing their creditors.

Shakespeare, in keeping with the common sentiment of his time, occasionally employs the word Jew as an insult, indicating miserly, sharp-dealing, or outright dishonest behavior. Falstaff insists he is truthful in his account of the robbery in *Henry IV, Part 1*, "or I am a Jew else, an Ebrew Jew." In *The Two Gentlemen of Verona*, Launce declares that if his fellow servant Speed fails to accompany him to the alehouse, he is "an Hebrew, a Jew, not worth the name Christian."* But in *The Merchant of Venice*, Shakespeare labors to depict Shylock as a believable human being rather than the caricature of a Jew or an outright villain, one who while he may be distasteful to the audience is yet able to arouse their sympathy.

We gain insight into the complexity of Shylock at his first entrance in the scene where young Bassanio and his friend Antonio, the "Merchant" of the title, apply to him for a loan. Bassanio, a likeable but profligate man-about-town, is deeply in debt and hopes to mend his fortunes by paying court to the wealthy Portia. He needs funds to equip himself properly, however, and asks Antonio for his help. The merchant is eager to assist his young friend, of whom he is especially fond, but as it happens all his wealth is committed to cargoes at sea. He suggests instead that Bassanio borrow the money elsewhere and he will stand surety for the loan.

The negotiations for the loan deserve close attention, as the scene establishes the tone of animosity between Christian and Jew that pervades the play. Bassanio approaches Shylock, who in this first encounter seems as intolerant as the Christians. When Bassanio invites him to dine with them, he rises indignantly: "I will buy with you, sell with you, talk with you . . . but I will not eat with you, drink with you, nor pray with you."† As Antonio enters, Shylock, in an aside, reveals his hatred of the merchant "for he is a Christian," one moreover who "lends out money gratis," keeping interest rates low. Behind this complaint was a doctrine of the church at the time that lending money at interest was sinful—Dante's Hell has a sepa-

---

*See also *Much Ado About Nothing*, where Benedick says of Beatrice, "if I do not love her, I am a Jew." And in *Macbeth* one of the ingredients of the witches' cauldron is "liver of blaspheming Jew."

†Later, apparently softening in his attitude, he accepts an invitation to dine with them.

rate circle for "usurers"—but Jews were exempt from such laws and many acquired wealth by doing so. "If I can catch him once upon the hip [at a disadvantage]," Shylock vows, "I will feed fat the ancient grudge I bear him."

It would appear that Shylock has good reason for his hatred. Turning heatedly on Antonio, he complains that the merchant unjustly reviles him "about my moneys and usuances," and, he goes on, "You call me misbeliever, cut-throat dog, / And spet upon my Jewish gaberdine." Should I lend money, he asks, to one "that did void his rheum upon my beard, / And foot me as you spurn a stranger cur?" The virtuous Christian Antonio apparently sees nothing improper about such behavior. Should Shylock agree to the loan, he answers evenly, "I am as like to call thee so again, / To spet on thee again, to spurn thee too."

Shylock abruptly changes his tone, protesting, "I would be friends with you, and have your love, / Forget the shames you have stained me with"; and he agrees to the loan, offering generously to charge no interest. In an apparent further gesture of amity, he proposes "in a merry sport," as he calls it, to accept as security for the money "an equal pound / Of your fair flesh." There is no reason to believe that Shylock intends harm to Antonio at this stage. There is nothing to be gained, as he says, "estimable, nor profitable" in "a pound of man's flesh." The offer is only "a merry bond," he insists, a gesture of friendship "to buy his favour."

Our response to Shylock at this point can only be described as mixed. He has admitted to a hatred of Antonio "for he is a Christian," and we cannot help but feel apprehensive that his "merry bond" is a subtle device to "catch him on the hip," however improbable it seems that he would ever collect should the merchant default on the loan. On the other hand, his overtures of friendship appear to be genuine, an effort to breach the centuries-long barrier of animosity that has separated Christian and Jew. He has had a rare opportunity to unburden himself of the resentment he feels at Antonio's degrading treatment and may indeed have purged his hatred, despite the merchant's uncompromising reply. It is safe to say that our sympathies lie more with the Jew, who despite his silent desire for revenge seems to sincerely desire friendship, rather than with the

Christians who are obdurate in their prejudice, consulting Shylock only because they have need of him at the moment. Antonio accepts him as sincere at any rate: "The Hebrew turns Christian, he grows kind." But Bassanio is not so sure: "I like not fair terms, and a villain's mind." Nor are we.

Whatever Shylock's purpose at the time, two developments shape his later decision, and Shakespeare is ambiguous as to whether they change his intent or merely confirm it. The first is the betrayal of his daughter Jessica, who elopes with the Christian Lorenzo, taking with her a quantity of his money and jewels. The Christians, again, see nothing wrong about stealing from her father, it being altogether proper in their minds to pilfer the ill-gotten gains of an acquisitive Jew. The second is the reported shipwrecks of Antonio's cargoes, leaving him unable to repay the debt. Jessica's betrayal, of course, has nothing to do with Antonio, but Shylock hears of the merchant's misfortune at the same time he is informed that his daughter is squandering his wealth in Genoa. The two developments come together in his mind, causing him to see his personal plight in the larger context of his people's suffering at the hands of intolerant Christians: "The curse never fell upon our nation till now. I never felt it till now." He determines to seek vengeance for this long history of oppression by pursuing a vendetta against one of the offending Christians, the merchant Antonio, who is now in his power. He will, he says, collect his "bond."

Shylock is confronted by two of Antonio's more virulent anti-Semitic young friends, and the Jew utters Shakespeare's most eloquent plea for tolerance, one that can only be fully appreciated if heard in its entirety:

> Hath not a Jew eyes? hath not a Jew hands, organs, dimensions, senses, affections, passions? fed with the same food, hurt with the same weapons, subject to the same diseases, healed by the same means, warmed and cooled by the same winter and summer as a Christian is? If you prick us do we not bleed? If you tickle us do we not laugh? If you poison us do we not die?

But Shylock compromises his plea by beginning and ending it with bitter words. When asked initially what benefit he will gain by collecting his bond, he replies sharply, "To bait fish withal,—if it will feed nothing else, it will feed my revenge." And he concludes his impassioned appeal for the equality of all mankind with yet one more trait that Christians and Jews have in common: "And if you wrong us shall we not revenge?"

The case is brought before the court of the duke, who solemnly counsels Shylock to be merciful; but he is adamant, arguing that the Venetian concern for material gain, the very vice they condemn him for, requires that they rule in his favor. If they deny his bond, he claims, "fie upon your law! / There is no force in the decrees of Venice"—or in other words, if they fail to enforce commercial contracts, their credit rating will suffer. Moreover he attacks the morality of their position, claiming that the bond is his property, no less so than their slaves are theirs, "because you have bought them." These are telling arguments, of course, but it cannot be forgotten that he marshals them to support his right to a pound of a man's flesh.

The sympathy of the Venetians is with Antonio, as is ours; but they impair their cause, at least in modern eyes, when they voice racial epithets in his defense. The duke counsels Antonio, characterizing Shylock as "a stony adversary, an inhuman wretch, / Uncapable of pity, void, and empty / From any dram of mercy," and the merchant despairs of trying "to soften that—than which is harder?— / His Jewish heart." Bassanio's friend Gratiano is most explicit: "O thou damned, inexorable dog! . . . thy desires are wolfish, bloody, starved, and ravenous." In the face of such invective, Shylock stands in contemptuous defiance.

Portia enters, disguised as the doctor of laws Balthazar; and empowered to adjudicate the case, she first advises Shylock to relent, pleading with him in famous lines to show mercy "that droppeth as the gentle rain from heaven / Upon the place beneath." He remains adamant, however, and Venetian law compels her to rule in his favor: "The court awards it, and the law doth give it."

There can be little doubt that Shylock fully intends to carve on Antonio's breast. During the course of the deliberations he has been sharpening his knife provocatively, and he approaches the task with malicious satisfaction. He is deterred only by Portia's sudden intrusion. She cites a somewhat more obscure law of Venice, which condemns to death an "alien" who seeks "the life of any citizen," and apportions half his wealth to his intended victim with the other half going to the state. Shylock, deemed an "alien" though he may have spent his entire life in Venice, must pay the penalty; but the duke is lenient, reducing the death sentence to a fine if he shows "humbleness." Antonio, offering the mercy to Shylock that the Jew denied him, asks the court "to acquit the fine" so long as he agrees to bequeath "of all he dies possessed / Unto his son Lorenzo and his daughter." His final condition is that Shylock "presently become a Christian." The Jew is forced to consent and leaves the court a broken man, stripped now of his dignity, his daughter, his wealth, and perhaps most painfully, his faith.

Does Shylock deserve his fate? Well, yes; he seeks the life of an innocent man, at fault only in that he demeans the Jew in public, which though reprehensible was by no means a crime in Renaissance Venice. On the other hand, in his attack on Antonio he strikes back at a culture that has oppressed and exploited his people for hundreds of years; and while we may not condone his actions, we can appreciate his anger. Shakespeare dared to portray a Jew as a complex human being torn by conflicting emotions, brought low in the end by a passion for revenge. This is no way, we must conclude, to seek redress of grievances, no matter how just or heartfelt they may be.

Shylock has been portrayed on the stage in various guises. For the first century and a half following his first appearance, we are told, he was enacted as a comic villain, the stereotypical miserly Jew, ridiculously avaricious. He was staged also in those early years as an abject villain, thirsting for Christian blood, devoid of any redeeming features. At the beginning of the nineteenth century the great English actor Edmund Kean offered a new Shylock, the "noble Jew" resolutely confronting his Christian oppressors, striking back at their hypocritical intolerance. And he has been so portrayed for the large part ever since, a sympathetic figure despite his malicious designs on the merchant Antonio.

It is tempting to speculate on, but of course impossible to say, which of these various Shylocks Shakespeare intended. The context of the play itself is suggestive, however, for it is crowded with racial and national stereotypes. Portia lists her tiresome suitors, dismissing each with what might be called today "ethnic slurs": the Neopolitan prince "doth nothing but talk of his horse," the German is always drunk, the Englishman is a "dumb-show," and the Count Palatine "doth nothing but frown." The princes of Aragon and Morocco are caricatures of their arrogant national types, and the two minor figures, Salerio and Solanio, are objectionable run-of-the-mill Jew-baiters, who in some productions physically abuse Shylock. It seems unlikely, then, that the Jew would be entirely exempt from this pattern of ethnic ridicule. Most probably Shakespeare would have endowed him with some of the characteristics that his audiences had come to expect of a Jewish figure. *The Merchant of Venice* is a comedy, and the poet was not above "playing to the pit," catering to the tastes of ordinary London citizens, the "groundlings" who paid their penny to stand and watch a performance. But Shakespeare gave them reason to reconsider their concept of the Jew, offering a Shylock who has been profoundly wronged and rebels against his oppressors in the only way open to him, turning their own laws against them. There is indeed a nobility in the figure, and there can be no moral satisfaction in his defeat.

# SILVIUS

*"Sweet Phebe pity me."*

SHAKESPEARE'S frequent portrayal of a young man in love draws much of it charm, and its humor, from the medieval tradition of the chivalric or courtly lover. The figure is largely a literary invention, spread by the songs of medieval troubadours who \entertained the high-born nobility in their castles on long winter evenings. As further entertainment the assembled lords and ladies engaged in lively debate about a knight's proper behavior toward the lady of his affections and her acceptable response to his attention. In time their discussions produced an elaborate code of love governing the courtesies and ceremonies appropriate to courtship.

Shakespeare gently satirizes this tradition, particularly those elements known as the "love-sickness," an affliction brought about by the suffering of a young man who is denied the favor of his lady as a result of separation or rejection. So deprived, it was said, he would sink into melancholy, seek isolation, weep at the sound of music, neglect his appearance, and in extreme cases wither away and die. To save him, it was further said, she need only show "pity" or "mercy" to relieve his pain and acknowledge his devotion, a delicate euphemism for satisfying his tortured desire for her. Of course, a young man in love is always a figure of fun to his unafflicted friends, and Shakespeare explores all the comic possibilities of those in that distracted state. Many of Shakespeare's figures exhibit symptoms of the "love-sickness" to one degree or another in a display of either antic behavior or ludicrous despondency, among them Romeo in his early infatuation for Rosaline, Orlando for Rosalind in *As You Like It*,

Orsino for Olivia in *Twelfth Night*, and the passion of Palamon and Arcite for Emilia in *The Two Noble Kinsmen*.*

Another such figure is the shepherd Silvius in *As You Like It*, who is pathetically in love with the shepherdess Phebe, who shuns his attentions. They appear but briefly in the play, but his pleas echo those of the chivalric lover distressed at his lady's indifference or outright rejection. When we first meet them, he has apparently just professed that she has "wounded" him. One of the elements of the tradition is that the man is transfixed by his first sight of his lady, whose single glance is sufficient to inflict a psychic wound, one which again might prove fatal to him if not attended to with a medicinal dosage of "pity." Phebe responds at length to the accusation, which she takes quite literally. "Thou tell'st me there is murder in mine eye," she says indignantly, and demands "now show the wound mine eyes hath made in thee." She is quite defensive about the notion: "I am sure, there is no force in eyes / That can do hurt." Silvius attempts to explain that he alludes to "the wounds invisible / That love's keen arrows make," but she remains unimpressed.

Another provision of the love code is that the lady is an object of silent adoration and desire, unattainable, worshipped from afar, as again is Emilia when Palamon and Arcite spy her from their prison window. Her inaccessibility does not discourage the young men's devotion, however, nor does Phebe's dismissal deter Silvius from pressing his suit. She is more accessible certainly, but no less unattainable, a harsh mistress who charges him, "Come thou not near me."

Rosalind comes upon them in the guise of the youth Ganymede and proceeds to scold Phebe for her aloofness, concluding with what is one of the most potent put-downs in literature:

> But mistress, know yourself. Down on your knees
> And thank heaven, fasting, for a good man's love;

---

*There is some question about how much of *The Two Noble Kinsmen* is Shakespeare's. It is generally thought to be the product of a collaboration between the poet and John Fletcher, and some editions of the complete works—David Bevington's, for example—omit it. I cite it here as yet another contemporary comic satire on the courtly love convention, one that Shakespeare certainly left his mark on.

> For I must tell you friendly in your ear,
> Sell when you can, you are not for all markets.

Rosalind's rebuke has an unexpected result: Phebe falls in love with Ganymede! Silvius detects her sudden affection and utters the plaintive plea of the chivalric lover: "Sweet Phebe pity me." Surprisingly, she seems to relent: "I will endure; and I'll employ thee too."

Thus enters another element of the tradition, the lover's desire to serve his lady. He strives, it is said, to prove his devotion by acts of valor, slaying Turks or rescuing distressed damsels. On other occasions he is content simply to enter her service, as Arcite does Emilia's in *The Two Noble Kinsmen*, though she has no idea who he is and is unaware of his devotion to her. Silvius is ecstatic when Phebe asks him to deliver a letter to Ganymede; he will serve her even though it is apparent that her affection has been captured by another:

> So holy and perfect is my love,
> And I in such a poverty of grace,
> That I shall think it a most plenteous crop
> To glean the broken ears after the man
> That the main harvest reaps. Loose now and then
> A scattered smile, and that I'll live upon.

He is far gone.

On receipt of the letter Rosalind, as Ganymede, puts Silvius to the severest test of a lover's service to his lady. Inform Phebe, she says, that "I will never have her, unless thou entreat for her." And the pitiful man, after a fashion, does just that when Phebe directs him to tell Ganymede "what 'tis to love." Speaking for himself as well as for her, he obediently invokes all the painful contradictions of the chivalric lover:

> It is to be all made of sighs and tears. . . .
> It is to be all made of faith and service. . . .
> It is to be all made of fantasy,
> All made of passion and all made of wishes,
> All adoration, duty and observance,

All humbleness, all patience and impatience,
All purity, all trial, all observance;[*]
And so am I for Phebe.

Shakespeare evokes a faded ideal, one he employs sympathetically to comic effect, but at the same time we detect in the poignant pleas of Silvius the poet's regret at its passing. It may be said in balance that this portrayal of a lover's distress could apply to any young man or woman so afflicted in any sector of the globe at any moment, past or present. Silvius may seem to us amusingly absurd in his pursuit of the scornful Phebe, but then what lover, real or imagined, isn't?

---

[*]Some editors, noting Shakespeare's uncharacteristic repetition of the word, substitute "obedience," which seems to make more sense.

# THERSITES

*"Now they are clapperclawing one another."*

IN *Troilus and Cressida*, Shakespeare retells Homer's *The Iliad*, faithfully following the epic poem's sequence of events from the initial conference of the Greek leaders to the death of Hector. But his is a comically satiric version of the ancient tale of Greek and Trojan heroes locked in battle over Helen, the beautiful wife of the Spartan king Menelaus, who deserts her husband and runs off with the Trojan prince Paris.[*]

The great majority of Shakespeare's plays are concerned to one degree or another with warfare. In all his histories, save only for *Henry VIII*, it is a prominent concern of the plot. Most of his tragic heroes are soldiers, and battles or sieges form a backdrop to the plots of all the tragedies, except perhaps for *Romeo and Juliet* where the violence takes the form of street fighting between feuding families. In some plays military action has a minor role, of course, as in Fortinbras's aborted invasion of Denmark in *Hamlet* and the sea battle interrupted by a storm in *Othello*, but even in such instances warfare moves the plot in significant ways. Even the aspirations of comic lovers are complicated by men-at-arms, as in *Cymbeline* and *All's Well That Ends Well*, and in *Much Ado About Nothing* the chief figures are soldiers returning from a military campaign.

But nowhere does Shakespeare ridicule warriors so sharply as he does in *Troilus and Cressida*, and the chief instrument of his derision is the acid wit of the common soldier Thersites. Many of the poet's plays are enlivened by clowns, often servants who question their masters' orders wittily—Grumio, for example, in *The Taming of the*

---

[*]The spelling of names here is Shakespeare's, not Homer's.

*Shrew*, and the brothers Dromio in *The Comedy of Errors*, or Lear's Fool who derides the king's actions with riddles and aphorisms, always at the risk of a beating or "the whip." Thersites takes the figure to a new level, however. He is a bitter clown who is incensed at his masters' stupidity; he sees the Greek warriors as so many posturing, brainless thugs on an ignominious mission whose only "argument is a whore and a cuckold."

Thersites is not reluctant to taunt a warrior to his face. When we first see him, he is raging at his master, the blunt-minded Ajax: "Thou mongrel beef-witted lord . . . thou hast no more brain than I have in mine elbows," and he receives a beating for his insolence. Later, when he has entered the service of Achilles, he is no less direct, calling the famed warrior an "idol of idiot-worshippers" whose wit also "lies in your sinews," and his companion Patroclus a "masculine whore." Fortunately for Thersites, Achilles is amused by his tirades and condones the invective.

More often though, Thersites ridicules the Greeks at a safer distance, railing against some of them out of their hearing and others in muttered asides, but none escape his acerbic derision. He is no less virulent about Ajax after he has left his service, mocking him to Achilles as a thickheaded fighting machine who wears "his wit in his belly and his guts in his head" and carries his "tongue in's arms." As for the others, Agamemnon "has not so much brain as ear-wax," and Menelaus is "the bull, the primitive statue and oblique memorial of cuckolds." Old Nestor he characterizes as a man "whose wit was moldy ere your grandsires had nails on their toes" and "that stale old mouse-eaten dry cheese." He dismisses Ulysses as "that same dog-fox," and Achilles with even more disdain: "I had rather be a tick in a sheep than such a valiant ignorance." Of Achilles and Patroclus together he says, "with too much blood and too little brain, these two may run mad." Watching Diomedes seduce Cressida, he calls him "a false-hearted rogue, a most unjust knave."

In the final act, when the two armies clash, he heaps scorn on the spectacle: "Now they are clapperclawing one another." For him the battle is no better than a catfight or an unseemly brawl. He is the omnipresent looker-on, popping up here and there, a choruslike figure who shapes our perception of the action. He watches the fight between Troilus and Diomedes, rivals for Cressida, and gleefully eggs them on: "Hold thy whore, Grecian! Now for thy whore, Trojan!" Observing Menelaus and Paris come to blows, he scoffs, "the cuckold and the cuckold-maker are at it." The whole scene is to him a sordid struggle between lustful men fighting over inconstant women: "Lechery, lechery; still wars and lechery; nothing else holds fashion."

Thersites himself, however, wants nothing to do with the fighting. When confronted by Hector, he insists that he is only a lowly soldier, an unworthy opponent for a high-born warrior: "No, no, I am a rascal, a scurvy railing knave, a very filthy rogue." Hector appears to agree that there can be no glory in killing such a coward, and Thersites escapes unharmed. When challenged by Margarelon, a bastard son of Priam, he pleads the common misfortune of their births—"I am a bastard too; I love bastards"—and argues that it "tempts judgment" for "the son of a whore [to] fight for a whore." Margarelon, momentarily taken aback by his gall, lets him go, but not without a curse: "The devil take thee, coward!"

Shakespeare makes no effort to explore the reasons for Thersites's distemper. There is a brief episode in which he claims that he is serving voluntarily, but Achilles quickly reminds him that he is "under an impress," that is, he was conscripted; but that is the only hint we have of the source of his bitter resentment. Thersites is quite simply an angry man, of a sort that we have all encountered at one time or another. So we recognize the type and have no need to ask what made him that way, especially since his diatribes provide occasion for us to enjoy Shakespeare's inexhaustible store of insults.

Across the spectrum of his plays, Shakespeare portrays the soldier in many guises. We admire the valiant resolve of Henry V and the chivalric loyalty of Talbot in *Henry VI, Part 1*. But we also witness the impotent posturing of the *miles gloriosus*, the "braggart soldier," in the figures of Parolles in *All's Well That Ends Well* and *Henry V's* Pistol, and we watch in dismay the haughty arrogance of Coriolanus. So Shakespeare adds to this galley of warriors the common soldier Thersites, who heaps scorn on the Greeks and Trojans and, we may assume, would hold them all in derision.

# TIMON

*"I am wealthy in my friends."*

*Timon of Athens* is the tale of a man who is generous to a fault, who in his innocence assumes that all humanity is as altruistic as himself, and who on discovering that this is not the case is transformed into a bitter misanthrope, convinced that the human race is irredeemably foul. When we first meet him, Timon plays host to a succession of sycophant guests who exploit his generosity.

His bounty seems bottomless. He pays the debt of a friend and refuses repayment. He provides a dowry for a young woman who wants to wed against her father's wishes, and serves as patron to a poet and a painter. He hosts lavish feasts with elaborate entertainment, welcoming anyone who appears at his door, and distributes jewels to his guests as favors. All praise him—"The noblest mind he carries / That ever governed man." "Long may he live in fortunes!"— and he relishes their goodwill: "I am wealthy in my friends."

But, as soon becomes clear, Timon's bounty is not bottomless. His faithful steward Flavius, who keeps the books, is distressed at his master's profligate generosity and worries that his gifts come "all out of an empty coffer." "His promises fly so beyond his state," Flavius fears, "that what he speaks is all in debt." Timon's debtors soon cluster at his door, clamoring for payment, and Flavius attempts to impress on him the fact that his largesse has bankrupted him. But Timon is unconcerned; he has friends, he says confidently, and sends servants out to secure loans from them. They all refuse, citing one reason or another, the last, Sempronius, with a pretentious show of hurt and indignation that Timon had not called on him first.

Timon invites them all to a feast, welcoming each with his customary geniality; but when the dishes are uncovered they are found to hold only warm water. He douses his guests and hurls the dishes at them, raging that they are "smiling, smooth, detested parasites, / Courteous destroyers, affable wolves, meek bears." He chases them from the house, proclaiming his newfound philosophy: "Henceforth hated be / Of Timon man and all humanity!"

Shakespeare does not explore Timon's inner turmoil in his abrupt transition from generous patron to a man whose only wish is that "his hate may grow / To the whole race of mankind, high and low!" In later plays the poet will portray similar transformations in more profound depth, as in Othello's change from a loving husband to a vengeful murderer, or Macbeth's from a loyal thane to a tyrannical monster. It must be said, however, that Timon's reversal rings true. Friendship, or love, that is based on the charity of only one partner can prove shallow, the poet tells us, and when the giving fades, loyalty and affection can be transitory. Flavius laments the paradox of Timon's fall:

> Poor, honest lord, brought low by his own heart,
> Undone by goodness! Strange, unusual blood,
> When man's worst sin is, he does too much good!
> Who then dares to be half so kind again?

The Timon we see in the latter half of the play is a different man entirely. Retiring to a hermit's existence in the forest, he grows wild and hirsute in appearance, scarcely resembling the polished patrician of Athens (Alcibiades does not recognize him at first). He manifests his hatred of mankind in a desire to shun all human company. Timon is plagued by a constant stream of visitors, however, each of whom he berates savagely for disturbing his solitude. His fondest wish is to be left alone, and their intrusion only inflames his anger, goading him into a resolve to strike back; and, providentially, he comes into possession of a means to do so. While digging for roots to feed upon, he unearths a horde of gold! He has wealth once again, but ironically such is his hatred of mankind that he uses it now not to benefit others, as he had before, but to torment them.

The first intruder is the general Alcibiades, who has been banished unjustly by the Athenians and is leading an army against them in retaliation. Learning of his purpose, Timon gives him gold to pay his soldiers, urging him to sack the city mercilessly: "Let not thy sword skip one. / Pity not honored age for his white beard. . . . Strike me the counterfeit matron. . . . Let not the virgin's cheek / Make soft thy trenchant sword. . . . Spare not the babe [nor] priests in holy vestments."* Alcibiades is accompanied by two women, whom Timon brands as whores. But he gives them gold as well, providing them with the means to corrupt and spread disease among men. A group of thieves comes upon him, and he presses some of his horde on them, charging them to "cut throats" and "break open shops" in Athens. Word of his discovery soon spreads, and the poet and painter pay a visit, seeking his patronage once again. He pays them to seek out villains whom they love and feed, as he had his Athenian "friends," and "hang them, or stab them, drown them in a draught, / Confound them by some course."

The faithful Flavius seeks him out, asking only that he may continue in his service. Timon is temporarily taken aback by what he calls "one honest man" and provides him with the means to "live rich and happy," but only on condition that he "hate all, curse all, show charity to none" and never "relieve the beggar." The Athenian senators appear and, threatened by the approaching army of Alcibiades, they entreat him to return and assume "the captainship" of the city. He dismisses them harshly, replying that "If Alcibiades kill my countrymen . . . if he sack fair Athens . . . I care not."

We are not witness to Timon's death; we hear of it only when a soldier stumbles on his grave and reports it to Alcibiades. We learn of his legacy to mankind when the general reads the epitaph on his solitary, seaside tomb: "Here lie I, Timon, who, alive, all living men did hate; / Pass by and curse thy fill, but pass and stay not here thy gait." It cannot be said that his death has the same tragic effect on an audience as do Lear's or Hamlet's or Othello's final moments, which are played out before our eyes. If there is tragedy in his death, it is more general than particular, a sorrow that a man could hold so fierce an aversion to his fellow humans that he would discourage any

*The lines call to mind the speech of Henry V before Harfleur.

one of them from pausing at his grave. He wants to be forgotten, preferring that no one give so much as a fleeting thought to the fact that he had ever lived. And that is tragic.

So Timon gives his wealth away, at first to benefit others, later to ravage them. In portraying a character so dramatically transformed from one state of mind to its opposite, Shakespeare is perhaps demonstrating that we need not resort to either. Human beings are capable paradoxically of mindless altruism and vengeful malice, but they may hope to lead lives that shun both extremes. And the poet reminds us of an ancient truth: wealth has no moral value in itself; it may be used for good or ill. Gold, in Timon's words, can make "foul fair, wrong right, / Base noble, old young, coward valiant," the contrasting qualities of the human condition; but it is only a lifeless metal.

# TITUS ANDRONICUS

*"When will this fearful slumber have an end?"*

SHAKESPEARE'S earliest tragedy, *Titus Andronicus*, is a bloodbath.
We witness or hear report of fourteen deaths, a carnage that wipes
out all but two of the principal characters, leaving only Titus's
brother Marcus and his last surviving son Lucius alive. Completing
this grizzly catalogue are a rape, two mutilations, one of them carried out in full view of the audience, and a final sentence on Aaron
the Moor, who is to be buried alive. This spectacle of bloodletting
stems from two early decisions by Titus. He returns triumphantly to
Rome after ten years of service in his country's wars, bringing with
him as prisoners Tamora, the queen of the Goths, and her three sons,
along with the body of one of his own, killed in battle. In a pagan
ritual he has one of Tamora's sons slaughtered so that, as he puts it,
the spirit of his own son can "sleep in peace," thus incurring the
fierce enmity of the mother. Next, in recognition of his long service
the people of Rome elect him emperor, but he declines the office,
stepping aside in favor of Saturninus, the late emperor's son.

His troubles start immediately, arising at first from a soldier's
blind devotion to Rome and its institutions. Saturninus declares
grandly that he will take as his empress Lavinia, Titus's daughter,
but she rejects the offer since she is already betrothed to Bassianus,
the emperor's brother. The two flee the scene and Titus pursues
them, enraged at their refusal to submit to the imperial will. One of
his sons springs to their defense, however, and blocks his way, only
to be killed by his infuriated father, the first in a series of seemingly
unconscionable acts. But Titus has been a Roman soldier for forty
years, and in his mind any defiance of the imperial authority to
which he has devoted his entire adult life discredits those decades of

faithful service. He does so without regret, he insists; his son in attempting to protect his disobedient sister has "dishonored all our family" and deserves his fate. The death proves needless, however, because meanwhile Saturninus has taken a fancy to Tamora and announces that he will marry her instead.

The troubles of Titus quickly multiply. Tamora's two remaining sons develop a passionate desire for Lavinia; they encounter her in the company of Bassianus, murder him, and drag her off. Having had their pleasure, they cut off her hands and sever her tongue so that she will be unable to identify her assailants. To complete the treachery, Tamora and her lover, Aaron the Moor, arrange to have two of Titus's remaining sons accused of the murder of Bassianus and sentenced to death.

Titus is reduced from the triumphant figure of the early scenes, revered by the Roman people, to a plaintive supplicant, entreating the senators and judges to spare his sons. They pass him silently by, deaf to his pleas. Despairing, he sinks to the ground, where, he says, he will "tell my sorrows to the stones," which are "in some sort better than the tribunes" for they at least will "receive my tears and seem to weep with me." But he soon suffers an even greater sorrow. Confronted with his mutilated daughter, he laments at length her anguish and the accumulated burden of his losses:

> Thou hast no hands to wipe away thy tears,
> Nor tongue to tell me who hath martyred thee.
> Thy husband he is dead, and for his death
> Thy brothers are condemned, and dead by this [by now].

And there is yet more to come. Saturninus sends a message stating that he will pardon Titus's sons if presented with the severed hand of one of their family. Titus sacrifices his and sends it to the emperor, who in a cruel jest returns it with the heads of his executed sons.

At this, the lowest point of his despair, Titus wonders if there can be more tribulations ahead: "When will this fearful slumber [nightmare] have an end?" Once the emperor and the Senate turn against him, both symbols of an ideal he has served with reverence over his long years in arms, it is as if they have dismissed that service as valueless, and in consequence, to echo another soldier's lament, Titus's "occupation's gone."* No longer a soldier of the empire now, he rises as a father, seeking vengeance on the powers responsible for the unjust murder of his children. He begins with a simple expression of his resolve, "Come, let me see what task I have to do." He sends Lucius to raise an army of Goths to assault Rome, and later, learning that Tamora's sons are responsible for Lavinia's mutilation, his resolve hardens. As he plots his course, however, some of his acts seem random—sending a gift of arms to the sons, for example—and his wits seem to turn as his speech is reduced to incoherent ramblings. He imagines that Astraea, the goddess of justice, has left the earth, and he speaks of sending his followers out in search of her. Some he dispatches to sea—"Go sound the ocean, and cast your nets"—others to the earth—"'Tis you must dig with mattock and with spade." Although his mind seems distracted and his thoughts chaotic, at their core is a single imperative: he will have "Justice for to wreak [avenge] our wrongs."

The revenge of Titus is terrifying. He orchestrates it by turning a scheme of Tamora to his advantage. Lucius is advancing on Rome at the head of a Gothic army, and she plots to have him meet with the emperor at Titus's house, where she is confident she can persuade the father to convince his son to abandon his campaign. Pretending to be mad, Titus lures her sons into his house, kills them, and bakes their remains in a pie in anticipation of a banquet when the parties convene. The guests arrive, and in a ludicrous scene Titus, in a cook's apron, greets them in the guise of a genial host. Suddenly, once they all sit down to the feast, the bloodshed begins. Titus stabs Lavinia, so as, he says, to end her shame. He then informs Tamora that she has been dining on her sons and stabs her. Saturninus stabs Titus, and Lucius in turn kills him. Four bodies litter the stage, as well as the two cooked in the pie, a bitter cost for Titus's rejection of the offer to rule Rome. Lucius, who survives the carnage, is declared emperor.

*Titus Andronicus* has many flaws as a play. It is a savage spectacle with an episodic plot, dubious motives for thinly drawn characters, and few memorable poetic passages. But Titus is an unforgettably

---

*See "Othello," p. 221.

tragic figure in his several roles, as a soldier sternly loyal to his solemn oath of service to his country, then a grieving father, his mind distracted by a towering sorrow over his lost sons and ravished daughter, and finally a relentless nemesis, imposing vengeful justice on his vindictive foes. The play is seldom produced but, once seen, Titus remains in the playgoer's imagination as a compelling character, the product of Shakespeare's as yet unsure pen, which will in time fashion masterworks of tragedy.

# Epilogue

*"Last scene of all,*
*That ends this strange eventful history."*
—*Jaques,* As You Like It

ASIDE FROM Shakespeare's extraordinary poetic powers, it is the range and depth of his characters that is most astonishing. Among his many figures may be found:

- The young, in careless pursuit of pleasure or as innocent victims of their elders' ambitions, some tragically, some comically scheming to evade parental designs.
- The aged, some wise, some foolish, in their fading years either cursing the trick that time has played on them or bowing with dignity to a destined end.
- Figures of authority, such as Roman emperors, monarchs of many realms, lordly dukes, senators, generals, a fairy king, and a godlike wizard.
- Villains, both those who act out of inbred evil and those who, though not innately wicked, are drawn to treachery by lust, envy, hatred, or ambition.
- Mothers, some fiercely ambitious and protective of their children, others sunk in sorrow at their loss.
- Soldiers, some young and untried, eagerly seeking fame "even in the cannon's mouth," some seasoned warriors dauntless in combat, and some braggart cowards shrinking from the heat of battle.
- Lovers, those who are young, innocent, and vulnerable, the pathetic youth, composing "a woeful ballad / To his mistress' eyebrow," and those more seductively mature, ripe in their passion.

The list includes simple peasants and common citizens, at times wise in the ways of the mighty, at others raging in unruly mobs, as well as fawning courtiers, arrogant lords, saucy servants, inept police, court fops, jesters, clowns, and bastards, the high and low of the Renaissance social structure.

If we add to Shakespeare's remarkable diversity in characters the matchless poetry with which he describes the emotions that move them, we gain an even greater gauge of his achievement:

• Love, whether youthful ardor or mature passion, comic in the lovesick suitor, tragic in those torn apart by chance or death.

• Hatred, arising from ancient grievances or personal affronts.

• Anger, provoked by frustrated hopes, arrogant enemies, challenges to honor, turncoat friends, or faithless lovers.

• Ambition for riches, fame, or a crown, at times commendable, at others a spur to treachery, betrayal, and murder.

• Desire, either blatant lust or fanciful adoration.

• Envy of a rival in love, an older brother in line to inherit, a superior in social or military rank, or others blessed with wealth or handsome features.

• Joy in the realization of a dream long delayed or the happy end of a time of trial and suffering.

• Grief at the loss of a loved one, the dashing of hope, or in general lamentation over the misery of life itself.

• Fear of injury, death, and the supernatural—ghosts, harpies, fairies, "the gods," or simply the threat of the unknown.

• The cheerful abandon of a carefree youth reveling in life or a dissolute elder losing himself in drink, and dance, and song.

Such a catalogue, admittedly sketchy, gives us some notion of the breathtaking scale of Shakespeare's achievement. How could one man know so much about the human condition, and how could he relate it all so convincingly, in a manner that strikes us instantly as the truth of his characters, persuading us that, yes, this is the way they are and this is how they must act, though we may never have faced a king, a cardinal, a madman, or a peasant, or felt the fury of the battlefield?*

---

*We have all encountered our share of others he portrays: lovers, fathers, brothers, tyrants, bullies, dandies, drunks, dupes, and stone-faced bureaucrats.

Any survey of Shakespeare's characters is bound to be inadequate. Aside from the sheer numbers, the range and depth of them is so rich, so vast, so varied that mere summary must fall short of satisfaction. So only a few of his hundreds are offered here in the hope, again, that these brief sketches will help theatergoers to find the figures more familiar and render the experience of a performance more enjoyable.

# Index I: Characters by Play

*Boldface numbers indicate where the entry is featured in the text.*

# Index II: Other Subjects

# A NOTE ON THE AUTHOR

Robert Thomas Fallon is emeritus professor of English at La Salle University in Philadelphia. Born in New York City, he studied at the United States Military Academy at West Point, Canisius College, and Columbia University, where he received a Ph.D. in English. For many years he has written and lectured on Shakespeare to a variety of audiences, including those at the Stratford (Ontario) Shakespeare Festival. His *A Theatergoer's Guide to Shakespeare's Characters* is a companion volume to *A Theatergoer's Guide to Shakespeare* and *A Theatergoer's Guide to Shakespeare's Themes*, both of which have drawn wide praise. Mr. Fallon has also written extensively on the life and work of John Milton, and has served as president of the Milton Society of America. He lives in Lumberville, Pennsylvania.